Market Power Handbook

Competition Law and Economic Foundations

Second Edition

SECTION OF

ANTITRUST LAW

Promoting Competition
Protecting Consumers

**Defending Liberty
Pursuing Justice**

This volume should be officially cited as:

ABA SECTION OF ANTITRUST LAW,
MARKET POWER HANDBOOK: COMPETITION
LAW AND ECONOMIC FOUNDATIONS, SECOND EDITION (2012)

Cover design by Dan Mazanec/ABA Publishing.

ISBN: 978-1-61438-069-6

Discounts are available for books ordered in bulk. Special consideration is given to state bars, CLE programs, and other bar-related organizations. Inquire at Book Publishing, ABA Publishing, American Bar Association, 321 N. Clark Street, Chicago, Illinois 60654-7598.

www.ShopABA.org

16 15 14 13 12   5 4 3 2 1

CONTENTS

FOREWORD

The Section of Antitrust Law is pleased to present the second edition of the *Market Power Handbook,* a comprehensive review of the market power issues that arise in antitrust analysis. The goal of the *Handbook* is to address market power from both a legal and an economic standpoint; it is designed to serve as a nontechnical resource rather than an economic text. Nonetheless, the *Handbook* provides an introduction to and summary of the economic concepts that are critical to an understanding of market power.

The Section is indebted to the many attorneys and economists who contributed to this *Handbook*. In particular, the Section's Economics Committee devoted a great deal of time and attention to this project. We are especially grateful to Mary Coleman and Bruce Hoffman, who coordinated the drafting and editing of the *Handbook*; and to Edwin Fountain, who edited the *Handbook* for publication.

March 2012   Richard M. Steuer
Chair, Section of Antitrust Law
American Bar Association
2011-2012

PREFACE

Market power is one of the essential concepts of antitrust law. At its core, antitrust policy is aimed at preventing firms from improperly obtaining, retaining, or utilizing market power. Although a plaintiff can, in some cases, win an antitrust case without showing that the defendant has or could obtain market power, those situations are the exception rather than the rule. As a result, the ability to determine if a firm or group of firms has or could obtain market power is an essential skill for every antitrust attorney.

The *Market Power Handbook* is designed to provide an overview of the fundamental market power issues that arise in antitrust cases. It attempts to offer an accessible description of the existing economic literature, including how that literature relates to the legal issues that arise in litigated cases and agency investigations, updating the discussion and references from the original edition. Where possible, the book identifies emerging issues which will shape future law.

Chapter I frames the discussion by explaining the various definitions of market power that have been used by economists and courts, including the distinction between market power and monopoly power. Chapter II summarizes the varying market power standards that are applied under the federal antitrust statutes. Chapter III introduces the fundamental economic doctrines related to market power, including the economic theories of perfectly competitive markets and of monopoly.

With that background, the *Handbook* turns to the realities of building a market power analysis. Chapter IV describes the role market power plays in market definition, and Chapter V discusses the measurement and interpretation of market shares and concentration as well as other empirical approaches for measuring market power. Chapter VI provides an overview of market power analysis as applied to markets that present special challenges, including differentiated product markets, cluster markets, and network industries. Finally, Chapter VII describes the analysis of barriers to entry.

The *Handbook* is the product of many dedicated lawyers and economists. Mary Coleman and Bruce Hoffman coordinated the editing and drafting of this book. The following economists and lawyers worked under their leadership to draft it:

Greg Adams	Robert Kneuper
Paul Godek	Henry McFarland
Margaret Guerin-Calvert	Richard Rapp
Stuart Gurrea	Michael Salinger
Matthew Hendricksen	David Scheffman
Bruce Hoffman	Evan Schouten
Gloria Hurdle	Robert Stoner
Guillermo Israelivich	David Weiskopf
Brian Keating	

In addition, Jonathan Bowater and Amanda Wait, with assistance from Kristina Van Horn, Hillary Maki, and Leslie Kostyshak, spent many countless hours editing and preparing the material for publication. Numerous reviewers provided extensive and helpful comments, often under very tight deadlines. Reviewers included: David Weiskopf, Piu Banerjee, James Nieberding, and Henry McFarland. Finally, Edwin Fountain systematically edited the draft and prepared it for publication.

March 2012

Jeffrey Schmidt
Co-Chair, Economics Committee
Section of Antitrust Law
American Bar Association
2009-2012

Mary Coleman
Co-Chair, Economics Committee
Section of Antitrust Law
American Bar Association
2011-2014

CHAPTER I

DEFINITION OF MARKET POWER

The definition of market power is often critical to antitrust analysis, but the term has been used differently by economists and courts depending on the circumstances presented. This Chapter sets a framework for the rest of the *Handbook* by describing the definition generally used by economists, as well as the varying formulations used in antitrust law. The Chapter then considers how antitrust law differentiates between two terms often used interchangeably—"market power" and "monopoly power."

A. Economic Concept of Market Power

"Market power" exists when an industry's behavior "deviates from perfect competition."[1] Economists often define market power as the ability of a firm or group of firms within a market[2] to *profitably* charge prices[3] above the *competitive level* for a *sustained period of time.*

---

1.   *See, e.g.*, Dennis W. Carlton, *Market Definition: Use and Abuse*, COMP. POL'Y INT'L, Spring 2007, at 3, 5.
2.   Economists and antitrust lawyers alike typically have analyzed market power in the context of well-defined markets. In antitrust law, these are referred to as "relevant markets." Chapter IV provides a discussion of the definition of relevant markets. The 2010 revisions to the *Merger Guidelines* suggest that the agencies may be moving away from defining relevant markets in all cases. *See* U.S. DEP'T OF JUSTICE & FED. TRADE COMM'N, HORIZONTAL MERGER GUIDELINES § 4 (2010), *available at* http://www.justice.gov/atr/public/guidelines/hmg-2010.html [hereinafter MERGER GUIDELINES]. Courts, on the other hand, may not be amenable to divorcing market power from market definition. *See, e.g.*, City of New York v. Group Health, No. 06 Civ. 13122, 2010 WL 2132246, at *2 (S.D.N.Y. 2010) ("To state claims under any of the statutes identified above, Plaintiffs must identify the product market in which competition will be impaired.").
3.   Although the economic definition of market power typically does not mention reductions in product or service quality, economists generally would expand the meaning of price to include the increases in real price

1

Although any firm can raise the price of its product, not every firm can do so profitably and for a sustained period of time. As a result, a distinguishing characteristic of a firm or group of firms with market power is that they can raise product prices without losing so many sales that the price increase is unprofitable. If close substitutes for a firm's product exist or others could easily begin producing close substitutes,[4] the firm will not profit from a price increase and thus, by definition, lacks market power.

Economists typically define market power by focusing on the ability to raise price relative to the competitive price level, rather than the current price level.[5] The reason for this is that a firm with market power might have already exercised its market power and raised the price of its product above the competitive level (to a "supracompetitive" level). Defining a market based on a hypothetical small, but significant and nontransitory increase in price (SSNIP) over that supracompetitive price could distort the market to include products that would not be substitutes and, therefore, included in the relevant market definition, if the SSNIP were calculated based on a competitive price.[6] As a result, if one focuses

---

that result from reductions in quality. *See, e.g.*, George A. Hay, *Market Power in Antitrust*, 60 ANTITRUST L.J. 807 (1992). Similarly, some economists include the notion of "restricting output" in the definition of market power. *See, e.g.*, PHILLIP AREEDA ET AL., ANTITRUST LAW ¶ 501, at 109 (3d ed. 2007) (defining market power as "the ability to raise price profitably by restricting output"). Generally, a monopolist will reduce sales to increase price (resulting in a net welfare loss). However, this is not always the case. For example, a monopolist need not restrict output to raise prices if it can employ perfect price discrimination (resulting in a welfare transfer). *See infra* ch. III. Whether this circumstance raises issues under antitrust law is a complex question.

4.   The identification of close substitutes is central to market definition. The ability of a firm quickly to begin producing a product can be included as part of a market definition exercise, as a "supply-side substitution," or as part of the entry analysis. *See infra* ch. IV.

5.   *See generally* MERGER GUIDELINES, *supra* note 2, § 1.

6.   *See Id.* § 4.1.2. For example, a profit-maximizing monopolist that faces a linear (straight-line), downward-sloping demand curve will increase its price until it reaches a point on the elastic portion of the demand curve at which further price increases would be unprofitable. *See infra* ch. III. For a similar discussion of this point, see Robert Pitofsky, *New Definitions of Relevant Market and the Assault on Antitrust*, 90 COLUM. L. REV. 1805 (1990).

on the ability of a firm to profitably raise prices above current levels, one may conclude that the firm does not have market power, when in fact it has already successfully exploited substantial market power.[7]

The notion that market power requires that prices remain above the competitive price for a sustained period of time is important to distinguish the exercise of market power from "opportunistic behavior."[8] Opportunistic behavior involves the temporary elevation of prices above competitive levels. For example, a firm might be able to use minor transaction costs or imperfections in information flows to raise prices temporarily above competitive levels, but might not be able to sustain supracompetitive prices over the long run.[9]

While economists often use the terms "market power" and "monopoly power" interchangeably,[10] some scholars distinguish between the two terms. Those scholars point out that firms might have trivial amounts of market power, perhaps because the products of competing firms differ slightly or because the firm has transitory advantages that will be competed away as other firms innovate. That market power

---

7.   *See* Eastman Kodak Co. v. Image Tech. Servs., 504 U.S. 451, 471 (1992); *see also infra* ch. IV (discussing the so-called Cellophane Fallacy).

8.   *See* AREEDA ET AL., *supra* note 3, ¶ 801d, at 387 (discussing the durability of market power).

9.   Severe structural imperfections in the market, such as incomplete information, can lead to sustained prices above competitive levels. As a result, it is important to determine what supply-side and demand-side responses are likely, and to assess whether structural characteristics permit only temporary supracompetitive pricing, or whether they permit prices to rise above competitive levels over the long run.

10. As Carlton and Perloff explained:

> It is common practice to say that whenever a firm can profitably set its price above its marginal cost without making a loss, it has *monopoly power* or *market power*. One might usefully distinguish between the terms by using *monopoly power* to describe a firm that makes a profit if it sets its price optimally above its marginal cost, and *market power* to describe a firm that earns only the competitive profit when it sets its price optimally above its marginal cost. However, people do not always make this distinction, and generally use the two terms interchangeably, sometimes creating confusion.
>
> DENNIS W. CARLTON & JEFFREY M. PERLOFF, MODERN INDUSTRIAL ORGANIZATION 93 (4th ed. 2005).

should not raise antitrust concerns.[11] In contrast, firms with a substantial amount of market power may be said to have monopoly power or "antitrust monopoly power," which can raise antitrust concerns. [12] Distinguishing among levels of market power often requires detailed economic analysis of the relevant market. The analysis of markets containing differentiated products is illustrative.

Economists recognize that a firm that sells a differentiated product is somewhat insulated from competitors. Economists formalize this insulation in their theoretical models by using a demand curve for differentiated products which slopes downward, implying that a firm can maximize its profits by charging a price that is above its marginal costs.[13] Moreover, some economists have argued that product differentiation itself can be a barrier to entry, which suggests that situations may exist in which the firm could earn sustained profits as a result of its unique position. [14] Nonetheless, prices charged by a firm that sells a differentiated product could be limited by other competitive factors. As a result, determining whether a firm that sells a differentiated product has market power rising to the level of antitrust monopoly power is very fact-

11.   *See* AREEDA ET AL., *supra* note 3, ¶¶ 501-08, at 109-35; *see also* William M. Landes & Richard A. Posner, *Market Power in Antitrust Cases*, 94 HARV. L. REV. 937, 939 (1981) (arguing that only substantial market power is a cause for concern).

12.   *See* Landes & Posner, *supra* note 11, at 937 (explaining that monopoly power involves "a high degree of market power"); AREEDA ET AL., *supra* note 3, ¶ 501, at 110-11; PHILLIP AREEDA & HERBERT HOVENKAMP, ANTITRUST LAW ¶¶ 800-03, at 382-402 (3d ed. 2008) (emphasizing that antitrust case law requires market power to be substantial to invoke a Section 2 remedy).

13.   The demand curve for a firm that sells a homogeneous product is horizontal (even when the market demand curve for that product slopes downward) because customers will not buy the firm's product if it is priced higher than the price of competitors' perfectly substitutable products. In contrast, a differentiated product such as a brand of premium coffee may have a downward sloping demand curve because some consumers do not view other brands of coffee as perfect substitutes. *See infra* ch. III.

14.   *See infra* ch. VII (discussing barriers to entry, including barriers to entry due to product differentiation).

specific and can, particularly in close cases, depend on the standards that are used.[15]

Some economists have suggested that the definition of antitrust monopoly power should include the requirement that the firm or group of firms alleged to have market power is earning "supranormal economic profits."[16] However, firms that have market power might not earn supranormal economic profits if they expend these profits on costly efforts to insulate themselves from competition.[17] As a result, market power might be present even if supranormal economic profits are absent.

In sum, while they are not always clear about it, many economists would distinguish antitrust monopoly power as a circumstance in which a firm (or group of firms) has substantial market power. As will be discussed more in this *Handbook*, the presence of substantial market power is reflected in the firm's (or group of firms') ability to raise a price significantly above competitive levels for a sustained period of time, and the firm's (or group of firms') insulation from competition over the long run by significant barriers to entry as opposed to minor differences in product attributes.

B. Market Power in Antitrust Law

The economic concept of market power is central to the legal analysis of most antitrust cases.[18] Some courts have defined market

---

15. As is explained in more detail in ch. VI, *infra*, fundamental questions include whether the firm's product, while differentiated, still faces close substitutes and whether other firms can easily reposition products or introduce new products that are close substitutes. With respect to the latter issue, relevant factual questions include: (i) how large are the sunk costs that must be invested to differentiate a product; (ii) is market demand large enough to allow profitable recovery of these sunk costs; (iii) how long does it take to communicate reliability or other attributes that differentiate a particular product; and (iv) can the consumer experiment with new products without incurring significant costs or risks? *See* MERGER GUIDELINES, *supra* note 2, § 6.1.
16. *See* Hay, *supra* note 3, at 814.
17. *See, e.g.*, Richard A. Posner, *The Social Costs of Monopoly and Regulations*, 83 J. POL. ECON. 807 (1975) (describing costly activities designed to secure profits).
18. Whether antitrust law should be concerned with anything in addition to market power and its economic consequences is often debated. *See* Neil W. Averitt & Robert H. Lande, *Using the "Consumer Choice" Approach*

power using terminology that is very close to that used in economic definitions. For example, in *Jefferson Parish Hospital District No. 2 v. Hyde*,[19] the Supreme Court wrote: "[M]arket power exists whenever prices can be raised above the levels that would be charged in a competitive market."[20] Said another way, market power is the ability to impose anticompetitive effects.[21] As courts and commentators have recognized, however, the antitrust laws require varying amounts of market power, depending on the nature of the allegations.[22] For a

---

> *to Antitrust Law*, 74 ANTITRUST L.J. 175 (2007); *see also* Eastman Kodak Co. v. Image Tech. Servs., 504 U.S. 451, 488 (1992) (Scalia, J., dissenting) ("The concerns . . . that have led the courts to heightened scrutiny both of the 'exclusionary conduct' practiced by a monopolist and of tying arrangements subject to *per se* prohibition[] are completely without force when the participants lack market power."). *Cf.* Rothery Storage & Van Co. v. Atlas Van Lines, Inc., 792 F.2d 210, 230-31 (D.C. Cir. 1986) (Wald, J., concurring) ("I do not believe that the debate over the purposes of the antitrust laws has been settled yet. Until the Supreme Court provides more definitive instruction in this regard, I think it premature to construct an antitrust test that ignores all other potential concerns of the antitrust laws except for restriction of output and price raising."). The Third Circuit has stated that market power is not a requirement in rule of reason tying cases that do not rely on a leverage theory. Town Sound & Custom Tops, Inc. v. Chrysler Motors Corp., 959 F.2d 468, 483 (3d Cir. 1992). This is perhaps a result of the Supreme Court stating that market power was a prerequisite for a per se rule in tying cases, but that a rule of reason analysis is still applicable even when a per se violation cannot be found. Jefferson Parish Hosp. Dist. No. 2 v. Hyde, 466 U.S. 2, 18 (1984), *abrogated on other grounds by* Illinois Tool Works v. Indep. Ink, 547 U.S. 28 (2006).

19.   466 U.S. 2 (1984).

20.   *Id.* at 27 n.46; *see also* Eastman Kodak Co. v. Image Tech. Servs., 504 U.S. 451, 464 (1992) (citing the ability of a single seller to raise prices and restrict output); Fortner Enters. v. United States Steel Corp., 394 U.S. 495, 503 (1969) (same); SCFC ILC, Inc. v. Visa USA, Inc., 36 F.3d 958, 965 (10th Cir. 1994) (same); Ball Mem'l Hosp. v. Mut. Hosp. Ins., 784 F.2d 1325, 1331 (7th Cir. 1986) (same).

21.   *See Jefferson Parish*, 466 U.S. at 28-29.

22.   *See, e.g.*, AREEDA & HOVENKAMP, *supra* note 12, ¶ 802c, at 392 (observing that "[t]he quantum of power required for judicial intervention varies with the nature of the antitrust challenge"). Areeda, Hovenkamp and Solow also argue that "[m]arket power exists in degrees. Power is small when more than a slight increase in price would lead to an

plaintiff to prevail on a tying claim under Sherman Act Section 1,[23] for example, the plaintiff must prove that the defendant possesses market power in the market for the tying product,[24] i.e., that it has the ability to impose anticompetitive effects. Price-fixing cases under Section 1, on the other hand, typically do not require proof of market power.[25] Instead of requiring a showing of market power to infer likely anticompetitive effects, courts in price-fixing cases directly infer anticompetitive effects from the conduct itself because the types of behavior that fall into the per se category are those almost always likely to have adverse price and output effects.[26] A monopolization claim under Sherman Act Section 2,[27] in contrast, expressly requires the possession of *monopoly* power,[28] and attempted monopolization under Section 2 requires that the defendant have a "dangerous probability of success" in achieving monopoly

---

unacceptable loss of sales. It is large when a firm can profit by raising prices substantially without losing too many sales." AREEDA ET AL., *supra* note 3, ¶ 501, at 109.

23.   15 U.S.C. § 1.

24.   *See, e.g., Illinois Tool Works*, 547 U.S. at 42-43 (holding tying arrangements involving patented products require proof of power in the relevant market).

25.   Court apply per se treatment in cases in which experience has shown that the conduct at issue "always or almost always tend[s] to restrict competition and decrease output." Northwest Wholesale Stationers v. Pac. Stationery & Printing Co., 472 U.S. 284, 289-90 (1985) (citation omitted). Such cases normally dispense with formal proof of market power based on a legal presumption of anticompetitive effects and lack of justification. *See* Arizona v. Maricopa County Med. Soc'y, 457 U.S. 332, 350-51 (1982); *see also* NCAA v. Bd. of Regents, 468 U.S. 85, 111-13 (1984).

26.   *See* Broad. Music v. CBS, 441 U.S. 1, 19-20 (1979) (explaining that the inquiry must focus on "whether the practice facially appears to be one that would always or almost always tend to restrict competition and decrease output").

27.   15 U.S.C. § 2.

28.   *See* Verizon Commc'ns v. Law Offices of Curtis V. Trinko, 540 U.S. 398, 407 (2004) (The monopolization offense requires (i) "the possession of monopoly power in the relevant market"; and (ii) "'the willful acquisition or maintenance of that power as distinguished from growth or development as a consequence of a superior product, business acumen, or historic accident . . . .'") (internal citation omitted).

power.[29] However, courts analyzing whether monopoly power exists use the same basic concepts as those used in evaluating market power.[30]

The concept of market power is also central to the analysis of mergers and acquisitions under the Clayton Act.[31] Since the Clayton Act is intended to be prophylactic, the merging firms do not need to have market power for the merger or acquisition to be found anticompetitive. However, a Clayton Act violation requires a showing that the transaction raises a substantial likelihood of subsequent anticompetitive behavior, such as the ability to sustain a small but significant increase in price above competitive levels, which typically involves a detailed (albeit prospective) market power analysis.[32] Higher market share concentration levels generally will reflect the extent to which a merger will raise prices.[33]

---

29. *See* Spectrum Sports v. McQuillan, 506 U.S. 447, 455 (1993). The amount of market power sufficient to satisfy the "dangerous probability of success" element for the attempted monopolization claim translates into less *current* market power than is required for monopolization under the same statute. According to some commentators, the defendant need not have present market power, but its "position must be sufficiently 'proximate' to monopoly that the challenged conduct threatens success." AREEDA & HOVENKAMP, *supra* note 12, ¶ 807a, at 429. Similarly, the Supreme Court has indicated that a plaintiff must show that the defendant has the "ability to lessen or destroy competition" in the relevant market. *Spectrum Sports*, 506 U.S. at 455-56. This suggests that the defendant does not have to have monopoly power at the time it attempts to monopolize.

30. Courts have characterized monopoly power as "substantial" market power. *See, e.g.*, Bacchus Indus. v. Arvin Indus., 939 F.2d 887, 894 (10th Cir. 1991); *see also* Deauville Corp. v. Federated Dep't Stores, 756 F.2d 1183, 1192 n.6 (5th Cir. 1985).

31. 15 U.S.C. § 18; *see* MERGER GUIDELINES, *supra* note 2, § 1 ("The unifying theme of these Guidelines is that mergers should not be permitted to create, enhance, or entrench market power or facilitate its exercise.").

32. *See infra* ch. IV.

33. *See* Jonathan B. Baker, *Market Concentration in the Antitrust Analysis of Horizontal Mergers*, *in* ANTITRUST LAW AND ECONOMICS 234, 246-47 (Keith Hylton ed., 2010). The *Merger Guidelines* also focus more on the closeness of competition between merging firms (and diversion ratios) and less on measures of marketwide concentration than did prior versions of the *Guidelines*. *See* MERGER GUIDELINES, *supra* note 2, § 6.1.

C. Differentiating Between Market Power and Monopoly Power in Antitrust Law

Although similar in concept, as noted above, the U.S. antitrust laws recognize a difference between market power and monopoly power. The Supreme Court has defined monopoly power as "the power to control prices or exclude competition,"[34] and has acknowledged that monopoly power is "something greater than market power."[35] A number of appellate courts have also recognized a distinction,[36] as have leading antitrust commentators.[37]

---

34. United States v. E.I. du Pont de Nemours & Co., 351 U.S. 377, 391 (1956); *accord* Aspen Skiing Co. v. Aspen Highlands Skiing Corp., 472 U.S. 585, 596 n.20 (1985).

35. *See* Eastman Kodak, 504 U.S. at 481; *see also* N. Pac. Ry. Co. v. United States, 356 U.S. 1, 6 (1958) (for tying violation, finding only sufficient economic power with respect to tying product is needed, rather than monopoly power).

36. *See* Port Dock & Stone Corp. v. Oldcastle Ne., Inc., 507 F.3d 117, 123 (2d Cir. 2007) (citing *Eastman Kodak*, 504 U.S. at 464, which defined market power as the ability of a single seller to raise price and restrict output, and AD/SAT v. Associated Press, 181 F.3d 216, 227 (2d Cir. 1999), which defined monopoly power as the ability to sustain price substantially above competitive level for a significant time); Spirit Airlines v. Northwest Airlines, 431 F.3d 917, 935 (6th Cir. 2005) (observing that "'[a]s an economic matter, market power exists whenever prices can be raised above the levels that would be charged in a competitive market'" whereas monopoly power is "the defendant's power 'to raise prices or to exclude competition whenever it is desired to do so'") (citations omitted); Reazin v. Blue Cross & Blue Shield, Inc., 899 F.2d 951, 967 (10th Cir. 1990) (observing that "[m]arket [power] and monopoly power only differ in degree—monopoly power is commonly thought of as 'substantial' market power"—and that in the Tenth Circuit, market power is the power to control prices *or* to exclude competition, whereas monopoly power requires proof of *both* power to control prices *and* exclude competition).

37. *See* AREEDA & HOVENKAMP, *supra* note 12, ¶ 801, at 382 ("[T]he Sherman Act § 2 notion of monopoly power" is "conventionally understood to mean 'substantial' market power."). Areeda and Hovenkamp suggest that in defining "substantial" market power, the tests applied "must be fairly demanding," for "[o]therwise, the power requisite will fail to impose limits on § 2's scope, which must be restricted to

Despite the differing legal standards that may be important in some circumstances, many courts use the terms "market power" and "monopoly power" interchangeably, or are imprecise in defining and distinguishing between the two concepts.[38] Such imprecision can lead to confusion when a firm arguably possesses a small degree of market power in the economic sense, but is still a long way from acquiring monopoly power in the legal sense. Even when courts apply the terminology precisely, however, the difficulty still lies in determining when a firm has crossed the applicable market power or monopoly power threshold (or is dangerously close to doing so) such that antitrust liability for certain types of conduct may begin to attach.[39] The chapters that follow provide an in-depth review of the factors that economists and courts consider when evaluating the nature and degree of a firm's market power.

While many firms may possess "market power" in an economic sense, they should not be considered to possess monopoly power so as to be at risk under Section 2, or "sufficient economic power" to be at risk

---

activities reasonably calculated to reduce marketwide output and increase price to supracompetitive levels." *Id.*

38.   *See, e.g.*, Sheridan v. Marathon Petroleum Co., 530 F.3d 590, 594-95 (7th Cir. 2008) (observing that market power is key for a tying claim, but defining monopoly power); Heerwagen v. Clear Channel Commc'ns, 435 F.3d 219, 226-27 (2d Cir. 2006) (recognizing that monopoly power is "a high degree of 'market power'" but stating that in order to prevail on her Section 2 claims, plaintiff had to prove that defendant created or maintained market power), *overruled in part on other grounds by In re* Initial Pub. Offerings Sec. Litig., 471 F.3d 24 (2d Cir. 2006); United States v. LSL Biotech., 379 F.3d 672, 696 (9th Cir. 2004) (Aldisert, J., dissenting) (observing, in connection with a Sherman Act Section 1 claim, that "[a]ntitrust is concerned with the power of market participants to distort the competitive process. . . . The power relevant to antitrust is market power, or as some economists put it, 'monopoly power.'"); Tops Mkts. v. Quality Mkts., 142 F.3d 90, 97-98 (2d Cir. 1998) ("Monopoly power, also referred to as market power, is 'the power to control prices or exclude competition.'") (citation omitted); *see also* MCI v. AT&T, 708 F.2d 1081, 1107 (7th Cir. 1983) (share in excess of 70-80 percent sufficient to infer the existence of monopoly power); Valley Liquors v. Renfield Imps., 822 F.2d 656, 667 (7th Cir. 1987) (absent other factors, share of 17-25 percent is the minimum that is legally sufficient to sustain a finding of monopolization). For more discussion, see *infra* ch. II.

39.   *See infra* ch. II for a discussion of the difficulty courts have had defining monopoly power.

under Section 1 for conduct that may be ubiquitous and generally procompetitive in many circumstances. Courts, recognizing this, have tended to use market shares as a screen to identify antitrust violations—a high share may imply the power substantially to increase price or decrease price. But, in fact, such screens may insulate firms with market or monopoly power from antitrust liability.[40]

---

40.   *See Eastman Kodak*, 504 U.S. at 464-80. *But see* Landes & Posner, *supra* note 11 (arguing that only the possession of substantial market power should raise antitrust concerns).

CHAPTER II

THE ROLE OF MARKET POWER IN STATUTORY ANTITRUST OFFENSES

The economic concept of market power plays a significant role in the analysis of potentially anticompetitive conduct under the antitrust laws. Courts have tailored the analysis of market power to fit the differing demands of various antitrust statutes. This Chapter explores the fundamental role that market power plays under each of the primary federal antitrust laws.

A. Market Power Under Section 1 of the Sherman Act

Sherman Act Section 1 provides that "[e]very contract, combination in the form of trust or otherwise, or conspiracy, in restraint of trade or commerce among the several States . . . is declared to be illegal."[1] However, because every agreement restrains trade to some degree, the Supreme Court has interpreted Section 1 to reach only concerted activity between separate entities that *unreasonably* restrains competition.[2] As explained more fully below, the analysis of market power in Section 1 cases is often integral to the court's assessment of whether a defendant's conduct unreasonably restrains trade by, for example, raising prices, restricting output, or impairing consumer choice.[3] However, the role of market power varies significantly between per se and rule of reason cases.

---

1. 15 U.S.C. § 1.
2. In *Standard Oil Co. v. United States,* 221 U.S. 1, 58-60 (1911), the Court concluded that it was not Congress' intention to prohibit contracts that impose insignificant restraints of trade, but only those that "unreasonably" restrain competition.
3. *See, e.g.*, United States v. Visa U.S.A., Inc., 344 F.3d 229, 238 (2d Cir. 2003) (holding that a plaintiff "must demonstrate that the defendant conspirators have 'market power' in a particular market for goods or services"); Sullivan v. NFL, 34 F.3d 1091, 1096-97 (1st Cir. 1994) ("Anticompetitive effects . . . are usually measured by a *reduction in output* and an *increase in prices* in the relevant market.").

1. The Role of Market Power in Per Se Cases

The per se rule applies to those practices that are "so plainly anticompetitive" that they are deemed illegal without analysis of market power and market effects.[4] The most commonly recognized of these per se offenses are horizontal price fixing,[5] bid rigging,[6] and horizontal market allocation.[7] Although these per se offenses under Sherman Act Section 1 do not require proof of market power,[8] they are nonetheless strongly influenced by the concept. Both anticompetitive effects and procompetitive justifications are defined and identified by reference to actual or expected price and output effects.[9] In this way, the economic

---

4.   *See* Nat'l Soc'y of Prof'l Eng'rs v. United States, 435 U.S. 679, 692 (1978). In *Continental T.V., Inc. v. GTE Sylvania Inc.*, 433 U.S. 36, 49-51, 58-59 (1977), the Supreme Court made it clear that the per se rule is a "demanding standard" and that any departure from the rule of reason must be based on "demonstrable economic effect rather than . . . upon formalistic line drawing." However, historically, courts have found per se violations even for conduct that may benefit consumers. For example, maximum price restraints may limit the prices consumers pay, yet were at one time viewed as per se illegal. *See, e.g.*, Albrecht v. Herald Co., 390 U.S. 145 (1968) (finding vertical maximum price fixing per se illegal). Courts have moved away from this in more recent cases. *See, e.g.*, Leegin Creative Leather Prods., Inc. v. PSKS, Inc., 551 U.S. 877 (2007) (holding all vertical price restraints are judged by the rule of reason and overturning the former per se treatment from *Dr. Miles Med. Co. v. John D. Park & Sons Co.*, 220 U.S. 373 (1911)); State Oil Co. v. Khan, 522 U.S. 3, 10 (1997) (finding "most antitrust claims are analyzed under a rule of 'reason'" and overturning the holding from *Albrecht v. Herald Co.*, 390 U.S. 145 (1968), that maximum resale price maintenance was per se illegal).

5.   *See, e.g.*, United States v. Socony-Vacuum Oil Co., 310 U.S. 150, 223 (1940).

6.   *See, e.g.*, United States v. Heffernan, 43 F.3d 1144, 1145-46 (7th Cir. 1994); United States v. Reicher, 983 F.2d 168, 170 (10th Cir. 1992); United States v. Koppers Co., 652 F.2d 290, 294 (2d Cir. 1981); United States v. Bensinger Co., 430 F.2d 584, 589 (8th Cir. 1970).

7.   *See, e.g.*, Palmer v. BRG of Ga., Inc., 498 U.S. 46, 49-50 (1990).

8.   *See* NCAA v. Bd. of Regents, 468 U.S. 85, 109-10 (1984).

9.   *See NCAA*, 468 U.S. at 114-15 (finding that many more games would be televised in a free market than under the NCAA plan); Jefferson Parish Hosp. Dist. No. 2 v. Hyde, 466 U.S. 2, 31 (1984) (finding "no evidence that the price, the quality, or the supply or demand . . . has been adversely

concept of market power remains central even when no formal proof of market power is required to establish a technical violation. For two other types of conduct that courts have deemed per se illegal under Sherman Act Section 1—tying[10] and group boycotts[11]—courts have explicitly introduced the concept of market power into their analyses. Courts have justified the inclusion of market power based on the notion that "tying arrangements and group boycotts may have valid business justifications and procompetitive effects."[12]

In *Jefferson Parish Hospital District No. 2 v. Hyde*,[13] the Supreme Court restated the basic concept that tying is per se unlawful, but added that the firm imposing the tie must have market power in the tying product market.[14] As a result, in subsequent cases tying arrangements only have been held per se unlawful if the seller has "appreciable economic power" in the tying product market.[15] "Appreciable economic power" has been defined as the power "to force a purchaser to do something that he would not do in a competitive market."[16]

Group boycotts, which are also known as "concerted refusals to deal," also sometimes involve market power analysis.[17] In cases in which it is not clear that the group boycott has achieved its objective of raising

affected"); SCFC ILC, Inc. v. Visa USA, Inc., 36 F.3d 958, 971-72 (10th Cir. 1994) (finding no evidence that the rule at issue harmed competition); Gen. Leaseways, Inc. v. Nat'l Truck Leasing Ass'n, 744 F.2d 588, 595-96 (7th Cir. 1984) (finding that evidence of higher prices suggests an absence of competition).

10. "A tying arrangement is 'an agreement by a party to sell one product but only on the condition that the buyer also purchases a different (or tied) product, or at least agrees that he will not purchase that product from any other supplier.'" Eastman Kodak Co. v. Image Tech. Servs., 504 U.S. 451, 461-62 (1992) (citing N. Pac. Ry. Co. v. United States, 356 U.S. 1, 5-6 (1958)).

11. Group boycotts (also known as concerted refusals to deal) involve agreements not to purchase or sell particular products or services. *See, e.g.,* Klor's, Inc. v. Broadway-Hale Stores, 359 U.S. 207, 212-14 (1959).

12. *NCAA,* 468 U.S. at 104 n.26; *see* 1 ABA SECTION OF ANTITRUST LAW, ANTITRUST LAW DEVELOPMENTS 55 (6th ed. 2007).

13. 466 U.S. 2 (1984).

14. *Id.* at 16-18.

15. *See, e.g., Eastman Kodak,* 504 U.S. at 460-62.

16. *Jefferson Parish,* 466 U.S. at 14.

17. *See, e.g.,* Northwest Wholesale Stationers v. Pac. Stationery & Printing Co., 472 U.S. 284, 296-97 (1985).

prices, courts have often required the plaintiffs to define a market and measure the defendants' combined market power before applying a per se standard.[18]

2. The Role of Market Power in Rule of Reason Cases

The majority of Sherman Act Section 1 cases are analyzed under the rule of reason, which requires the factfinder to determine "whether the restraint imposed is such as merely regulates and perhaps thereby promotes competition or whether it is such as may suppress or even destroy competition."[19] In such cases, the plaintiff must generally provide some evidence of market power. Although the amount of market power required under Section 1 is subject to different definitions in various courts of appeal, in general, the plaintiff must show that the defendants have sufficient market power to adversely affect competition in the relevant market.[20] However, the Supreme Court has made clear that market power under Section 1 need not rise to the level of monopoly power under Sherman Act Section 2.[21]

In some cases, courts have applied a hybrid between a full rule of reason analysis and the per se rule called a "quick look" or "truncated rule of reason."[22] This quick look abbreviates the analysis of conduct for which per se condemnation is inappropriate but for which an elaborate industry analysis is not required. In these cases, "[b]ecause competitive

---

18. *See id.* at 296 ("Unless the cooperative possesses market power or exclusive access to an element essential to effective competition, the conclusion that expulsion is virtually always likely to have an anticompetitive effect is not warranted.").
19. Bd. of Trade v. United States, 246 U.S. 231, 238 (1918).
20. *See, e.g.*, Levine v. Cent. Fla. Med. Affiliates, 72 F.3d 1538, 1555 (11th Cir. 1996); K.M.B. Warehouse Distribs. v. Walker Mfg. Co., 61 F.3d 123, 130 (2d Cir. 1995).
21. Eastman Kodak Co. v. Image Tech. Servs., 504 U.S. 451, 481 (1992) ("Monopoly power under § 2 requires, of course, something greater than market power under § 1."); *see also* Reazin v. Blue Cross & Blue Shield of Kan., Inc., 899 F.2d 951, 967 (10th Cir. 1990) ("Market and monopoly power only differ in degree—monopoly power is commonly thought of as 'substantial' market power.").
22. The use of the quick look has been rare. As the Ninth Circuit has pointed out, in the absence of a naked restraint, full rule of reason analysis generally applies. Am. Ad Mgmt., Inc. v. GTE Corp., 92 F.3d 781, 789-90 (9th Cir. 1996).

harm is presumed, the defendant must promulgate 'some competitive justification' for the restraint . . . ."[23] In cases involving a quick look analysis, the Supreme Court has established the plaintiff does not have to undertake a complete analysis of the market to establish market power, but may satisfy its burden of proof through direct evidence of anticompetitive effects. Specifically, in *FTC v. Indiana Federation of Dentists*,[24] the Court explained:

> Since the purpose of the inquiries into market definition and market power is to determine whether an arrangement has the potential for genuine adverse effects on competition, "proof of actual detrimental effect, such as a reduction in output," can obviate the need for an inquiry into market power, which is but a "surrogate for detrimental effect."[25]

Although some courts have applied *Indiana Federation of Dentists*,[26] some courts of appeals (including the Seventh and Tenth Circuits) continue to require proof of market power as a "filter" for all rule of reason cases.[27] Similarly, the Federal Trade Commission (FTC) and Antitrust Division of the U.S. Department of Justice (DOJ) (collectively, the "agencies") may use a market power filter to create a "safe harbor"

---

23. United States v. Brown Univ., 5 F.3d 658, 669 (3d Cir. 1993) (citing NCAA v. Bd. of Regents, 468 U.S. 85, 110 (1984)).

24. 476 U.S. 447 (1986).

25. *Id.* at 460-61 (1986)   (quoting VII PHILLIP AREEDA, ANTITRUST LAW ¶ 1511, at 429 (1986)).

26. *Eastman Kodak*, 504 U.S. at 477 ("It is clearly reasonable to infer that Kodak has market power to raise prices and drive out competition in the aftermarkets, since respondents offer direct evidence that Kodak did so."); *see also* Schering-Plough Corp. v. FTC, 402 F.3d 1056, 1065 n.13 (11th Cir. 2005); Todd v. Exxon Corp., 275 F.3d 191, 206 (2d Cir. 2001) ("If a plaintiff can show that a defendant's conduct exerted an actual adverse effect on competition . . . this arguably is more direct evidence of market power than calculations of elusive market share figures.").

27. *See, e.g.*, Menasha Corp. v. News Am. Mktg. In-Store, 354 F.3d 661, 663 (7th Cir. 2004) ("The first requirement in every suit based on the Rule of Reason is market power, without which the practice cannot cause those injuries (lower output and the associated welfare losses) that matter under the federal antitrust laws."); SCFC ILC, Inc. v. Visa USA, Inc., 36 F.3d 958, 965 (10th Cir. 1994) ("Proof of market power, then, for many courts is a critical first step, or 'screen,' or 'filter,' which is often dispositive of the case.") (internal citations omitted).

for defendants who do not possess dominant shares by presuming that they do not have market power without any further inquiry into market structure or effects.[28]

When a plaintiff cannot show direct evidence of market power, Section 1 requires examination of circumstantial evidence.[29] The analysis starts by defining a relevant product and geographic market, and then turns to an evaluation of the defendants' share of the relevant market.[30] In calculating market shares, aggregating the shares of the conspirators to assess their collective power may be appropriate.[31]

Although courts have not adopted a consistent minimum standard for the market share sufficient to support a finding of market power for purposes of Section 1, de minimis market shares clearly will be insufficient. Many courts have held that market shares less than 30 percent cannot alone support an inference of market power.[32] Courts

---

28. *See, e.g.*, FED. TRADE COMM'N & U.S. DEP'T OF JUSTICE, ANTITRUST GUIDELINES FOR THE LICENSING OF INTELLECTUAL PROPERTY § 4.3 (1995); *see also* FED. TRADE COMM'N & U.S. DEP'T OF JUSTICE, ANTITRUST GUIDELINES FOR COLLABORATIONS AMONG COMPETITORS § 4 (2000); FED. TRADE COMM'N & U.S. DEP'T OF JUSTICE, STATEMENTS OF ANTITRUST ENFORCEMENT POLICY IN HEALTH CARE 5 (1996).

29. *See, e.g.*, Flegel v. Christian Hosp., 4 F.3d 682, 688-91 (8th Cir. 1993) (analyzing circumstantial evidence of market power after finding insufficient direct evidence).

30. *See, e.g.*, Times-Picayune Publ'g v. United States, 345 U.S. 594, 611-13 (1953).

31. *See* Wilk v. Am. Med. Ass'n, 895 F.2d 352, 360 (7th Cir. 1990) (finding district court appropriately held that market share of association consists of combined shares of members). See *infra* ch. V for a discussion of concentration analyses that are used by economists to aggregate market shares. In some cases, considering both concentration statistics and individual firm market shares may be helpful, since both provide insight into market structure.

32. *See, e.g.*, Capital Imaging Assocs. v. Mohawk Valley Med. Assocs., 996 F.2d 537, 547 (2d Cir. 1993) (market shares ranging from 1.15 percent to 6.75 percent are insufficient to survive summary judgment); Virtual Maint. v. Prime Computer, 11 F.3d 660, 664 (6th Cir. 1993) (11 percent share insufficient as a matter of law to support inference of market power); Valley Liquors v. Renfield Imps., 822 F.2d 656, 667 (7th Cir. 1987) ("Without a showing of special market conditions or other compelling evidence of market power, the lowest possible share legally sufficient to sustain a finding of monopolization [or substantial market power] is between 17% and 25%.").

recognize that high market shares by themselves do not mean that the firms involved in the concerted activity have market power and, accordingly, they will consider multiple factors pertaining to the structure of the market at issue.[33]

B. Market Power Under Section 2 of the Sherman Act

Sherman Act Section 2[34] makes it illegal to monopolize, attempt to monopolize, or combine or conspire to monopolize.[35] Thus, Section 2 captures both unilateral conduct (monopolization and attempted monopolization) and collusive behavior (joint agreements that create monopoly power and incipient conspiracies to obtain monopoly power).

Although antitrust law does not prevent firms from obtaining market power through business acumen, skill, diligence, or foresight, it does target exclusionary activities that allow firms to obtain or enhance market power.[36] As a result, antitrust law attempts to undertake a certain amount of sorting of procompetitive "sheep" from predatory "wolves."

Courts have applied Section 2 to a wide range of exclusionary conduct, including refusals to deal, exclusive dealing, tying, predatory pricing, and nonprice predation. In each case, economic principles, including analyses of monopoly power, can be used to help distinguish procompetitive activities from exclusionary ones.

Monopoly power is an essential element of any violation of Sherman Act Section 2.[37] The requisite finding of "monopoly" power under

---

33. *See, e.g.*, K.M.B. Warehouse Distribs. v. Walker Mfg. Co., 61 F.3d 123, 128-30 (2d Cir. 1995) ("[A] showing of market power . . . is not sufficient. There must be other grounds to believe that the defendant's behavior will harm competition market-wide, such as the inherent anti-competitive nature of defendant's behavior or the structure of the interbrand market.").

34. 15 U.S.C. § 2.

35. "Every person who shall monopolize, or attempt to monopolize, or combine or conspire with any other person or persons, to monopolize any part of the trade or commerce among the several States, or with foreign nations, shall be deemed guilty of a felony. . . ." *Id.*

36. *See* United States v. Grinnell Corp., 384 U.S. 563, 570-71 (1966).

37. *See* Am. Tobacco v. United States, 328 U.S. 781, 811 (1946) ("[T]he material consideration in determining whether a monopoly exists is . . . that power exists to raise prices or to exclude competition when it is desired to do so.").

Section 2 requires "something greater" than a finding of market power under Section 1.[38]

The Supreme Court has defined monopoly power as the "power to control prices or exclude competition."[39] A plaintiff can show monopoly power through both direct and circumstantial evidence.

1. Direct Evidence of Monopoly Power

A Section 2 plaintiff can prove monopoly power by proffering direct evidence of the defendant's ability to control price or to exclude competition.[40] Consistent with this approach, courts also have relied on evidence of the defendant's actual *inability* to control prices or to exclude competition to reject a claim that the defendant possesses market power.[41] Some courts considering direct evidence of monopoly power

---

38. *See* Eastman Kodak Co. v. Image Tech. Servs., 504 U.S. 451, 481 (1992).
39. United States v. E.I. du Pont de Nemours & Co., 351 U.S. 377, 391 (1956); s*ee also Eastman Kodak,* 504 U.S. at 481; *Grinnell,* 384 U.S. at 571; MCI v. AT&T, 708 F.2d 1081, 1106 (7th Cir. 1983) ("According to the Supreme Court, monopoly power may be defined as 'the power to control prices or exclude competition' in a relevant market.").
40. *See* U.S. Football League v. NFL, 842 F.2d 1335, 1362 (2d Cir. 1988 (explaining that "[a]bsent market share data, definite evidence of monopoly power is needed"); Moore v. Jas. H. Matthews & Co., 550 F.2d 1207, 1219 (9th Cir. 1977) ("Even in the absence of empirical proof of market shares (usually the best indicator of monopoly power), the requisite power also can be demonstrated by evidence of the exercise of actual control over prices or exclusion of competitors."). *Cf.* Ball Mem'l Hosp. v. Mut. Hosp. Ins., 784 F.2d 1325, 1338 (7th Cir. 1986) ("We assume without deciding that a court sometimes may infer market power from a sufficiently clear demonstration that a firm believes that it possesses [market] power."). The role of intent in monopolization cases is controversial, but some courts have suggested that intent evidence could shed light on the monopoly power question by indicating whether the defendant believed its conduct would enable it to acquire or maintain monopoly power. *See, e.g.,* Aspen Skiing Co. v. Aspen Highlands Skiing Corp., 472 U.S. 585, 602 (1985).
41. *See* United States v. Syufy Enters., 903 F.2d 659, 664 n.6 (9th Cir. 1990) (inference of market power can be rebutted by evidence of defendant's inability to control prices or to exclude competitors); Richter Concrete Corp. v. Hilltop Concrete Corp., 691 F.2d 818, 823-26 (8th Cir. 1982).

have required "unambiguous evidence" that the defendant has the power to control price or to exclude competition.[42]

2. Circumstantial Evidence of Monopoly Power

The most common method by which a plaintiff may prove monopoly power is to offer circumstantial evidence pertaining to market structure.[43] To demonstrate monopoly power through such indirect proof, "a plaintiff must (1) define the relevant market, (2) show that the defendant controls a dominant share of that market, and (3) show that there are significant barriers to entry and show that existing competitors lack the capacity to increase their output in the short run."[44] A court may infer monopoly power from the existence of a large market share. However, additional market factors may be relevant to the inference of monopoly power. Firms with large market shares may not have market power if entry or expansion by other firms is easy, because any effort to increase price will be unsuccessful and met by increased competition.[45]

In practice, courts continue to use market share as a principal proxy both for measuring monopoly power in a monopolization case, and for determining the defendant's probability of acquiring monopoly power in an attempted monopolization case.[46] Courts have not yet identified a

---

42. *See, e.g., U.S. Football League*, 842 F.2d at 1362 (upholding an instruction that a jury find "unambiguous evidence" of defendants' market power).

43. *See MCI*, 708 F.2d at 1106-07 ("In many cases . . . courts have eschewed examination of the ostensible monopolist's actual degree of control over prices or competition, and have relied solely on statistical data concerning the accused firm's share of the market.").

44. *See* Rebel Oil Co. v. Atl. Richfield Co., 51 F.3d 1421, 1434 (9th Cir. 1995).

45. *See infra* ch. VII.

46. *See* U.S. Anchor Mfg. v. Rule Indus., 7 F.3d 986, 999 (11th Cir. 1993); *see also* Spectrum Sports v. McQuillan, 506 U.S. 447, 455-56 (1993) (dangerous probability element of attempted monopolization requires inquiry into relevant markets and defendant's power in that market); Eastman Kodak Co. v. Image Tech. Servs., 504 U.S. 451, 481-82 (1992) (evidence of defendant's high market shares was sufficient to show a genuine issue of material fact and to survive summary judgment); United States v. Grinnell Corp., 384 U.S. 563, 571 (1966) ("The existence of [monopoly] power ordinarily may be inferred from the predominant share of the market."); Del. & Hudson Ry. Co. v. Consol. Rail Corp., 902 F.2d

precise level at which monopoly power will be inferred.[47] In *United States v. E.I. du Pont de Nemours & Co.*,[48] the Supreme Court unanimously stated that control of 75 percent of a relevant market containing cellophane wrapping material "may be assumed" to constitute monopoly power, had the market been so defined.[49] In subsequent decisions, the Court has relied on shares in excess of 75 percent to support a finding that the defendant had the power to control price or to exclude competition.[50] In the lower courts, proof of market share in excess of 70 percent in a well-defined market often has been sufficient to support a finding of monopoly power.[51] Conversely, at market shares below 30 percent, courts generally conclude that monopoly power does not exist or, in the case of an attempted monopolization claim, that there is not a dangerous probability of monopolization.[52] In cases in which a

---

174, 179 (2d Cir. 1990) ("While market share is not the sole factor in the determination of market power, it is a highly significant one."). Additional measures of market power are discussed, *infra*, ch. V.C.

47.   In fact, the Supreme Court has recognized that exclusive focus on market share percentages can produce a distorted picture of market power because "[t]he relative effect of percentage command of a market varies with the setting in which that factor is placed." United States v. Columbia Steel Co., 334 U.S. 495, 527-28 (1948).

48.   351 U.S. 377 (1956).

49.   *Id.* at 379, 391.

50.   *See, e.g., Grinnell*, 384 U.S. at 571 (87 percent share deemed sufficient); Int'l Boxing Club v. United States, 358 U.S. 242, 249 (1959) (93 percent share deemed sufficient to prove monopoly power); *Eastman Kodak,* 504 U.S. at 481 (80 percent to 95 percent share sufficient to survive summary judgment under the "more stringent monopoly standard of § 2").

51.   *See* MCI v. AT&T, 708 F.2d 1081, 1107 (7th Cir. 1983) ("Where that data reveals a market share of more than seventy to eighty percent, the courts have inferred the existence of monopoly power."); Weiss v. York Hosp., 745 F.2d 786, 827 (3d Cir. 1984) (market share in excess of 80 percent confers monopoly power); Greyhound Computer Corp. v. IBM, 559 F.2d 488, 496-97 (9th Cir. 1977) (market share in the range of 65 percent to 83 percent sufficient to confer monopoly power); Pac. Coast Agric. Exp. Ass'n v. Sunkist Growers, Inc., 526 F.2d 1196, 1204 (9th Cir. 1975) (market share in the range of 45 percent to 75 percent sufficient to confer monopoly power based, in part, on presence of other facts supporting finding, even though recognizing that "[s]ome past decisions have required larger percentages").

52.   *See, e.g.,* Dimmitt Agri Indus. v. CPC Int'l, 679 F.2d 516, 529-31 (5th Cir. 1982) (market shares in the range of 16 percent to 25 percent were

defendant's market share is between 40 percent and 70 percent, courts are less willing to infer monopoly power absent some other evidence of power.[53]

In addition to market share, in determining whether an inference of monopoly power from market shares is appropriate, courts regularly consider the relative size and strength of the competition, the stability of market shares over time, a firm's ability to sustain supracompetitive profits, and the presence and degree of regulatory or other barriers to entry or expansion.[54] Monopoly power also may be evidenced by a

---

insufficient to confer monopoly power "at least absent other compelling structural evidence"). For attempted monopolization, market shares in excess of 30 percent have been found to be sufficient in combination with other evidence from the market supporting the dangerous probability of monopoly power. *See* Rebel Oil v. Atl. Richfield Co., 51 F.3d 1421, 1438 (9th Cir. 1995) (holding 44 percent share sufficient in attempted monopolization case).

53.   *Compare* PepsiCo Inc. v. Coca-Cola Co., 315 F.3d 101, 108-09 (2d Cir. 2002) (absent other evidence, a 64 percent market share is insufficient to infer market power), *and* Hunt-Wesson Foods v. Ragu Foods, 627 F.2d 919, 924-25 (9th Cir. 1980) (reversing ruling that a 65 percent market share was sufficient to prove market power), *with Sunkist Growers,* 526 F.2d at 1204 (upholding actual monopolization claim for shares ranging from 45 percent to 70 percent when there were numerous other factors signaling monopoly power).

54.   *See, e.g.,* United States v. Columbia Steel, 334 U.S. 495, 527 (1948) (considering "the strength of the remaining competition, whether the action springs from business requirements or purpose to monopolize, the probable development of the industry, consumer demands, and other characteristics"). Declining shares are relevant to an assessment of the defendant's market strength. *See* Richter Concrete Corp. v. Hilltop Concrete Corp., 691 F.2d 818, 826 (8th Cir. 1982) (declining share from 40 percent to 30 percent insufficient to show monopoly power). Some courts have suggested that the presence of supracompetitive profits may support a finding that the defendant has the ability to control price without attracting entry. *See In re* IBM Peripheral EDP Devices Antitrust Litig., 481 F. Supp. 965, 981 (N.D. Cal. 1979), *aff'd sub nom.* Transamerica Computer Co. v. IBM, 698 F.2d 1377 (9th Cir. 1983). However, other courts and commentators have rejected attempts to infer monopoly power from profits. *See, e.g.,* Blue Cross & Blue Shield of United of Wis. v. Marshfield Clinic, 65 F.3d 1406, 1412 (7th Cir. 1995). When considering a regulated defendant, inferences of monopoly power from high market shares are drawn cautiously. *See* Metro Mobile CTS,

firm's ability to maintain its market share despite an inferior product or service.[55]

Courts regularly consider barriers to entry and expansion as integral components of monopoly power analysis.[56] Examples of such barriers include licensing or permitting requirements,[57] entrenched buyer

---

Inc. v. NewVector Commc'ns, 892 F.2d 62, 63 (9th Cir. 1989) (holding that in cases in which a predominant market share is the result of regulation, the court should focus directly on the regulated firm's ability to control prices or to exclude competition). *Compare* Mid-Texas Commc'ns Sys. v. AT&T, 615 F.2d 1372, 1386-87 (5th Cir. 1980) (regulatory control may preclude a finding of monopoly power), *with* Hartigan v. Panhandle E. Pipe Line Co., 730 F. Supp. 826, 905 (C.D. Ill. 1990) (finding regulations are not a barrier to liability when the conduct at issue is left to the monopolists' discretion or the regulating agency is not able to respond to the defendant's abuses "promptly or effectively"), *aff'd sub nom.* Burris v. Panhandle E. Pipe Line Co., 935 F.2d 1469 (7th Cir. 1991).

55. *See* Byars v. Bluff City News Co., 609 F.2d 843, 853 & n.26 (6th Cir. 1979) (noting that maintenance of a 90 percent share, despite evidence of "inferior service at greater cost," would be "strong support" for a finding of monopoly power).

56. *See, e.g.*, Oahu Gas Serv. v. Pac. Res., 838 F.2d 360, 366 (9th Cir. 1988) (noting that a firm can only maintain a high market share if the market has "significant and continuing" entry barriers); *see also Rebel Oil,* 51 F.3d at 1438 n.10 (noting that the tell-tale factors of market power include market share, entry barriers, and the inability of existing competitors to expand output); Ball Mem'l Hosp. v. Mut. Hosp. Ins., 784 F.2d 1325, 1335 (7th Cir. 1986) ("[T]he lower the barriers to entry, and the shorter the lags of new entry, the less power existing firms have."). Courts have defined barriers to entry using differing formulations:

> Barriers to entry have been defined as either a cost that would have to be borne by an entrant that was not and is not borne by the incumbent or any condition that is likely to inhibit other firms from entering the market on a substantial scale in response to an increase in the incumbent's prices.

ABA Section of Antitrust Law, *supra* note 12, at 233 (collecting cases); *see infra* ch. VII.

57. *See Rebel Oil,* 51 F.3d at 1439.

preferences for established brands,[58] limited demand for a particular product or service,[59] possession of patents or other intellectual property,[60] economies of scale,[61] and the need for large capital outlays or capital market evaluations that impose higher capital costs on new entrants.[62] In evaluating entry barriers, courts also consider frequency and success of competitors who have sought to enter the market.[63]

C. Market Power Under the Robinson-Patman Act

The Robinson-Patman Act, which was passed as an amendment to the Clayton Act in 1936, prohibits discriminating in price to different purchasers of the same commodity when the effect would be to lessen competition or to create a monopoly.[64] Historically, analysis of market

---

58.   See S. Pac. Commc'ns v. AT&T, 740 F.2d 980, 1001-02 (D.C. Cir. 1984) (referring to "the need to overcome brand preference established by [defendants]" as a barrier to entry).

59.   See Union Leader Corp. v. Newspapers of New Eng., 284 F.2d 582, 583-84 (1st Cir. 1960) ("The court found that by nature of circumstances . . . [the relevant geographic market] cannot support two good daily newspapers under present-day conditions.").

60.   Image Tech. Servs. v. Eastman Kodak Co., 125 F.3d 1195, 1208 (9th Cir. 1997) (finding barriers to entry where defendant had 220 patents and controlled its designs and tools); United States v. United Shoe Mach., 110 F. Supp. 295, 339, 344 (D. Mass. 1953) (listing the "capacity to invent around patents" as a requirement for entry).

61.   See *Rebel Oil*, 51 F.3d at 1439 (finding that the minimum scale needed for pipeline shipments constituted barrier to entry).

62.   See *S. Pac. Commc'ns*, 740 F.2d at 1001-02 (finding barriers to entry resulting from the need for large capital outlays); see also In re Cal. Dental Ass'n, 121 F.T.C. 190 (1996), aff'd sub nom. Cal. Dental Ass'n v. FTC, 128 F.3d 720, 730 (9th Cir. 1997), rev'd on other grounds, 526 U.S. 756 (1999) (finding high barriers to entry where cost of dental school education ranged from $50,000 to $100,00, cost of opening a dental practice ranged from $75,000 to $100,000, and thereafter it took a new dentist 18 months to two years to become profitable); see also Avery Dennison Corp. v. ACCO Brands, No. 99-1877, 2000 WL 986995, at *14 (C.D. Cal. 2000).

63.   See, e.g., Davis v. S. Bell Tel. & Tel. Co., No. 89-2839, 1994 WL 912242, at *15 (S.D. Fla. 1994) ("[T]he fact that few competitors have actually entered the market indicates that there must be some barrier to entry.").

64.   15 U.S.C. §§ 13, *et seq.*

power has not played a significant role in Robinson-Patman Act cases because courts have not required plaintiffs to prove that the alleged discriminatory pricing adversely affected competition.[65] Instead, courts have tended to infer anticompetitive effect from a showing of injury to a disfavored buyer.[66] This approach, which is rooted in the legislative history of the Robinson-Patman Act,[67] largely relieved plaintiffs of the need to engage in detailed economic analyses to demonstrate the defendant's market power, as is typical in other areas of antitrust law.[68]

In modern cases, however, market power has played an increasingly important role in some Robinson-Patman Act analyses. The Supreme Court's decision in *Brooke Group v. Brown & Williamson Tobacco*[69] moved Robinson-Patman Act law closer to Sherman Act Section 2 precedent.[70] *Brooke Group* expressly incorporated market power analysis into "primary line" cases[71]—*e.g.*, those cases based on claims that discriminatory pricing by one seller has anticompetitive effects on another seller of the same product. Indeed, to a significant extent, the Court's holding appears to have incorporated the law of predatory pricing under the Sherman Act wholesale into primary line Robinson-

---

65. *See* Hugh C. Hansen, *Robinson-Patman Law: A Review and Analysis*, 51 FORDHAM L. REV. 1113, 1133-38 (1983).

66. *See* FTC v. Morton Salt Co., 334 U.S. 37, 46-47 (1948) (explaining that the injury to competition was "obvious" when certain merchants had to pay "substantially more for their goods than their competitors had to pay").

67. *See* Boise Cascade Corp. v. FTC, 837 F.2d 1127, 1153-58 (D.C. Cir. 1988) (Mikva, J., dissenting) (explaining that aspects of the Act's legislative history "set Robinson-Patman apart from the rest of antitrust law" such that an "inherent tension" exists between them).

68. *Cf.* Hansen, *supra* note 65, at 1135 (noting that "the whole issue of competitive injury [in Robinson-Patman Act section 2(a) cases] has become something of a semantic exercise").

69. 509 U.S. 209 (1993).

70. *See id.* at 220 ("Thus, 'the Robinson-Patman Act should be construed consistently with broader policies of the antitrust laws.'") (citing Great Atl. & Pac. Tea Co. v. FTC, 440 U.S. 69, 80 n.13 (1979)).

71. *See id.* at 220, 224-27 (incorporating consideration of "the structure and conditions of the relevant market" into the analysis of the probability of recoupment). The Supreme Court previously had made similar but less explicit statements. *See* Great Atl. & Pac. Tea Co. v. FTC, 440 U.S. 69, 80 n.13 (1979); Automatic Canteen Co. v. FTC, 346 U.S. 61, 63, 74 (1953).

Patman Act jurisprudence.[72] Although recognizing differences between the Robinson-Patman Act and Sherman Act Section 2, the Court explained that "the essence of the claim under either statute is the same . . . ."[73] In *Brooke Group*, the Court appeared to support the notion that the Robinson-Patman Act should be interpreted in a manner that promotes consumer welfare and allocative efficiency.[74]

"Secondary line" Robinson-Patman Act cases, which focus on the effects of price discrimination between the favored and disfavored customers of the discriminating seller, have not experienced a similar shift. In those cases, Robinson-Patman Act plaintiffs continue to benefit from historical inferences relieving them of the need to demonstrate the defendant's market power.[75] For example, the Supreme Court has noted that, in a Robinson-Patman Act secondary line case, "a permissible inference of competitive injury may arise from evidence that a favored competitor received a significant price reduction over a substantial period of time."[76]

D. Market Power Under Section 7 of the Clayton Act

Clayton Act Section 7[77] addresses business combinations, including mergers and acquisitions, that have the potential to create or enhance market power or to facilitate its exercise, outlawing the acquisition of assets or stock that may "substantially . . . lessen competition, or . . . tend

---

72.   *See Brooke Group,* 509 U.S. at 222.
73.   *Id.*
74.   *See id.* at 223-27, 254.
75.   *See* FTC v. Morton Salt, 334 U.S. 37, 46-47 (1948); Coastal Fuels v. Caribbean Petroleum Corp., 79 F.3d 182 (1st Cir. 1996) (affirming verdict of secondary line price discrimination, while reversing monopolization verdict on the grounds that plaintiff failed to show monopoly power by defendant). However, this does not mean that market power analysis plays no role in secondary line cases. In particular, even before *Brooke Group*, Robinson-Patman Act defendants were able to rebut the inference of injury to competition. Falls City Indus., Inc. v. Vanco Beverage, 460 U.S. 428, 451-52 (1983) (vacating judgment against the defendant to determine on remand whether defendant could rebut inference of injury by demonstrating that conduct was a "well-tailored response to the competitive circumstances").
76.   Volvo Trucks N. Am. v. Reeder-Simco GMC, Inc., 546 U.S. 164, 177 (2006)
77.   15 U.S.C. § 18.

to create a monopoly."[78] The central question in most merger cases is "whether the effect of the merger 'may be substantially to lessen competition' 'in any line of commerce in any section of the country.'"[79] At the heart of this analysis is a determination of whether the merger creates market power or entrenches existing market power. Two sources of market power are distinguished in modern merger analyses: coordinated effects and unilateral effects.[80] Coordinated effects measure the ability of competitors within a market to maintain supracompetitive prices by cooperating with one another, while unilateral effects refer to a single firm's ability to maintain above-market prices regardless of the behavior of competitors.

1. *Market Shares and Market Structural Characteristics*

As in the market power inquiry underlying Sherman Act rule of reason cases, the analysis of market power in merger cases starts with defining the relevant market and calculating the concentration in that market.[81] At the heart of this structural analysis is the assumption that market concentration affects the likelihood that one firm, or a small group of firms, could successfully exercise market power.[82] A significant increase in a firm's market share in a concentrated market is presumed to reduce competition because it gives a firm unilateral market power.[83] In addition, a reduction in the number of competitors in a market may make it easier for the remaining competitors to coordinate pricing and other terms of sale, and consequently more likely that they will do so.[84] The agencies also have focused increasingly upon the degree to which the

---

78.   *Id.*
79.   United States v. Philadelphia Nat'l Bank, 374 U.S. 321, 355 (1963); *see* Brown Shoe Co. v. United States, 370 U.S. 294 (1962).
80.   U.S. DEP'T OF JUSTICE & FED. TRADE COMM'N, HORIZONTAL MERGER GUIDELINES § 1 (2010), *available at* http://www.justice.gov/atr/public/guidelines/hmg-2010.html [hereinafter MERGER GUIDELINES].
81.   *Id.* § 4. See *infra* Chs. IV and V for discussion of market definition and the measurement of market shares.
82.   *Id.* § 5.3.
83.   *Id.* § 2.1.3.
84.   *See* Hosp. Corp. v. FTC, 807 F.2d 1381, 1387 (7th Cir. 1986); FTC v. PPG Indus., 798 F.2d 1500, 1503 (D.C. Cir. 1986); MERGER GUIDELINES, *supra* note 80, § 1.

products or services of the two merging firms compete, and whether the acquiring firm will be able to raise prices unilaterally after the merger.[85]

Common devices for assessing market power include single-firm market shares and concentration statistics. Single-firm market shares help courts in assessing a firm's unilateral market power, while concentration statistics are used to analyze likely collusive effects of a proposed merger.[86] Large market shares (and associated concentration statistics) are "a convenient proxy for appraising the danger of monopoly power resulting from a horizontal merger."[87] Courts consistently have held that the government can establish a prima facie Clayton Act Section 7 violation through market share statistics that demonstrate a significantly more concentrated postmerger market.[88]

Courts recognize, however, that "market shares, while undeniably important, do not tell the whole story. The law is geared to economics, not mathematics."[89] Therefore, thorough market analysis demands an examination of other economic factors that may offset a firm's market power despite its share of the relevant market.[90]

---

85. *See* Jonathan B. Baker, *Product Differentiation Through Space and Time: Some Antitrust Policy Issues*, 42 ANTITRUST BULL. 177 (1997); Carl Shapiro, *Mergers with Differentiated Products*, ANTITRUST, Spring 1996, at 23.

86. *See infra* ch. V.

87. United States v. Waste Mgmt., 743 F.2d 976, 981 (2d Cir. 1984).

88. United States v. Citizens & S. Nat'l Bank, 422 U.S. 86, 120 (1975); FTC v. H.J. Heinz Co., 246 F.3d 708, 716 (D.C. Cir. 2001).

89. United States v. Tidewater Marine Serv., 284 F. Supp. 324, 341 (E.D. La. 1968).

90. *See* United States v. Marine Bancorp., 418 U.S. 602 (1974) (noting that "it is imperative" for a court to consider "competitive characteristics" of an industry rather than just market concentration); United States v. Gen. Dynamics Corp., 415 U.S. 486, 498 (1974) (recognizing that while market share is an important indicator of a firm's future competitive strength, other factors may discount its significance); Brown Shoe Co. v. United States, 370 U.S. 294, 344 (1962) (explaining that "other factors [must] be considered in evaluating the probable effects of a merger in the relevant market"); FTC v. Nat'l Tea Co., 603 F.2d 694, 700 (8th Cir. 1979) (finding it is appropriate to scrutinize the "probable future" of the market); *see also* MERGER GUIDELINES, *supra* note 80, § 4 ("Evidence of competitive effects can inform market definition, just as market definition can be informative regarding competitive effects."). For a discussion of other economic factors considered by courts, see, *infra*, ch. V.C.

The Supreme Court has considered other economic factors in analyses of market power and likely postmerger effects. For example, in determining the extent of a merging firm's market power, the Supreme Court has considered an industry's trends toward consolidation,[91] the degree of concentration in the industry,[92] the history of acquisitions of the merging firms,[93] barriers to entry in the industry,[94] and the strategic position of customers.[95] Once a plaintiff establishes its prima facie case through market concentration statistics, the burden of proof shifts to the defendant firms to show that the proposed acquisition will not lessen competition significantly.[96] A defendant may rebut the presumption of impermissible market power by presenting evidence sufficient to show "that the prima facie case inaccurately predicts the relevant transaction's probable effect on future competition."[97] A variety of factors considered pertinent to the analysis, including the possibility of new entrants in the market, concentration on the buying side of the market, and the "failing firm defense," are so well-established in the case law and the *Merger Guidelines* that they are now "hornbook law."[98] Each of these factors is discussed below.

---

91. *See Brown Shoe*, 370 U.S. at 320-21; United States v. Pabst Brewing Co., 384 U.S. 546, 550-53 (1966).

92. *See* United States v. Philadelphia Nat'l Bank, 374 U.S. 321, 363 (1963); *Brown Shoe*, 370 U.S. at 343 ("The market share which companies may control by merging is one of the most important factors to be considered when determining the probable effects of the combination on effective competition in the relevant market.").

93. *See Brown Shoe*, 370 U.S. at 345 n.72 (explaining that a "company's history of expansion through mergers presents a different economic picture than a history of expansion through unilateral growth.").

94. *See Brown Shoe*, 370 U.S. at 322; FTC v. Procter & Gamble Co., 386 U.S. 568, 579 (1967); FTC v. Cardinal Health, 12 F. Supp. 2d 34, 54-61 (D.D.C. 1998); FTC v. Staples, Inc., 970 F. Supp. 1066, 1086-88 (D.D.C. 1997).

95. *See Cardinal Health*, 12 F. Supp. 2d at 47 (explaining that a certain segment of customers would have no postmerger substitutes); FTC v. Owens-Illinois, Inc., 681 F. Supp. 27, 48-49 (D.D.C.) (discussing the ability to identify inelastic customers), *vacated as moot*, 850 F.2d 694 (D.D.C. 1988).

96. *See* United States v. Marine Bancorp., 418 U.S. 602, 631 (1974).

97. United States v. Baker Hughes, Inc., 908 F.2d 981, 991 (D.C. Cir. 1990).

98. *Id.* at 985.

a. Entry

Perhaps the most important mitigating factor is the possibility of market entry or expansion.[99] If entry barriers are low, it is unlikely that market power, whether individually or collectively exercised, will persist for long, because even with a large market share, a firm will be unable to maintain supracompetitive prices. High profits will prompt new firms to enter the market or existing firms to expand. In industries in which entry is easy, a firm can retain its market share only by pricing competitively. The *Merger Guidelines* indicate that entry barriers are low "if entry into the market is so easy that the merged firm and its remaining rivals in the market ... could not profitably raise price or otherwise reduce competition compared to the level that would prevail in the absence of the merger."[100] Should the combined firm attempt to exercise market power by raising prices, entry likely would occur, thereby likely creating new competitors and driving the price down to competitive levels.[101]

b. Buyer Power

The antitrust agencies have also considered the counterbalancing power of customers in market power analysis.[102] Courts recognize the competitive significance of large and sophisticated buyers even in markets with only a few sellers.[103] "Empirical studies have shown that the stronger and more concentrated the buyers' side of the market is, the less is any ability of sellers to elevate their prices."[104] Concentration on the buying side tends to inhibit collusion by sellers because it creates stronger incentives to cheat within the cartel: a single transaction may be able to increase dramatically the profits and sales of the cheating

---

99.   For additional discussion of entry, see *infra* ch. VII.
100. MERGER GUIDELINES, *supra* note 80, § 9.
101. *See* United States v. Waste Mgmt., 743 F.2d 976, 983-84 (2d Cir. 1984).
102. *See* FTC v. Cardinal Health, 12 F. Supp. 2d 34, 42-43 (D.D.C. 1998); FTC v. Owens-Illinois, Inc., 681 F. Supp. 27, 48-49 (D.D.C.), *vacated as moot*, 850 F.2d 694 (D.C. Cir. 1988).
103. *See Cardinal Health*, 12 F. Supp. 2d at 47-48; *see* United States v. Archer-Daniels-Midland Co., 781 F. Supp. 1400, 1422 (S.D. Iowa 1991); *Baker Hughes*, 908 F.2d at 986; FTC v. R.R. Donnelley & Sons Co., No. 90-1619, 1990 WL 193674, at *4 (D.D.C. 1990).
104. *Archer-Daniels Midland*, 781 F. Supp. at 1416; *see also* FTC v. Tenet Health Care Corp., 186 F.3d 1045, 1054 (8th Cir. 1999).

member. [105] This increases the monitoring costs of maintaining supracompetitive prices and discourages coordination among sellers. Sophisticated purchasers who can place large orders, use competitive bidding, and monitor prices are especially well situated to challenge attempts to increase price.[106] In addition, large buyers can sponsor entry into the supplier's market, which further discourages supracompetitive pricing.[107]

c. Consideration of Failing Firms and Failing Divisions

Courts and the antitrust agencies have recognized a so-called failing firm defense.[108] Simply stated, if one of the merging parties would be unlikely to continue as a competitive factor in the market, then the elimination of that firm is unlikely to create or enhance market power or facilitate its exercise beyond that which would have occurred once the firm exited the market on its own.[109] The *Merger Guidelines* recognize the failing firm defense, but impose rigid criteria for its use. A proponent of the defense must show:

> (1) the allegedly failing firm would be unable to meet its financial obligations in the near future; (2) it would not be able to reorganize successfully under Chapter 11 of the Bankruptcy Act; and (3) it has made unsuccessful good-faith efforts to elicit reasonable alternative offers that would keep its tangible and intangible assets in the relevant market and pose a less severe danger to competition than does the proposed merger.[110]

105. *See Owens-Illinois*, 681 F. Supp. at 49; *see also* Hosp. Corp. v. FTC, 807 F.2d 1381, 1391 (7th Cir. 1986); United States v. Country Lake Foods, 754 F. Supp. 669, 679 (D. Minn. 1990).
106. *See Baker Hughes*, 908 F.2d at 986-87 (affirming the district court's finding that consumer sophistication "was likely to promote competition even in a highly concentrated market").
107. *See Cardinal Health*, 12 F. Supp. 2d at 59.
108. *See* United States v. Gen. Dynamics Corp., 415 U.S. 486, 506 (1974); MERGER GUIDELINES, *supra* note 80, § 11.
109. *See* MERGER GUIDELINES, *supra* note 80, § 11.
110. *Id.*

Successful application of the failing firm defense is rare.[111] Similar findings are required for a defense for "failing divisions" within a firm.[112]

In addition to providing an affirmative defense to an otherwise anticompetitive merger, the weakened financial condition of one of the merging entities can be important to market power analysis in two other ways. First, evidence of financial problems can indicate that current "market-share statistics gave an inaccurate account of the acquisitions' probable effects on competition."[113] Second, the evidence bears upon the related proposition that, even accepting market share statistics as the primary index of market power, one must undertake "a further examination of the particular market . . . [to] provide the appropriate setting for judging the probable anticompetitive effects of the merger."[114] Therefore, the financial condition of the parties is relevant in determining whether a merger is likely to result in a substantial lessening of competition.

2. Efficiencies

Finally, a merger that creates or enhances market power might not necessarily lead to anticompetitive effects if the merger generates sufficient cost savings, generally referred to as "efficiencies."[115] The legislative history of Clayton Act Section 7 does not expressly address

---

111. *But see, e.g.*, Statement of Bureau of Competition Dir. Richard Feinstein on the FTC's Closure of Its Investigation of Consummated Hospital Merger in Temple, Texas (Dec. 23, 2009), *available at* http://www.ftc.gov/os/closings/091223scottwhitestmt.pdf.

112. *Id.; see generally* Amanda L. Wait, *Surviving the Shipwreck: A Proposal to Revive the Failing Division Defense*, 45 WM. & MARY L. REV. 429 (2003).

113. United States v. Citizens & S. Nat'l Bank, 422 U.S. 86, 120 (1975); *see also Gen. Dynamics Corp.*, 415 U.S. at 501; United States v. Int'l Harvester, 564 F.2d 769, 773-74 (7th Cir. 1977); FTC v. Great Lakes Chem. Corp., 528 F. Supp. 84, 87-90 (N.D. Ill. 1981).

114. *Gen. Dynamics*, 415 U.S. at 498 (citing Brown Shoe Co. v. United States, 370 U.S. 294, 322 n.38 (1962)); *see Great Lakes Chem.*, 528 F. Supp. at 90.

115. MERGER GUIDELINES, *supra* note 80, § 10; FED. TRADE COMM'N STAFF REPORT, ANTICIPATING THE 21ST CENTURY: COMPETITION POLICY IN THE NEW HIGH-TECH GLOBAL MARKETPLACE ch. 2 (1996), *available at* http://www.ftc.gov/opp/global/report/gc_v1.pdf.

whether efficiencies should be factored into the market power analysis.[116] Nonetheless, the *Merger Guidelines* clearly recognize that a merger might not have anticompetitive effects if significant efficiencies will keep postmerger prices at or below current levels.[117] Efficiencies are most likely to be useful in justifying a merger when the cost savings and increased size permit the combined firm to compete more effectively against an industry leader.[118] Although no court has relied exclusively on efficiency justifications to permit an otherwise anticompetitive merger, efficiency justifications often are credited in merger analysis by agencies.[119]

116. *See* IVA PHILLIP AREEDA & HERBERT HOVENKAMP, ANTITRUST LAW ¶ 970c, at 27 (2009).

117. *See* MERGER GUIDELINES, *supra* note 80, § 10.

118. *See, e.g.*, United States v. Country Lake Foods, 754 F. Supp. 669, 674 (D. Minn. 1990).

119. *See, e.g.*, U.S. Dep't of Justice, Statement of the Department of Justice's Antitrust Division on Its Decision to Close Its Investigation of the Merger of Delta Air Lines Inc. and Northwest Airlines Corporation, Oct. 29, 2008, *available at* http://www.justice/gov/opa/pr/2008/October/08-at-963.html; *see also* MALCOLM B. COATE & ANDREW J. HEIMERT, MERGER EFFICIENCIES AT THE FEDERAL TRADE COMMISSION 1997-2007 (2009).

CHAPTER III

THE ECONOMICS OF MARKET POWER

In antitrust litigation and merger review, the concept of market power is often in dispute. In economic theory, however, the subject is largely well-settled and uncontroversial. Market power disputes in antitrust litigation and merger review generally arise over differences in factual assumptions or over the multiple meanings of the phrase "market power." Thus, understanding both the underlying theory and the variety of commercial settings in which market power is analyzed has value. This Chapter introduces the core economic concepts relating to market power and discusses market power in both familiar and exceptional settings.

A. Core Concepts: Supply, Demand, Marginal Cost, and Price Elasticity

A prerequisite for intelligent reasoning about market power is an understanding of four core concepts of microeconomics: supply, demand, marginal cost, and price elasticity.

In economics, the term "supply" refers to a schedule that depicts the amounts a supplier will offer at various prices: "How much will you supply if the price is $1.50?"; "How much will you supply if the price is $1.75?"; and so forth. Market supply at a given price is the sum across all sellers of the amounts that they would be willing to supply at that price.[1]

---

1.   *See* DENNIS W. CARLTON & JEFFREY M. PERLOFF, MODERN INDUSTRIAL ORGANIZATION 61 (4th ed. 2005).

Figure 1   **A Perfectly-competitive Market**

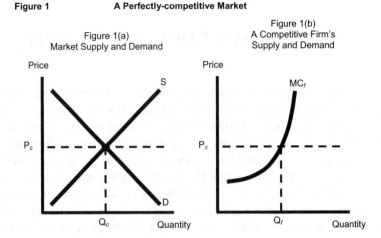

Figure 1(a)
Market Supply and Demand

Figure 1(b)
A Competitive Firm's
Supply and Demand

A supply curve generally slopes upward from left to right (although in principle it can be flat), as shown with curve S in Figure 1(a). Higher quantities are supplied at higher prices. The higher the price an individual supplier can obtain, the more it will supply because it can recover the extra cost of supplying the increased volume.

The term "demand" refers to a schedule that depicts the amounts a consumer would be willing to purchase at various prices. Market demand at a given price is the sum across all consumers of the amounts that they would be willing to purchase at that price.[2] One central idea in economics is the law of demand—the empirical fact that demand generally falls as price rises.[3] For consumer products, diminishing marginal utility can give rise to the law of demand. Viewed from the standpoint of consumers, we expect that as consumers purchase and consume more units of a product, the incremental value of additional consumption of the product diminishes. As this incremental value diminishes, so does willingness to pay.[4] Incorporating these demand conditions into a typical market demand schedule, we associate lower prices with larger quantities demanded. Demand curves therefore slope downwards, as shown with curve D in Figure 1(a).

The equilibrium price in a competitive market is determined by the intersection of the market's demand and supply curves. In Figure 1(a),

---

2.   *See* GEORGE J. STIGLER, THE THEORY OF PRICE 33-4 (4th ed. 1987).
3.   *See id.* at 19-25.
4.   *See id.* at 42-52.

this occurs at the price P$_c$ and the quantity Q$_c$. At the prevailing market price, the quantity supplied by an individual seller will be determined by that seller's marginal cost of production. The seller will supply a quantity such that the market price equals its marginal cost, as shown in Figure 1(b).

Marginal cost refers to the extra cost incurred to produce one additional unit of output. For most production processes, making more units of output becomes increasingly costly at some point because of forces such as the partial exhaustion of capacity (which can often be expanded in the long run), the need to bid for scarce resources, or congestion. Aggregating these effects across sellers in a market, we expect a typical market supply curve to slope upwards, indicating that higher prices are needed to call forth higher levels of output.[5] For simplicity, we often portray supply and demand curves as linear, but reality may be different. The idiosyncrasies of specific industries can be reflected in their demand and supply curves. For example, consider a ski resort that measures output as skiers per day on the mountainside. When the resort is operating well below peak capacity, the cost of serving an extra skier may be small, but at (or close to) maximum capacity, the cost of serving even a few extra skiers may increase significantly with increases in congestion and hazard.

The relative responsiveness of quantities demanded and supplied to changes in price is known as "price elasticity." Price elasticity is a synonym for price sensitivity. The price elasticity of demand is defined as the percentage change in quantity demanded that would arise from a 1 percent change in price.[6] Demand is "inelastic" when this ratio is less than one—i.e., when a 1 percent increase in price reduces the quantity demanded by less than 1 percent. This reflects demand that is relatively insensitive to price. Demand is "elastic" when a 1 percent price increase reduces demand by more than 1 percent—i.e., demand is relatively price sensitive.

---

5. *See* CARLTON & PERLOFF, *supra* note 1, at 61-64. In the long run, the industry-wide marginal cost curve for a manufactured product may be relatively flat if its production does not depend on specialized inputs and if capacity expansion is feasible. For such an industry, short-run marginal cost may nonetheless increase as production nears capacity.
6. *See id.* The price elasticity of demand is often expressed as a positive number even though (given the law of demand) a price increase will normally cause a decrease in demand.

The price elasticity of market demand measures the extent to which market demand responds to changes in the market price. The price elasticity of the demand facing an individual supplier similarly measures the extent to which that supplier-specific demand responds to changes in that supplier's price.

Price elasticities of supply can be similarly calculated for market supply and for supply to an individual purchaser. The price elasticity of demand (or supply) need not be constant at all price levels; it may (but need not) change as prices change.[7] With a linear demand curve, each dollar price increase is met with a specific decrease in the number of units demanded (e.g., a $1 price increase leads to a 10 unit decrease in quantity demanded). Thus, the price elasticity increases as the price increases because at a higher price-lower quantity starting point a given dollar price increase will be a lower percentage increase, while a given unit quantity decrease will be a higher percentage decrease, giving a lower elasticity.

B. The Perfect Competition Model: The Absence of Market Power

The phrase "perfect competition" describes a hypothetical market in which no buyer or seller has market power. In other words, all sellers and all buyers are pure price-takers; none has any influence over the market price. Also, in these hypothetical, perfectly-competitive markets, any seller can bring to the market and sell at the market price as many units as it can produce while, symmetrically, any buyer can purchase its full requirement at the market price. A perfectly-competitive market achieves optimal resource allocation, maximum consumer welfare, and (for producers at the margin) profit no greater than the cost of capital.

The conditions of market structure necessary to obtain this ideal level of market performance include:

(i)   A large number of both buyers and sellers exist, such that each buyer or seller is so small relative to the overall market that no buyer or seller believes that it can individually affect market price by changing the quantity that it buys or sells;

(ii) The relevant product is homogeneous, so any firm's product is a perfect substitute for every other firm's product;

(iii) There are no barriers to entry or exit; and

---

7.   *See* STIGLER, *supra* note 2, at 346-51.

(iv) Market participants have complete market information.[8]

Perfect competition also requires that consumers maximize utility, producers maximize profit, and, importantly, decisions are made independently by all market participants—in other words, there is no collusion. The conditions for perfect competition are rarely, if ever, found in reality and are not intended to be the objective of antitrust laws. Rather, perfect competition acts as a guiding theoretical construct.

A competitive supplier takes the competitive market price as a given because it is not able to affect that price by expanding or contracting its own output. The firm maximizes its profits by producing the quantity at which its marginal cost equals the market price. Thus, the competitive supplier's interest is to produce that quantity, but no more and no less.

Figure 1(b), above, illustrates this relationship: P_c represents the competitive market price, and MC_f is the competitive firm's marginal cost, which in this example depends on the quantity produced. Q_f shows the output level where the firm's marginal cost (MC_f) equals the competitive price (P_c), i.e., Q_f is the firm's profit-maximizing production quantity. At quantities below Q_f, the firm could increase its profits by expanding output because the additional revenue (P_c) that it would receive from the sale of one additional unit of output would exceed the additional cost (MC_f) of supplying that unit. Similarly, at quantities above Q_f, the firm would not receive enough income for the extra unit to justify producing it because MC_f would exceed P_c.

The market supply curve in a perfectly-competitive market is the sum of quantities across all suppliers at each price. If all markets were perfectly competitive, nothing would cost more or less than the extra cost necessary to make it—a resource allocation optimum.

The horizontal line at the competitive price (P_c) can be viewed as the perfectly elastic demand curve facing a competitive supplier. By definition, in a perfectly-competitive market, the sale of any amount by a single firm will be too small to affect the market price. With a perfectly elastic demand curve, the competitive firm will be able to sell any amount it desires at the competitive market price (P_c), but nothing at any higher price.

Some of the earliest and most important findings of experimental economics demonstrate the robustness of the perfect competition model. Economist Vernon Smith's experiments, reported in the early 1960s,

---

8.   *See* JEFFREY M. PERLOFF, MICROECONOMICS 228 (6th ed. 2012).

overturned the widely-held belief that (nearly) perfect competition in the real world required large numbers of buyers and sellers. Smith showed that, in situations involving few traders, each with no direct information of the others' costs or values, outcomes could approximate perfect competition.[9] Later work confirmed Smith's finding that experimental markets can produce competitive outcomes even when very few traders are involved.[10] In other words, so long as collusion among buyers is prohibited, large numbers of buyers and sellers are not necessary to come very close to the price and quantity that the model of perfect competition predicts for homogeneous products.

C. The Pure Monopoly Model: Extreme Market Power

When a single seller supplies a market and there is no real threat of entry, the seller is a monopolist. Monopolists have the ability to charge prices above the competitive level, which they accomplish by limiting their own output and thus the market's output. The monopolist's marginal revenue, not market demand, determines the profit-maximizing price and quantity.[11]

---

9.   *See* Charles A. Holt & Alvin E. Roth, *The Nash Equilibrium: A Perspective*, 101 PNAS (PROCEEDINGS OF THE NAT'L ACAD. OF SCI. OF THE U.S. OF AM.) 3999, 4001 (2004). Smith was a co-winner of the 2002 Nobel Prize in Economics for this work.

10.   *See* Charles R. Plott, *Industrial Organization Theory and Experimental Economics*, 20 J. ECON. LIT. 1485, 1486 (1982) (focusing on market institutions rather than numbers of firms). Auction markets are a special case. Extensive literature in auction theory, experimentation, and empirical observation has developed around the question of how market design (i.e., the rules and institutions governing auctions) affects outcomes. For additional discussion of auction markets, see several articles on these subjects in THE NEW PALGRAVE DICTIONARY OF ECONOMICS, *available at* www.dictionaryofeconomics.com.

11.   *See* CARLTON & PERLOFF, *supra* note 1, at 89-93.

Figure 2   **A Monopolist's Profit Maximization**

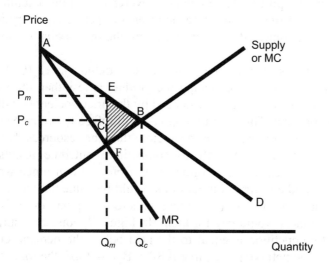

With only a single seller in a market, the demand curve faced by the seller is the market demand curve, and the marginal cost curve of the seller is the market marginal cost curve. Figure 2 illustrates the standard economic model of profit maximization by a monopolist. As in a perfectly-competitive market, the demand curve slopes downward and is shown as curve D. Marginal revenue, or the incremental revenue the monopolist will earn if it sells one more unit, is shown as curve MR. Because the firm must reduce its price on all units in order to sell an additional unit, the marginal revenue is lower than the price at which the incremental unit is sold. Accordingly, the marginal revenue (MR) curve lies below the demand (D) curve.[12]

Under these conditions, the difference between a monopoly outcome and a perfectly-competitive market outcome (with the same industry marginal cost curve as the monopolist) is clear. As shown in Figure 2, the competitive market outcome is the point where price equals the marginal cost of production, leading to quantity Q_c and price P_c. The monopoly outcome, however, has a higher price and lower market output. A monopolist maximizes profit by producing output at the point Q_m where its marginal revenue equals its marginal cost. The demand curve shows that the market will pay a price of P_m when the output is Q_m.

---

12.   *Id.*

By restricting its output below the perfectly-competitive output level (Q_c), the monopolist is able to raise its price above the competitive level and earn monopoly profits. The monopoly overcharge in this example is measured by the difference in price between the perfectly-competitive and monopoly outcomes (P_m-P_c) multiplied by the monopolist's optimal output (Q_m).[13]

Figure 2 shows that at the monopolist's output level (Q_m) the marginal cost to society of producing the product is less than the value society places on the product, as evidenced by the price society is willing to pay for the product. Thus, the monopolist will refuse to produce some product that is valued more highly by society than the resources that are needed to produce it. The perfectly-competitive outcome results in consumer surplus because the marginal unit of product consumed would be valued at P_c and all inframarginal units would be valued at more than P_c. Thus, the value of these inframarginal units to consumers exceeds the price that consumers would pay for them. In Figure 2, consumer surplus under perfect competition is equal to the area below the demand curve and above the competitive price (area ABP_c). By contrast, the monopoly model results in reduced consumer surplus. The monopolist will produce fewer units (Q_m) at a higher price (P_m), leading to a lower consumer surplus corresponding to the area AEP_m. Some of the consumer surplus under perfect competition (area P_mECP_c) will be converted into profit for the monopolist.

The rest of the lost consumer surplus, the striped area (EBC), is lost to all—even the monopolist—as a result of the output restriction. The triangle BCF is lost producer surplus arising from output reduction. The combined shaded triangle EBF is the entire welfare loss—the total social impact of monopoly. This welfare loss is referred to as "dead weight loss."[14] The wealth transfer between consumers and the monopolist (area P_mECP_c) can also raise concerns of welfare loss. For one thing, consumers lose the value of the consumer surplus transferred to the monopolist. For another, the acquisition and maintenance of a monopoly may be costly—part of the captured consumer surplus may be consumed by wasteful expenditures on deterring the entry of potential rivals.[15]

---

13.   *Id.*
14.   *Id.* at 95-96.
15.   *Id.* at 96-97.

Output restriction is the key device by which monopolists achieve monopoly pricing.[16] For example, OPEC, a cartel that accounts for about 40 percent of world crude oil output,[17] tries to behave as much like a monopolist as it can. OPEC engages in monopoly conduct by attempting to regulate market output.[18] In another example, the lysine cartel that was active in the 1990s attempted to raise and maintain prices through output restrictions, including sales allocation plans based upon the investment levels and market power of the participants.[19] In the same way, a single-firm monopolist withholds its output from the market to achieve its profit-maximizing price.

The market power of even a pure monopolist is not absolute. The limitation in the price it can charge comes from the reduction in consumer purchase volumes at higher prices. Thus, the amount of market power the monopolist enjoys varies inversely with the price sensitivity of consumers—the price elasticity of market demand.

---

16. In principle, a perfectly discriminating monopolist could extract the full consumer surplus from each purchaser, thereby achieving the maximum possible monopoly profits without reducing output below the competitive level. Although, in practice, perfect price discrimination is rarely achievable, less-than-perfect discrimination reduces the monopolist's incentive to restrict output. More consumers will be served when a firm with market power can segment its market by customer demand because even less-than-perfect discrimination can enable a monopolist to capture additional rents. For example, pharmaceutical companies frequently price discriminate across countries, charging higher prices in the United States and lower prices in other countries around the world, as a means of expanding output. *See* CARLTON & PERLOFF, *supra* note 1, at 293-308 (on price discrimination).

17. U.S. Energy Info. Admin., *Issues in Focus: World Oil Prices and Production Trends in AE02011*, in ANNUAL ENERGY OUTLOOK 2011, at 23 (2011), *available at* http://www.eic.gov/forecasts/apo/index.com.

18. For example, OPEC cuts output rather than announces price increases directly. *See, e.g.*, *OPEC Set for Major Output Cut Later This Week*, ASSOC. PRESS, Dec. 16, 2008. In certain other cartel arrangements such as bid-rigging in auction markets or customer allocation schemes, reduced output is more a consequence then a cause of monopoly pricing; in other words, prices set at monopoly levels cause output to fall as less is demanded.

19. *See* United States v. Andreas, 216 F.3d 645, 651-54 (7th Cir. 2000).

A powerful statement of the relationship between a firm's market power, its marginal cost of production, and the price elasticity of demand of its customers (ε) is the Lerner equation.[20]

$$L = (P\text{-}MC)/P = 1/\varepsilon$$

The Lerner Index (L) varies from zero to one. L equals zero when price equals marginal cost—the outcome in perfect competition. L equals (nearly) one when marginal cost is a very small fraction of price, indicating a great deal of market power. The relationship to the price elasticity of demand arises because marginal revenue is inversely related to the price elasticity of demand[21] and from the fact that marginal revenue equals marginal cost at the monopolist's profit-maximizing price.

Thus, the Lerner equation describes the relationship among the key determinants of market power: price, marginal cost, and price elasticity of demand. It teaches that the ability of a firm to exceed the competitive price depends upon the price sensitivity of its customers. Understanding the nature of market power requires understanding that the availability and prices of substitutes are the key determinants of the price elasticity of demand and thus of the seller's power over price. The more numerous, closer in nature, and less expensive the substitute products available to consumers, the higher the price elasticity of demand, the lower the Lerner Index (L), and the weaker the market power of the seller.

D. The Market Power of a Dominant Firm

While the model of a single-firm monopolist is central to the economic analysis of market power, pure monopolists are relatively rare in real markets. The perfectly-competitive situation is also rare. Economists have constructed models to clarify the nature of competitive interaction in intermediate markets. One such intermediate market model is of a single dominant firm and a group of smaller firms, the latter described as the "competitive fringe."

A common approach to modeling dominant firm behavior is to assume that the fringe firms respond to the dominant firm's price in the same way that competitive firms respond to market-determined

---

20. *See* A.P. Lerner, *The Concept of Monopoly and the Measurement of Monopoly Power*, 1 REV. OF ECON. STUDIES 157 (1934).
21. MR = $P(1-1/\varepsilon)$.

competitive prices in the perfect competition model—as pure price-takers. This approach also assumes that the dominant firm takes the competitive fringe into account when determining its price and output levels. Under these circumstances, the price elasticity of demand facing the dominant firm (that is, market demand minus the supply from the competitive fringe) depends on the price elasticity of market demand, the price elasticity of supply of the competitive fringe, and the share of the dominant firm. This dominant firm's price elasticity of demand can be substituted into the Lerner equation, making the Lerner Index (i.e., the dominant firm's variable margin) a function of these three elements: the price elasticity of market demand, the price elasticity of fringe supply, and the dominant firm's share.[22]

The Lerner Index for the dominant firm tells us that the bigger the dominant firm's share, the greater its market power will be. Conversely, the higher the price elasticity of market demand, the higher the price elasticity of fringe supply, and the higher the fringe share, the lower the dominant firm's market power will be. In other words, the availability of alternatives to the dominant firm's products, whether in the form of substitute products or as a supply response by other sellers, reduces the market power of the dominant firm, all else equal. Understanding these forces and how they work helps us to move from the theoretical world of

---

22. The price elasticity of demand for the dominant firm is expressed by the following equation:

$$\varepsilon = [\varepsilon_m + \eta(1\text{-}s)]/s$$

This equation says that the price elasticity of net demand facing the dominant firm equals the market price elasticity of demand plus the price elasticity of supply of the competitive fringe multiplied by the share of the fringe, with the sum divided by the share of the dominant firm. Importing this equality into the original Lerner equation, the Lerner Index becomes:

$$(P\text{-}MC)/P = 1/\varepsilon = s/[\varepsilon_m + \eta(1\text{-}s)]$$

Articulated in writing, this becomes:

$$\text{Lerner index} = \frac{\text{dominant firm's share}}{\left(\begin{array}{c}(\text{market price elasticity of demand}) + \\ (\text{fringe price elasticity of supply}) \times \\ (\text{fringe share})\end{array}\right)}$$

pure competition and pure monopoly to realistic settings in which the market power of sellers—ubiquitous in varying degrees in the economy—is constrained by consumers' alternatives, either from suppliers of similar products who can expand their output or from suppliers who are quickly able to enter or expand in response to the profit opportunities created by supracompetitive prices.

E. Market Power: A Business Perspective

While antitrust lawyers and economists regard market power as a wasteful departure from the competitive ideal, the creation, expansion, and exploitation of market powers is a ubiquitous business pursuit. Moreover, the pursuit of market power is widely understood to be a primary engine of economic growth.

Profit-maximizing businesses in imperfect competition seek supranormal returns by striving to create and exploit market power. In the 1970s, an industrial economist, Michael Porter, created a paradigm for the education of business leaders by translating the economics of market power into devices more easily consumed than the equations and diagrams of economists' market power models. Porter renamed market power "competitive advantage" and created diagrams like Figure 3 below that describe the forces that determine profitability:

- The potential for entry by competitors;
- The market power of suppliers;
- The market power of customers;
- The availability of substitutes; and
- The intensity of rivalry within the market.

Figure 3 **Michael Porter's Competitive Advantage Chart**

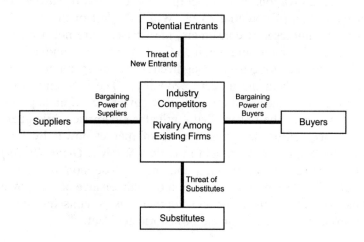

Many business people devote themselves to trying to control and harness these forces. They use several means to create competitive advantage:

- Creating protectable, value-enhancing product characteristics that set their products apart from competing products, thereby reducing the degree of substitution between products (e.g., the iPad and Wii);
- Creating "brand value" by advertising and promotion (e.g., Budweiser or Chanel);
- Creating many related products in order to occupy a segment of "product space" and deflect rivals from it (e.g., Cheerios, Honey Nut Cheerios, MultiGrain Cheerios, Banana Nut Cheerios, Cheerios Crunch, Berry Burst Cheerios, Frosted Cheerios, Apple Cinnamon Cheerios, Fruity Cheerios, and Yogurt Burst Cheerios); and
- Obtaining an advantage in location by paying real estate owners for prime selling space (e.g., Coke or Pepsi on supermarket aisle "end-caps").[23]

---

23. The last of these is less a matter of creating market power than of renting it. The owner of the scarce resource—the supermarket real estate—is the source of the market power. The firm selling the product merely hires it.

Supra-normal profits come from product differentiation, technological innovation, and, sometimes, the creation of barriers to the entry or expansion of potential rivals. While the last of these is clearly harmful to the interests of consumers, the first two are not. Consumers value product diversity and choice. Competition by innovation and technical change has long been recognized as the most important source of economic growth in the modern economy.[24] The U.S. antitrust laws recognize the Janus-faced nature of market power—even monopoly—by acknowledging it as the reward that motivates enterprise while guarding against the acquisition and maintenance of market power by harmful means. As the Supreme Court held in *United States v. Grinnell, Corp.*,[25] the antitrust laws do not prohibit the mere possession of monopoly power, but rather "the willful acquisition or maintenance of that power as distinguished from growth or development as a consequence of a superior product, business acumen, or historic accident."[26]

F. Models of Oligopoly

It may be tempting to think of perfect competition and single-firm monopoly as the ends of a spectrum of market structures, with an array of increasingly monopolistic markets in between. This temptation should be resisted—reality is more complicated, with a cloud rather than a spectrum of models describing competition among the few. Many markets are characterized by a small number of firms—an oligopoly structure. The common feature of oligopoly markets is that each competitor recognizes that its success depends in part upon the actions of

---

For discussion of these concepts, see FED. TRADE COMM'N, STAFF REPORT ON THE FEDERAL TRADE COMMISSION WORKSHOP ON SLOTTING ALLOWANCES AND OTHER MARKETING PRACTICES IN THE GROCERY INDUSTRY pt. IV (Feb. 2011), *available at* htpp://www.ftc.gov/-os/2001/02/slotting allowancesreportfinal.pdf.

24. The seminal contribution to this literature is Robert M. Solow, *Technical Change and the Aggregate Production Function*, 39 REV. OF ECON. & STATISTICS 312 (1957).
25. 384 U.S. 563 (1966).
26. *Id.* at 570-71; *see also* Verizon Commc'ns v. Law Offices of Curtis V. Trinko, 540 U.S. 398, 407 (2004) ("The opportunity to charge monopoly prices—at least for a short period—is what attracts 'business acumen' in the first place; it induces risk taking that produces innovation and economic growth.").

its rivals.[27] Within this framework, however, a number of models of exist for how firms interact.

An example of a model of price-setting competition that, unlike the dominant firm/competitive fringe model, is more realistically adaptable to representing competition among a few sellers with product differentiation is one by Joseph Bertrand. In its simpler, original form, Bertrand competition has two firms with identical products and identical constant average costs, each setting its own price while assuming that the price of its rival is fixed.[28] The equilibrium outcome under that particular Bertrand competition model is a competitive, zero economic profit solution as each price reduction wins the entire market and rivals bid down price to average cost.[29] In Bertrand models for differentiated products, the price of a given product depends upon the price elasticity of demand for that product, and a firm can increase its price in response to a rival's ventured price increase.

Bertrand devised the model that bears his name in 1883 as a criticism of his intellectual forebear, Augustin Cournot, who was the creator of the earliest and best known model of noncooperative oligopoly behavior.[30] Like Bertrand's original model, the original Cournot model assumes product homogeneity.[31] Under the Cournot model, firms are quantity-setting, taking each other's output as given. Using the Cournot model, economists have found that the weighted average price-cost margin in an equilibrium market is positively related to market concentration and inversely related to the price elasticity of market demand.[32] Another

---

27. The Supreme Court recognized that oligopolies have interdependent pricing in its decision in *Brooke Group Ltd. v. Brown & Williamson Tobacco Corp.*, 509 U.S. 209 (1993).

28. *See* CARLTON & PERLOFF, *supra* note 1, at 171-74 (describing Bertrand competition).

29. This reiterates in theory the observed result from experimental tests reported above. Absent collusion, markets with a few competitors can achieve competitive outcomes. *See infra* pt. J of this Chapter for a discussion of the different meanings of the word "competitive."

30. *See* CARLTON & PERLOFF, *supra* note 1, at 161.

31. Although in principle Cournot models can be extended to differentiated products, in practice they seldom are.

32. *See* Kenneth Hendricks et al., *Evaluating Likely Competitive Effects of Horizontal and Vertical Mergers: A New Approach*, 1-2 ANTITRUST REP. 2, 2 n.1 (2007); *see also* CARLTON & PERLOFF, *supra* note 1, at 283. Concentration is measured by the Herfindahl-Hirschman Index (HHI),

finding of the Cournot model is that, in equilibrium, a firm's price-cost margin divided by the market price is related to its market share divided by the elasticity of demand. That is, the model predicts that a lower-cost producer of a homogeneous product would have a higher market share.[33]

One weakness of simple Cournot and Bertrand analyses and other conjectural variation models—models that include a prediction about how a rival will respond—is that they specify that firms make output or price decisions only once, which ignores the reality that firms interact over time, learning about their rivals' competitive tactics.

The theory of noncooperative games has provided a rich source of modeling possibilities that can be tailored to specific assumptions about the nature of competition. Oligopolists, for example, can be characterized as players in a game whose outcome depends on each player's ability to anticipate the moves of its opponents, to assess its own strengths and weaknesses, and to develop "winning" strategies. Economists also employ models of repeated games, to describe more realistically the behavior of firms which can learn and be patient. An important concept in game theory is the "folk theorem" which teaches that, with repetition, if firms are sufficiently patient (i.e., discount the future very little), almost any result, from competitive to monopoly price, could be an equilibrium. Later developments in the theory add realism with refinements such as imperfections in the mechanisms of cooperation, notably in the detection and punishment of cheating.[34]

The oligopoly models that have most influenced antitrust policy in recent years have focused on differentiated products. The DOJ and FTC have analyzed mergers involving differentiated products based, in part,

---

which is the sum of the squared market share of each firm in the market. The higher the HHI, the more concentrated is the market. *See infra* ch. V.

33.   This relationship is expressed as a Lerner Index for an individual firm by the following equation for firm *i* with share s_i:

$$L_i = (P-MC_i)/P = s_i/\varepsilon.$$

34.   For surveys of the extensive literature of oligopoly theory, see Drew Fudenberg & Jean Tirole, *Noncooperative Game Theory for Industrial Organization: An Introduction and Overview, in* 1 HANDBOOK OF INDUSTRIAL ORGANIZATION ch. 10 (Richard Schmalensee and Robert D. Willig eds., 1989); Carl Shapiro, *Theories of Oligopoly Behavior, in* 1 HANDBOOK OF INDUSTRIAL ORGANIZATION, *supra*, ch. 6; Louis Kaplow & Carl Shapiro, *Antitrust, in* 2 HANDBOOK OF LAW AND ECONOMICS ch. 15 (A. Mitchell Polinsky & Steen Shavell eds., 2007).

on standard oligopoly modeling of a differentiated product industry—standard extensions of Bertrand price-setting.

When thinking about markets with relatively few sellers and differentiated products, "product space" is a useful concept.[35] Product space can be thought of as a multidimensional space in which goods are bundles of characteristics that determine each good's coordinates within the relevant product space. The characteristics of a good can include its brand and its specific features (for a laptop computer, potential customers might care about speed, weight, battery life, screen size, and so forth). Individual consumers have preferences about product characteristics, and producers use advertising to inform potential buyers of product characteristics as well as to influence buyer preferences. The connection to market power analysis is straightforward: producers strive to influence consumers' willingness to pay for their products by creating desirable characteristics (e.g., by adding features or merely adding advertising). These efforts create a "space-scape" of products and product clusters, and although there may be many products in the space, proximity in the characteristics space governs substitution by buyers and ultimately competition among sellers.

For example, although small cars with efficient gasoline engines may be available to automobile buyers in the same price range as the gas-electric hybrids, they may be imperfect substitutes despite their ability to transport their owners at approximately the same speed, comfort, and lifetime cost of ownership because they do not provide the same environmental benefits or display the same environmental image for the owner.[36]

Consumers are willing to pay premiums for desirable product characteristics that separate products from otherwise similar products in the product space. Economists typically draw no distinction between characteristics that arise in engineering or chemistry and those that arise in advertising-stimulated imagination.[37]

---

35.   *See* JEAN TIROLE, THE THEORY OF INDUSTRIAL ORGANIZATION 96-100 (1988).

36.   Indeed, Toyota's Prius could be distant from all of them because it was the most successful hybrid car at visually announcing by its body shape its hybrid technology, thus declaring more publicly than any of the other brands the good environmental intentions of its owners.

37.   *See, e.g.,* CARLTON & PERLOFF, *supra* note 1, at 202-03.

G. Buyers' Side Market Power

Buyers' side market power, or monopsony power, arises with less frequency than monopoly power as an antitrust issue. The canonical case of a single employer in a company town hiring workers whose only alternative is idleness does not directly implicate antitrust concerns. The same applies to a government in its role as a single buyer of military goods or, in the case of single payor health care system, medical goods and services. Subtracting these examples leaves us with the cases involving the bargaining power of wholesale purchasers, such as large retail chains or agricultural or natural resource businesses (e.g., meat packers or sawmills), and little else.[38]

Monopsony power arises when a buying firm faces an upward-sloping supply curve, meaning that suppliers require higher prices to call forth additional production. In this setting, a buyer large enough to be capable of affecting the *market* quantity demanded can reduce the market price of the good it is buying by reducing its *own* quantity demanded. The marginal outlay (MO) schedule in Figure 4, below, shows the marginal cost to a monopsonist of buying additional units (much as the marginal revenue curve in Figure 2 shows the marginal revenue to a monopolist of selling additional units). At any given purchase level, the marginal outlay lies above the supply curve because in order to acquire extra units of output, the monopsonist must raise the price of inframarginal (all other) units. Conversely, by restricting its own quantity demanded, it can keep the price below what it would be in a competitive market—an exercise of monopsony power. A profit-maximizing monopsonist's equilibrium is determined in two steps: (i) the intersection of the marginal outlay schedule (MO) and the demand curve (D) yields the buyer's profit-maximizing quantity (Q_m); (ii) the monopsony price (P_m) is determined by the supply cure at that quantity. The striped area in Figure 4 shows the deadweight loss arising from the use of that power.

---

38. *See, e.g.*, Telecor Commc'ns v. Sw. Bell Tel. Co., 305 F.3d 1133-36 1124, (10th Cir. 2002) (applying monopsony theory to provider of pay phone services); Houser v. Fox Theaters Mgmt. Corp., 845 F.2d 1225 (3d Cir. 1988) (first-run movie theatre market); United States v. Aetna, Inc., Proposed Final Judgment and Competitive Impact Statement, 64 Fed. Reg. 44,946, 44,955 (Aug. 18, 1999) (alleging that Aetna's acquisition of Prudential would allow it to exercise purchasing power over physician's services in Houston, Texas).

Figure 4   **A Monopsonist's Profit Maximization**

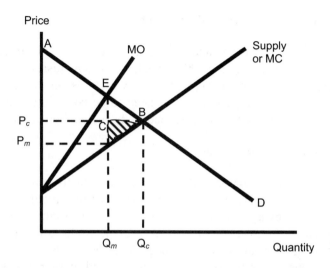

Like monopoly, the single buyer case is the extreme. A firm may possess at least some monopsony power even if it is not the sole buyer in a market. For homogeneous products, the dominant firm/competitive fringe models and the Cournot models, in principle, can be adapted to analyze monopsony power. A useful distinction can be drawn between monopsony pricing and the exercise of buyers' side bargaining power without output restriction. Consider first the hypothetical case of a large regional meatpacker or commercial dairy, alone or nearly so, confronting sellers who are numerous small ranchers or dairy farmers. Exercising monopsony power by restricting the quantity demanded will be profit-enhancing for the buyer because it keeps the regional market price for all cattle or milk below the competitive price.

Turn now to the case of a large (but not solitary) retailer confronting a packaged goods manufacturer that represents a modest fraction of the total market of whatever packaged goods market we are considering. The retailer may bargain by saying "I will take all that you can sell me if your price is very low." The implied threat is that the retailer will buy less from the manufacturer and more from others if the manufacturer does not price low. The manufacturer may profitably accept because of captured scale economies, saved selling costs, or the alleviation of uncertainty at the cost of a lower margin. In this case, although consumers may have fewer choices on this particular retailer's shelves, the retailer is not reducing the overall amount it buys to obtain the lower price—that is, there is no output restriction and no associated deadweight loss.[39]

H. Market Power in Idiosyncratic Markets

The preceding observations about market power will apply in most industrial and commercial settings. Nevertheless, idiosyncrasies in some markets create special cases, exceptions, and variations on the themes that economic theory illuminates and that need to be taken into account in an assessment of market power. This section discusses four examples.

1. Low Marginal Cost Industries

Industries such as movies, software, pharmaceuticals, music, and passenger air travel all have a high ratio of up-front fixed cost to marginal cost. It takes a substantial amount of money to launch a new drug, a commercial film, or a commercial airplane flight, although the differences among them are orders of magnitude: hundreds of millions for the drug, tens of millions for the movie, and perhaps tens of thousands for a single airplane flight. Once the up-front costs have been incurred, an extra DVD of the film, an extra dose of the drug, or an extra person sitting in an otherwise empty airplane seat is very nearly costless. This minimal marginal cost, once up-front costs are incurred, governs the economics of pricing in all these and other industries with similar characteristics. Among other things, it makes differential pricing profitable and perhaps necessary. This is why widespread diversity exists in the price of a movie ($10 for a first run viewing in a theater, or, later, watch for free on cable TV), a medicine (costs much more in the United States than in Canada, Germany, or Greece), or an air travel ticket (higher priced first class weekday versus weekend bargain fares).

In order to charge discriminatory prices across customers, firms must have some ability to control the prices they charge. This means that they

---

39. Price clubs may have fewer brands on their shelves and offer lower prices than supermarkets for a number of reasons: (i) they exercise this sort of bargaining power; (ii) they sell to buyers who are willing to buy in bulk and warehouse at home large quantities of products purchased; (iii) they operate low-rent operations with minimum-wage labor; and (iv) membership fees and restricted payment card policies minimize transaction costs. Bargaining power is on this list, but monopsony power is not.

can not be pure price takers and, thus, must have some market power. But it is rare that firms can control the market price, so they are not usually pure monopolists either. Unfortunately, the index that we use to measure market power does not apply in low marginal cost industries. Because so much of the average total cost is fixed and marginal cost is so low, the Lerner Index (P-MC/P) for thriving firms in these industries is likely to be astronomically high.[40] The Lerner Index and the definition of market power both depend upon the proposition that, through competition, price is driven down to marginal cost, while cost that is fixed and sunk in the past is irrelevant. Yet firms or industries that are unable to recover the full cost of operations, even if some of those costs occurred in the past, will fail. This needs to be taken into account in an assessment of market power. One need only look at the mergers over the last decade among large pharmaceutical firms and airlines to recognize this reality. While the surviving firms may have large margins over marginal cost (i.e., high Lerner Indexes), that does not speak to their ability to earn a supranormal or even a competitive rate of return.

2. Declining Marginal Cost Industries

Producers in some industries routinely experience declining marginal cost as a result of effects such as economies of cumulative production or rapid technological change. These do not always correspond to the low marginal cost industries described in the preceding subpart. The cost of making pills is not known to decline notably with manufacturing experience. In contrast, the marginal cost of semiconductor products such as microprocessors and computer memory does decline with cumulative volume because of the ability of manufacturers continually to improve yields and shrink the sizes of chips obtainable from a single silicon wafer. When marginal costs decrease, the Lerner Index becomes unreliable as an indicator of changes in the market power of manufacturers. This is true because a firm that expands output and sales may move to the less elastic portion of its demand curve, which would cause its Lerner Index to increase. A simple example shows that even if the entire marginal cost decrease were passed along to consumers in the form of lower prices, the Lerner Index would increase. Assume an initial price, P=1, and marginal cost, MC=0.5, so the Lerner Index described above is initially:

---

40.   *See supra* pt. C.

(1.0 - 0.5)/1.0 = 0.5

and the associated price elasticity of demand is 2 (1 divided by 0.5). If marginal costs decrease from 0.5 to 0.3 and the savings are entirely passed through to buyers,[41] the Lerner Index becomes:

(0.8 - 0.3)/0.8 = 0.625

implying a price elasticity of 1.6 (1 divided by 0.625). Although there has been no increase in the firm's market position, the Lerner Index has increased.[42] Such changes in marginal cost need to be taken into account in a market power assessment.

3. Durable Goods Industries

To restate a key point: consumer choice is the main governor of the sellers' power over price in a market. A ready availability of alternatives for customers in the form of competing suppliers reduces any supplier's ability to extract higher-than-competitive prices and to restrict the market output as a means to do so. A firm's market share is a measure of how much ability it has to move the market level of output and price. The ability of fringe suppliers to expand their sales quickly in the face of profit opportunities and the ability of new firms to enter markets quickly are also determinants of market power, but they are variations on the theme—the expansion of fringe suppliers and the entry of new sellers into the market also represent means by which alternatives become available to consumers. In settings in which goods do not depreciate quickly and are bought and sold used as well as new, buyers' choices are expanded providing a further limit on the market power suppliers of new goods can enjoy. Automobiles and boats are longstanding examples of goods frequently purchased both new and used. The requirements for this broader competition among used and new products include low transaction costs relative to the cost of the goods themselves, enabling efficient search and evaluation without the reputation-based guarantees

---

41.　There is no guarantee, of course, that a profit-maximizing firm would find it profit-maximizing to pass through the full amount of its decrease in marginal cost.

42.　If this price-reducing behavior is profit-maximizing, then the change in the Lerner Index implies that the demand curve has an elasticity that varies with the price.

that sellers of new products provide. The development of Internet-based markets for used goods of lesser value (e.g., eBay) has reduced transaction costs and created "used" alternatives to new products formerly immune to such competition.

4. Intellectual Property

Rights to make, use, and sell inventions can be the good traded in technology and pharmaceutical markets. Sometimes the rights are traded alone, and sometimes they are bundled with ancillary services such as the provision of manufacturing know-how or advice. For simplicity, this discussion is limited to a simple patent license. IP licensing in general and patent licensing in particular sometimes resemble transactions for goods or services in that they may involve providing many licensees with identical or similar rights. For example, licensing a patent that has been incorporated into an industry standard may involve a standard-setting body that requires participating patent holders to license on standard (e.g., reasonable and non-discriminatory) terms. But, sometimes the transactions are more idiosyncratic as a result of the intersection of the owner of a unique invention with a unique licensee.

The substitution possibilities available to buyers affect price sensitivity and sellers' market power as much in technology markets as in goods markets. When a licensor owns the patent to a useful invention for which viable substitute technologies are remote, the license fee will be high owing to the market power of the licensor. Most patents, on the other hand, while protecting inventions that are novel and useful (the requirements for obtaining a patent), are not valuable because numerous unpatented or patented substitutes exist in the market. The license fee for a better mousetrap would surely be high, but a merely better mousetrap competes with the variety of other mouse traps and pest management products on store shelves. Thus, the price of the invention is unlikely to be high.

Besides the availability of alternatives to the licensee, prices (license fees) in technology and pharmaceutical markets are also determined, in part, by the cost to the licensor of granting a license. These costs include opportunity costs, which do not show up in obvious ways in observable accounting statements.

Consider two possible inventors of a valuable patent, one a university professor, the other the chief executive of a small manufacturing firm. In considering how much to charge for a license, each considers what the market will bear, i.e., what potential licensees will pay, based upon the value of the license in increased revenue or reduced costs. But each also considers the cost of licensing, and here they arrive at very different conclusions. The professor's cost of licensing is close to zero. Whatever was expended in research cost is sunk in the past and irrelevant for price decision-making. His only forward-looking expenses will be monitoring and processing royalty reports and payments. The case of the manufacturer is different, particularly if that the firm's invention would be licensed to rivals in the same product market. In that case, the opportunity cost of licensing is potentially large. Opportunity cost is defined as the cost of a decision, measured as the value of the foregone next-best alternative. In this case, the next-best alternative is to not license, at least not to license to rivals. Since granting competitors a license to employ a valuable invention presumably enhances those competitors' prospects in the market by either improving their products or reducing their costs, the decision to do so could be costly to the licensor. But this cost is not a marginal cost of production and sale for the licensor/manufacturer, so while it is likely to play an important role in decision-making about whether to license and for how much, it does not have a role in determining how much market power the inventor has.

While the markets described above are idiosyncratic in their cost structures or demand characteristics, together with others like them they are large and important segments of industry. It is therefore worth emphasizing that the relationship between market power, margin over marginal cost, and market demand elasticity captured in the Lerner equation must be employed and reported thoughtfully, not mechanically. Marginal cost is often hard to identify, and even when accurate recognition of the relevant measure of cost can be achieved, high price-cost margins do not invariably imply weak competition.

I.   Market Power Anomalies

The industrial markets described in the preceding section are exceptional in their cost or demand characteristics. They do not, however, represent departures from the most fundamental assumption of industrial economics: that every firm seeks to maximize its profits. The recent rise to prominence of behavioral economics in policy circles, and a longer-standing interest among antitrust practitioners in possible non-price consequences of the exercise of market power, leads to questions that price theory alone may not always be able to answer, including: In what ways might an acquisition substantially lessen competition in service, quality, product variety or innovation, apart from any price and output effects?[43] Or, how can we tell whether apparently monopolizing actions arise from an agency problem—a sales manager striving for a bigger bonus—rather than a firm's drive for profitability?

Few would advocate turning a blind eye to real-world evidence about departures from rationality and profit maximization. But enthusiasm for the proposition that people (and therefore firms) sometimes do not obey perfectly their materialistic self-interest should not mislead us. The strength of price theory (and within it market power analysis) is its explanatory power. That power derives from the basic law-like statements of economics described at the beginning of this Chapter. Anomalies can be observed, counted and studied, but to date no one has come up with an alternate means for reliably understanding and forecasting, for example, the effect on a firm's sales of a change in its customers' substitution possibilities or the impact upon consumers of a merger.[44]

Price theory and the analysis of incentives will usually aid in understanding the non-price consequences of the exercise of market power. To understand how a firm will behave when competition diminishes, one could ask: Can profit be more readily increased by reducing quality, variety, or R&D, and saving production cost rather than by simply increasing price? Instances could exist in which conventional economic explanations would fail, but theories by which robust explanations for such cases (or predictions about future outcomes) could be made do not, at present, appear to be sufficiently developed for extensive use in antitrust analysis.

J. Conclusion: Market Power Misunderstandings

Since the definition and identification of market power are well settled concepts in economics, courtroom disputes about market power tend to arise from differences in assumptions, different views of the facts, or from ambiguous use of terms. When assumptions are explicitly

---

43. This paraphrases only slightly a concern voiced by FTC Commissioner J. Thomas Rosch. *See* J. Thomas Rosch, Statement of Commissioner J. Thomas Rosch on the Release of the 2010 Horizontal Merger Guidelines (Aug. 19, 2010), *available at* http://www.ftc.gov/os/2010/08/ 100819hmgrosch.pdf.

44. *See generally* Michael A. Salinger, *Behavioral Economics, Consumer Protection, and Antitrust*, 6 COMPETITION POL'Y INT'L 65, 77-79 (2010).

stated as part of the analysis, differences of opinion can contribute to a fact-finder's understanding. When different opinions arise from different usages of terms, the outcome is more likely to be confusion.

The adjective "competitive" has the potential to create confusion because it can refer either to the economist's concept of perfect competition or simply to marketplace rivalry. Consider, for example, the following statement: "If this market were competitive, then price would equal marginal cost (and marginal cost is very small)." This statement may be entirely correct or entirely incorrect depending upon whether the intended meaning of "competitive" matches the realities of the market. In an atomistic market, this would be true; in a rivalrous market of relatively few sellers of heterogeneous goods, it would be false.

Similarly, the term "monopoly" has multiple meanings. Firms may have monopoly power and not be single sellers. In contrast, a single seller in a market with no barriers to entry may have no monopoly power. Controversies about market power based on misunderstandings are unproductive. Ambiguities in the language of market power, when they appear, must be clarified to get to the heart of the issue.[45]

---

45.   The term "market" can create additional confusion based on how it is used in the ordinary course of business versus its use in antitrust, as discussed in ch. IV *infra*.

CHAPTER IV

MARKET DEFINITION

A. Introduction

Defining a relevant market is typically a critical issue in assessing market power, since market definition identifies the relevant competitors and provides the basis for estimating market shares.[1]

Courts have identified basic methodologies and factors to be considered in defining a market, but applying these principles in particular cases is often difficult. As the Supreme Court has noted:

> For every product, substitutes exist. But a relevant market cannot meaningfully encompass that infinite range. The circle must be drawn narrowly to exclude any other product to which, within reasonable variations in price, only a limited number of buyers will turn; in technical terms, products whose "cross elasticities of demand" are small.[2]

This identifies the key issue in market definition, i.e., would buyers shift their purchases sufficiently in the face of an attempted exercise of market power that the attempt would be thwarted. As the Ninth Circuit explained:

---

1. "Because market power is often inferred from market share, market definition generally determines the result of the case." Eastman Kodak Co. v. Image Tech. Servs., 504 U.S. 451, 469 n.15 (1992) (citation omitted). The agencies recently have downplayed the importance of market definition in assessing market power for differentiated products as well as reliance on market shares to make inferences about likely competitive effects. U.S. DEP'T OF JUSTICE & FED. TRADE COMM'N, HORIZONTAL MERGER GUIDELINES § 4 (2010), *available at* http://www.justice.gov/atr/public/guidelines/hmg-2010.html [hereinafter MERGER GUIDELINES]. Whether this approach will gain traction in the courts remains to be seen. *See* FTC v. Lundbeck, 650 F.3d 1236, 1239 (8th Cir. 2011) ("To prevail, the FTC bears the burden of identifying a relevant market."); City of New York v. Group Health, No. 06 Civ. 13122, 2010 WL 2132246, at *3 (S.D.N.Y. 2010) (relying on market definition and rejecting the upward pricing pressure (UPP) test).

2. Times-Picayune Publ'g v. United States, 345 U.S. 594, 612 n.31 (1953).

61

A "market" is any grouping of sales whose sellers, if unified by a monopolist or a hypothetical cartel, would have market power in dealing with any group of buyers.[3]

Thus, broadly speaking, the objective in defining the relevant market is to draw the boundary—which, of necessity, might be imprecise—between those products and services that compete to some substantial degree with the product being studied and those that do not.

A relevant market has two components, which reflect different dimensions in which competition occurs: (i) the relevant *product* market, which identifies the products or services that compete with the product of interest; and (ii) the relevant *geographic* market, which identifies the geographic area within which competition with the product of interest takes place.[4]

B. Product Market Definition

The relevant product market includes all products that substantially constrain the pricing of the product being studied. For example, in a case involving alleged monopolization of "widgets," product market analysis assesses whether "gadgets," which appear to be substitutes for purchasers

---

3.   Rebel Oil v. Atl. Richfield Co., 51 F.3d 1421, 1434 (9th Cir. 1995) (citing PHILLIP AREEDA & HERBERT HOVENKAMP, ANTITRUST LAW ¶ 518.1b, at 534 (Supp. 1993)). Several other courts have cited the Areeda & Hovenkamp definition of a relevant market (from various editions of their treatise). *See, e.g.*, AD/SAT v. Associated Press, 181 F.3d 216, 228 (2d Cir. 1999); Levine v. Cent. Fla. Med. Affiliates, 72 F.3d 1538, 1552 (11th Cir. 1996); H.J., Inc. v. ITT Corp., 867 F.2d 1531, 1537 (8th Cir. 1989); Piazza v. MLB, 831 F. Supp. 420, 439 (E.D. Pa. 1993). The FTC has used an almost identical definition, defining a market as "the smallest grouping of products whose sellers, if unified by a hypothetical cartel or merger, could profitably increase prices significantly above the competitive level." R.R. Donnelley & Sons Co., 120 F.T.C. 36, 153 (1995) (citing *H.J., Inc.*, 867 F.2d at 1537). Finally, the *Merger Guidelines* have been cited in analyzing the relevant market. FTC v. Whole Foods Mkt., 548 F.3d 1028, 1037-38 (D.C. Cir. 2008).

4.   *See, e.g.*, United States v. Marine Bancorp., 418 U.S. 602, 618 (1974); Brown Shoe Co. v. United States, 370 U.S. 294, 324 (1962); Eichorn v. AT&T, 248 F.3d 131, 147 (3d Cir. 2001); Bathke v. Casey's Gen. Stores, 64 F.3d 340, 345 (8th Cir. 1995); Los Angeles Mem'l Coliseum Comm'n v. NFL, 726 F.2d 1381, 1392 (9th Cir. 1984).

of widgets, are a sufficiently good substitute for widgets such that competition from gadgets substantially constrains widget prices, preventing the substantial exercise of market power.

Although courts have described the process of defining a relevant product market in a variety of ways, the core of such analysis is an effort to identify the products and the suppliers of those products that compete to some substantial degree with the product in question. The Third Circuit explained that "defining a relevant product market is a process of describing those groups of producers which, because of the similarity of their products, have the ability—actual or potential—to take significant amounts of business away from each other."[5]

Products may be included in the same market based on effective demand-side substitution or, in some instances, effective supply-side substitution. In defining the relevant market in which widgets compete, the issue of demand-side substitution involves the extent to which current buyers of widgets would switch to gadgets in response to a small increase in the price of widgets. The issue of supply-side substitution involves the extent to which producers of gadgets would switch to producing widgets in response to a small increase in the price of widgets. Thus, for example, cookies and cakes might be both demand-side and supply-side substitutes. By contrast, men's and women's apparel are usually not demand-side substitutes, although they may well be supply-side substitutes if the two can be produced using the same production facilities.

The case law does not provide a precise test for determining how attractive a demand-side substitute must be to be included in the relevant product market; rather, courts rely on numerous factors in making this assessment. The use of supply-side considerations to define markets is more rare, and a consensus on the appropriate standards has not yet emerged.[6]

---

5.   SmithKline Corp. v. Eli Lilly & Co., 575 F.2d 1056, 1063 (3d Cir. 1978); *see also* Harrison Aire, Inc. v. Aerostar Int'l, 423 F.3d 374, 383 (3d Cir. 2005); Spanish Broad. Sys. v. Clear Channel Commc'ns, 376 F.3d 1065, 1074 (11th Cir. 2004). Similarly, in the *Merger Guidelines*, the FTC and DOJ explain that they seek to identify products that are in substantial competition with one another by focusing on the consequences for pricing behavior in the market if such competition were to cease. *See* MERGER GUIDELINES, *supra* note 1, § 4.

6.   Even if not considered as part of the relevant market analysis, considerations of supply-side substitution are often taken into account in

1. Cross-Elasticity of Demand

Courts have considered cross-elasticity of demand in defining the relevant product market.[7] The cross-elasticity of demand between two products measures the extent to which the quantity demanded of the first product will change in response to a change in the price of the second product—all else being equal.[8] A high cross-elasticity value indicates that the products are good substitutes and are probably in the same product market. [9] Although cross-elasticity of demand has a

---

the analysis of potential entry. This is the approach taken by the revised *Merger Guidelines*. However, as discussed below, courts have frequently considered supply substitution in defining relevant markets.

7.   *See, e.g.*, PepsiCo, Inc. v. Coca-Cola Co., 315 F.3d 101, 105 (2d Cir. 2002) (finding that "[a] relevant product market consists of products that have reasonable interchangeability for the purposes for which they are produced" and that are treated by consumers as "acceptable substitutes") (citations and quotations omitted); Virtual Maint. v. Prime Computer, 11 F.3d 660, 664-65 (6th Cir. 1993) (in remanding case for new trial, rescinding conclusion in earlier decision that the alleged tying market could not be predicated on the "demand side" alone); United States v. Archer-Daniels-Midland Co., 866 F.2d 242, 246 (8th Cir. 1988); Borden, Inc. v. FTC, 674 F.2d 498, 507-10 (6th Cir. 1982) (product market analyzed principally in terms of demand cross-elasticity to determine interchangeability), *vacated & remanded for entry of consent judgment*, 461 U.S. 940 (1983); Columbia Metal Culvert Co. v. Kaiser Aluminum & Chem., 579 F.2d 20, 29-30 (3d Cir. 1978) (noting that perceptions of consumers, not manufacturers, are most salient in determination of market boundaries); Auburn News v. Providence Journal Co., 504 F. Supp. 292, 302 (D.R.I. 1980) (defining product markets primarily with reference to cross-elasticity of demand), *rev'd on other grounds*, 659 F.2d 273 (1st Cir. 1981); Donald B. Rice Tire v. Michelin Tire, 483 F. Supp. 750, 755 (D. Md. 1980) (same), *aff'd*, 638 F.2d 15 (4th Cir. 1981); Murphy Tugboat Co. v. Shipowners & Merchs. Towboat Co., 467 F. Supp. 841, 849 (N.D. Cal. 1979) ("The relevant product market consists of commodities or services reasonably interchangeable by consumers for the same purpose . . . .") (citation omitted), *aff'd sub nom.* Murphy Tugboat Co. v. Crowley, 658 F.2d 1256 (9th Cir. 1981).

8.   *See* Eastman Kodak Co. v. Image Tech. Servs., 504 U.S. 451, 469 (1992).

9.   *See, e.g.*, United States v. E.I. duPont de Nemours & Co., 351 U.S. 377, 400, 404 (1956); Forsyth v. Humana, Inc., 114 F.3d 1467, 1483 (9th Cir. 1997), *aff'd*, 525 U.S. 299 (1999); *Archer-Daniels-Midland*, 866 F.2d at 248; Rothery Storage & Van v. Atlas Van Lines, Inc., 792 F.2d 210, 218

mathematically precise meaning in economics,[10] courts often use the term in a more general, nonquantitative manner to refer to the tendency of an increase in the price of one product to increase the quantity demanded of a second product within a reasonably short time.[11] In effect, courts usually use the term as a synonym for "reasonable interchangeability of use." As market definition analyses have become more sophisticated and expert-driven, however, courts increasingly have looked at quantitative measures of elasticity.[12]

(D.C. Cir. 1986); *SmithKline Corp.*, 575 F.2d at 1063; United States v. Empire Gas, 537 F.2d 296, 303 (8th Cir. 1976); *In re* Coca-Cola Co., 117 F.T.C. 795, 925 & n.48 (1994), *modified*, 119 F.T.C. 724 (1995).

10. The cross-elasticity of demand between two products is the percentage increase in the quantity demanded of the second product divided by the percentage increase in the price of the first product, holding all else constant. Thus, if a 5 percent increase in the price of *A* leads to a 10 percent increase in the quantity demanded of *B*, the cross-elasticity would be 10 percent divided by 5 percent, or 2. *See Coca-Cola Co.*, 117 F.T.C. at 925 & n.48.

11. There is relatively little judicial discussion of the time period during which the switch in demand must be made in order to be meaningful. In *United States v. Cont'l Can Co.*, 378 U.S. 441, 455 (1964), the Supreme Court considered customer responses to competitive conditions over the "long run." In *U.S. Anchor Manufacturing v. Rule Industries*, 7 F.3d 986, 996 (11th Cir. 1993), the Eleventh Circuit found two types of anchor products to be in separate markets despite some evidence correlating one of the product's rising prices with falling sales over a five-year measuring period. The court held that the plaintiff's correlation evidence failed to "take account of factors other than price (or quality) which may have affected demand" over the five-year period. *Id.* The *Merger Guidelines* do not specify a fixed time period for measuring shifts in demand. *See* MERGER GUIDELINES, *supra* note 1, § 4.1.3.

12. *See, e.g.*, Geneva Pharm. Tech. v. Barr Labs., 386 F.3d 485, 497 (2d Cir. 2004) citing inelastic demand by branded drug consumers as evidence that generic drugs were a separate market from branded drugs where the generic substitution rate was only 30 percent despite the fact that generic drug prices were 40 percent lower than the branded drug prices); FTC v. Staples, Inc., 970 F. Supp. 1066, 1080 (D.D.C. 1997) (defining a product market based on retail sales channels where pricing evidence indicated a low cross-elasticity of demand between consumable office products sold by office superstores and those same products sold by other sellers of office supplies); New York v. Kraft Gen. Foods, 926 F. Supp. 321, 333 (S.D.N.Y. 1995) (finding "statistically significant" cross-price elasticities

2. Cross-Elasticity of Supply

Courts have also considered the cross-elasticity of supply, defined by one court as "the extent to which producers of one product would be willing to shift their resources to producing another product in response to an increase in the price of the other product."[13]

---

between "highly differentiated" ready-to-eat cereals confirmed that the relevant product market consisted of all ready-to-eat cereals); *see also* McLaughlin Equip. v. Servaas, No. IP98-0127, 2004 WL 1629603, at *6, (S.D. Ind. 2004) ("It is insufficient for an expert to merely mention cross-elasticity of demand or supply; an analysis is required.").

13.   AD/SAT v. Associated Press, 181 F.3d 216, 227 (2d Cir. 1999) (citation omitted); *see also* Brown Shoe Co. v. United States, 370 U.S. 294, 325 n.42 (1962) (acknowledging relevance of supply substitutability but finding record insufficient to establish it); United States v. Columbia Steel Co., 334 U.S. 495, 510-11 (1948) (relying on supply substitution); Lucas Auto. Eng'g v. Bridgestone/Firestone, Inc., 275 F.3d 762, 768 (9th Cir. 2001) (genuine issue of fact existed as to whether the relevant market was limited to original equipment major brand vintage tires or included all tire manufacturing capacity that can be used to produce replacement tires for vintage automobiles); Rebel Oil v. Atl. Richfield Co., 51 F.3d 1421, 1436 (9th Cir. 1995) ("[D]efining a market on the basis of demand considerations alone is erroneous. A reasonable market definition must also be based on 'supply elasticity.'") (citations omitted); Virtual Maint. v. Prime Computer, 11 F.3d 660, 664 (6th Cir. 1993); *In re* Mun. Bond Reporting Antitrust Litig., 672 F.2d 436, 441 (5th Cir. 1982) (claiming that the sought limitation to relevant market "fails to give due accord to the significance of elasticity of supply"); Kaiser Aluminum & Chem. v. FTC, 652 F.2d 1324, 1330 (7th Cir. 1981) ("Cross-elasticity of supply, or production flexibility among sellers, is another relevant factor... in defining a product market."); United States v. Empire Gas, 537 F.2d 296, 303 (8th Cir. 1976) ("The cross-elasticity of supply would seem to be as important as the demand factor in determining relevant product market."); Calnetics Corp. v. Volkswagen, 532 F.2d 674, 691 (9th Cir. 1976) (holding, in claim under Clayton Act Section 7, district court's failure to consider cross-elasticity of production was error); Creative Copier Servs. v. Xerox Corp., 344 F. Supp. 2d 858, 864-65 (D. Conn. 2004) (plaintiff alleged sufficient facts to support inference that supply interchangeability was not possible); Nobody In Particular Presents, Inc. v. Clear Channel Commc'ns, 311 F. Supp. 2d 1048, 1085 (D. Colo. 2004) (low cross-elasticity of supply supported plaintiffs' allegations of relevant market); United States v. Syufy Enters., 712 F. Supp. 1386, 1398 (N.D. Cal. 1989) (noting that, although the vast majority of cases have used

Courts have found products to be in the same market if firms can readily switch their production capabilities between them,[14] but the ease

only cross-elasticity of demand in determining the relevant product market, it is appropriate to use both cross-elasticity of demand and cross-elasticity of supply), *aff'd*, 903 F.2d 659 (9th Cir. 1990); *In re* Air Passenger Computer Reservations Sys. Antitrust Litig., 694 F. Supp. 1443, 1457-58 (C.D. Cal. 1988) (analyzing both demand and supply cross-elasticity), *aff'd sub nom.* Alaska Airlines v. United Airlines, 948 F.2d 536 (9th Cir. 1991); United States v. AT&T, 524 F. Supp. 1336, 1375-76 n.163 (D.D.C. 1981) ("Supply cross-elasticity, no less than demand cross-elasticity, is an important factor in the definition of economic markets."); Sci. Prods. Co. v. Chevron Chem. Co., 384 F. Supp. 793, 798 (N.D. Ill. 1974) (considering production facilities).

14. *See, e.g.*, Blue Cross & Blue Shield United v. Marshfield Clinic, 65 F.3d 1406, 1410-11 (7th Cir. 1995) ("Even if two products are completely different from the consumer's standpoint, if they are made by the same producers an increase in the price of one that is not cost-justified will induce producers to shift production from the other product to this one in order to increase their profits by selling at a supracompetitive price."); Yoder Bros. v. California-Florida Plant Corp., 537 F.2d 1347, 1367-68 (5th Cir. 1976) (ability of growers to switch among different types of flowers precludes a chrysanthemum-only market); *Calnetics Corp.*, 532 F.2d at 691 (lower court erred by failing to consider cross-elasticity of production facilities or capacity in defining product market); Telex Corp. v. IBM, 510 F.2d 894, 915-17 (10th Cir. 1975) (cross-elasticity of supply requires that relevant market not be limited to peripherals that are plug-compatible with IBM's central processing unit); New York v. Kraft Gen. Foods, 926 F. Supp. 321, 361 (S.D.N.Y. 1995) (conclusion that relevant product market includes all "ready to eat" cereals is "reinforced by the court's consideration of supply substitutability in the RTE cereal industry"); Cmty. Publishers v. Donrey Corp., 892 F. Supp. 1146, 1164 (W.D. Ark. 1995) (all local daily papers have potential to compete in regional market and should be included in market definition), *aff'd sub nom.* Cmty. Publishers v. DR Partners, 139 F.3d 1180 (8th Cir. 1998); FTC v. Occidental Petroleum Corp., No. 86-900, 1986 WL 952, at *6 (D.D.C. 1986) (attempted price increase by copolymer producers would cause homopolymer producers to switch); United States v. Calmar, Inc., 612 F. Supp. 1298, 1304 (D.N.J. 1985) (rejecting proposed market and including several kinds of consumer-product sprayers and dispensers made with almost identical procedures); Frank Saltz & Sons v. Hart Schaffner & Marx, No. 82-Civ.-2931, 1985 WL 2510, at *5 (S.D.N.Y. 1985) (rejecting "better quality" men's suits market based, in part, on finding of an unspecified level of supply-side substitutability in suit

with which they can do so is a determinative factor.[15] For example, after
noting that two products with a high degree of substitutability in use

---

market); Carter Hawley Hale Stores v. Limited, Inc., 587 F. Supp. 246,
253 (C.D. Cal. 1984) (garment manufacturers can easily switch
production to different quality and sizes of clothing and retailers can
similarly change types of clothing sold); J.H. Westerbeke Corp. v. Onan
Corp., 580 F. Supp. 1173, 1186 (D. Mass. 1984) (modification of
production facilities "could be performed easily by any reasonably
competent mechanic"); *In re* ITT, 104 F.T.C. 280, 411 (1984) (captive
bakers included in market with wholesale bakers since former could
readily divert production to other retail groceries in response to an
increase in wholesale baker prices). *Cf.* NicSand, Inc. v. 3M Co., 457
F.3d 534, 547 (6th Cir.) ("Both supply substitution and demand
substitution . . . factor into the ultimate definition of an economic
market. . . . [I]f, on a motion for summary judgment, [plaintiff] does not
put forth facts supporting its alleged market that account for the
possibility of supply substitution, its claims will have to be dismissed."),
vacated on other grounds, No. 05-3431, 2006 U.S. App. LEXIS 32342
(6th Cir. 2006); *Kaiser Aluminum & Chem.*, 652 F.2d at 1330 (noting that
while "economic theory would envisage defining a market solely on the
basis of cross-elasticity of supply . . . such [a] possibility is not
meaningful") (citations omitted).

15.   *See, e.g., Nobody In Particular Presents*, 311 F. Supp. 2d at 1085
(inability of suppliers to switch supported relevant market for rock
concert tickets); Ansell, Inc. v. Schmid Labs., 757 F. Supp. 467, 475-76
(D.N.J. 1991) (product market limited to retail brand name condoms
despite production flexibility where shift in production would not be
profitable), *aff'd mem.*, 941 F.2d 1200 (3d Cir. 1991); United States v.
Ivaco, Inc., 704 F. Supp. 1409, 1416-17 (W.D. Mich. 1989) (product
market properly limited to automatic tampers where manufacturers of
maintenance of way equipment could not be expected to switch quickly
to production of automatic tampers due to differences in technology and
engineering); Slocomb Indus. v. Chelsea Indus., No. 82-2546, 1984 WL
2945, at *5 (E.D. Pa. 1984) (supply substitutability not established
because of unique production facilities that would take three to six
months to change); *In re* B.A.T. Indus., 104 F.T.C. 852, 932 (1984)
(separate markets where production required unique facilities,
custom-designed equipment, specialized raw materials, specially trained
personnel, extensive research efforts, and rigorous quality control and
testing procedures); *In re* Tenneco, Inc., 98 F.T.C. 464, 580-81 (1981)
(original equipment and replacement shock absorbers in separate markets
despite production flexibility because of differences in the marketing and
distribution of the products), *rev'd on other grounds*, 689 F.2d 346 (2d

should be included in the same market, the Ninth Circuit, in *Twin City Sportservice v. Charles O. Finley & Co.*,[16] observed that:

> A like analysis applies when the market is viewed from the production rather than the consumption standpoint. . . . Where the degree of substitutability in production is high, cross-elasticities of supply will also be high, and again the two commodities in question should be treated as part of the same market.[17]

3. Price Differences

Courts have often considered price differences between products in evaluating the extent to which the products are substitutes.[18] For example, in *United States v. Aluminum Co. of America*,[19] the Supreme Court relied heavily upon a greater than 50 percent price differential between copper and aluminum and held that aluminum cable constituted a submarket separate from copper cable, even though "each does the job equally well" and "the class of customers is the same."[20]

The mere fact of price differences, however, will not preclude placing products in the same market. In *United States v. E.I. duPont de Nemours & Co.*,[21] for example, the Supreme Court held that cellophane was in the same market as other flexible packaging materials despite

---

Cir. 1982). *Cf.* U.S. Anchor Mfg. v. Rule Indus., 7 F.3d 986, 997 (11th Cir. 1993) (supply substitutability does not justify broader market where company that produced premium product could switch to produce generic product but where it would be economically irrational for it to do so).

16. 512 F.2d 1264 (9th Cir. 1975).
17. *Id.* at 1271.
18. *See, e.g.*, CDC Techs. v. IDEXX Labs., 7 F. Supp. 2d 119, 126-27 (D. Conn. 1998) (denying defendants' motion for summary judgment as to the relevant product market because the significant price difference between in-clinic hematology analyzers for veterinarians and outside laboratory services providing the same information raised a material issue of fact whether outside laboratory services belonged in the same product market as in-clinic analyzers), *aff'd on other grounds*, 186 F.3d 74 (2d Cir. 1999).
19. 377 U.S. 271 (1964).
20. *Id.* at 276-77; *see* Rebel Oil v. Atl. Richfield Co., 51 F.3d 1421, 1436 (9th Cir. 1995) ("A price differential between two products may reflect a low cross-elasticity of demand, if the higher priced product offers additional service for which consumers are willing to pay a premium.").
21. 351 U.S. 377 (1956).

costing two or three times as much.[22] Because packaging accounted for a very small portion of the entire cost of the wrapped article—and because of quality differences among the packaging materials—the Court concluded that they were reasonably interchangeable notwithstanding the price difference.[23] Similarly, in *Nifty Foods v. Great Atlantic & Pacific Tea Co.*,[24] the Second Circuit determined that despite persistent differences in price, brand name frozen waffles and private label frozen waffles were in the same product market where the products appeared side-by-side in supermarket frozen food displays.[25]

In *FTC v. Staples, Inc.*,[26] the district court rejected the merging parties' claim that the relevant market was "the *overall* sale of office

---

22. *Id.* at 401.
23. *Id.* ; *see also* United States v. Cont'l Can Co., 378 U.S. 441, 455 (1964) ("That there are price differentials ... [is] relevant ... but not determinative of the product market issue."); Twin City Sportserv. v. Charles O. Finley & Co., 512 F.2d 1264, 1274 (9th Cir. 1975) (citing *duPont*); Buehler AG v. Ocrim S.p.A., 836 F. Supp. 1305, 1325 (N.D. Tex. 1993) (relevant market included both American and European roller mills sold in the United States, because while the American mills had higher labor costs, the European mills had higher capital costs, so that both types of mills "perform the same function at about the same overall cost"), *aff'd mem.*, 34 F.3d 1080 (Fed. Cir. 1994).
24. 614 F.2d 832 (2d Cir. 1980).
25. *Id.* at 840; *see also* AD/SAT v. Associated Press, 181 F.3d 216, 228 (2d Cir. 1999) (holding that the price difference between one-hour delivery services for newspaper advertisements ($40) and overnight transmission services ($8) was insufficient to demonstrate that the two delivery services were in different product markets); Tarrant Serv. Agency v. Am. Standard, Inc., 12 F.3d 609, 614-15 (6th Cir. 1993) (holding that relevant market in sale of heating, ventilating, and air conditioning equipment included genuine parts, duplicator parts, and generic parts); Liggett & Myers, Inc. v. FTC, 567 F.2d 1273, 1274-75 (4th Cir. 1977) (economy and premium dog foods in single market); Acme Precision Prods. v. Am. Alloys Corp., 484 F.2d 1237, 1240-44 (8th Cir. 1973) (various alloys in same product market despite price differences); United States v. Joseph Schlitz Brewing Co., 253 F. Supp. 129, 133-34 (N.D. Cal. 1966) (finding "premium beer" is in same product market as "popularly priced beer" and "private label beer"), *aff'd per curiam*, 385 U.S. 37 (1966). *But see* Geneva Pharms. Tech. v. Barr Labs., 386 F.3d 485, 498 (2d Cir. 2004) (rejecting district court holding that relevant market included generic and branded warfarin sodium).
26. 970 F. Supp. 1066 (D.D.C. 1997).

products" in favor of a narrower market for "consumable office supply products sold through office superstores."[27] The court based its decision on "cross-elasticity of demand" analysis—in that case, the responsiveness of the sales of consumable office supply products sold by other retailers to price changes in consumable office supply products sold through office supply superstores.[28] The *Staples* court relied heavily on documents of the merging parties and statistical analyses of price comparisons across geographic markets to find that prices were about 13 percent higher in cities with one chain superstore than in cities with three chain superstores.[29] From these comparisons, the court inferred a high cross-elasticity of demand between consumable products offered by the three competing superstore chains, and a low cross-elasticity of demand between products offered at superstores and similar consumable office supply products offered by other retail sellers.[30]

4. Price Discrimination

In certain situations, price discrimination provides a basis for concluding that sales of a product to a particular group of customers constitute a relevant product market separate from sales of the same product to other customers. Successful price discrimination can occur only if a few conditions are met. First, the seller or group of sellers must be able to distinguish between a group of customers who have a less elastic demand for a product and another group of customers who have a more elastic demand for the same product. Second, the seller must be able to charge a higher price to the first group than to the second. Third, it must not be possible for a significant share of customers who are able to purchase at the lower price to resell to customers who are otherwise able to purchase only at the higher price. When these conditions are met,

---

27. *Id.* at 1073 (emphasis added).
28. *Id.* at 1080. Although relying on economic concepts rather than intuition, the court did note that "it is difficult to overcome the first blush or initial gut reaction of many people to the definition of the relevant product market as the sale of consumable office supplies through office supply superstores." *Id.* at 1075.
29. *Id.* at 1076-80.
30. *Id.* at 1078.

the group of customers with relatively inelastic demand may constitute a relevant market.[31]

5. Price Trends

In addition to comparing the existing prices of two products, courts sometimes have compared the movements of their prices over time, reasoning that changes in price should be similar for products in the same

---

31.　This discussion refers to what economists call "third-degree price discrimination." *See, e.g.*, United States v. Grinnell Corp., 384 U.S. 563, 571-75 (1966) (finding a relevant price discrimination product market for class of inelastic buyers); United States v. Rockford Mem'l Corp., 898 F.2d 1278, 1283-84 (7th Cir. 1990) (Posner, J.) (explaining that each category of customers identified with a specific hospital service (i.e., a specific medical indication) could represent a separate relevant product market if a hypothetical monopolist could discriminate in price (or other terms of competition) between such categories based on identified demand elasticities); R.R. Donnelley & Sons Co., 120 F.T.C. 36, 153 (1995) (explaining that the FTC will define a relevant market for a group of buyers for which a hypothetical monopolist could profitably impose a "small but significant and nontransitory" increase in price); Owens-Illinois, Inc., 115 F.T.C. 179, 295-96 (1992) (same). *But see* AD/SAT v. Associated Press, 181 F.2d 216, 228 (2d Cir. 1999) ("[W]here a 'market' itself is insubstantial, made up of only a few buyers with extremely strong preferences, antitrust law is not implicated."). In *R.R. Donnelley*, the FTC concluded that a profitable discriminatory price increase would be possible, and therefore sufficient to define a relevant market, if three conditions were satisfied:

> (1) the hypothetical monopolist can identify gravure customers with sufficiently inelastic demand for gravure printing (*i.e.*, those who will not switch to offset printing in response to a five percent price increase); (2) the hypothetical monopolist can selectively and profitably increase prices to those gravure customers; and (3) arbitrage of gravure printing (resale by favored elastic customers to targeted inelastic customers) would not be sufficient to undermine the price increase.

120 F.T.C. at 158 (footnotes omitted). More recently in *FTC v. Whole Foods Market*, 548 F.3d 1028, 1038 (D.C. Cir. 2008), the D.C. Circuit found that a group of "core" customers for which a supplier can price discriminate can constitute a relevant market. *Id.* at 1041.

market. For example, in *United States v. Aluminum Co. of America*,[32] the Supreme Court relied on the fact that "aluminum and copper conductor prices do not respond to one another" in concluding that aluminum and copper cable belonged in separate submarkets.[33] Such evidence can be difficult to interpret, however, especially because parallel price movements of different products might result from separate responses to common costs or marketing conditions.[34]

6. The "Cellophane Fallacy"

Courts have warned against the "Cellophane [*duPont*] fallacy," cautioning that cross-elasticity of demand should be measured at a competitive price level, rather than at a higher market price that might

---

32. 377 U.S. 271 (1964).
33. *Id.* at 276; *see also* U.S. Anchor Mfg. v. Rule Indus., 7 F.3d 986, 996 (11th Cir. 1993) ("If changes in relative prices had been more closely correlated in time with shifting purchases then it might have been reasonable to infer that the demand shifts were caused by the price differences."); Ad-Vantage Tel. Directory Consultants v. GTE Directories Corp., 849 F.2d 1336, 1342 (11th Cir. 1987) (finding that fact that increases in prices of yellow pages advertising were not commensurate with increases in prices for other forms of advertising supported jury finding that yellow pages advertising was a relevant product market); Avnet, Inc. v. FTC, 511 F.2d 70, 77 (7th Cir. 1975) (noting the lack of "substantial interaction in price" between reconditioned and new parts); FTC v. Swedish Match, 131 F. Supp. 2d 151, 165 (D.D.C. 2000). *Cf.* Yoder Bros. v. California-Florida Plant Corp., 537 F.2d 1347, 1368 (5th Cir. 1976) (finding that consumer responsiveness to price differences between chrysanthemums and carnations was not negated by facts that prices of carnations did not change at "same instant" as chrysanthemum prices and that prices for the two ornamental flowers did not change by "precisely the same amounts"). *But see* Gordon v. Lewistown Hosp., 272 F. Supp. 2d 393, 420-24 (M.D. Pa. 2003) (finding products in same market despite no cross-elasticity of demand on the ground that price is an insufficient measure of consumer preference in medical markets), *aff'd*, 423 F.3d 184 (3d Cir. 2005).
34. *See, e.g., In re* Coca-Cola Co., 117 F.T.C. 795, 936 n.67, 940 (1994), *modified*, 119 F.T.C. 724 (1995) (finding separate product markets for branded and nonbranded carbonated soft drink concentrate despite evidence that prices "have trended together over time," noting that the parallel price trends could be attributable to other factors such as "changes in the costs of common ingredients").

reflect the presence of pre-existing market power. For example, in *Eastman Kodak Co. v. Image Technical Services*,[35] the Court indicated that the fact that the price of a product is currently restrained by the ability of buyers to substitute other goods or services does not necessarily disprove the existence of market power in the market for that product because its sellers might already be charging a monopoly price.[36]

C. Geographic Market Definition

The Supreme Court has described the relevant geographic market as "the 'area of effective competition . . . in which the seller operates, and to which the purchaser can practicably turn for supplies.'"[37] As with

---

35.   504 U.S. 451 (1992).
36.   *Id.* at 471; *see also* Santa Cruz Med. Clinic v. Dominican Santa Cruz Hosp., No. C93-20613, 1995 WL 853037, at *10 & n.10 (N.D. Cal. 1995) (discussing Cellophane fallacy in context of geographic market definition).
37.   United States v. Philadelphia Nat'l Bank, 374 U.S. 321, 359 (1963) (quoting Tampa Elec. Co. v. Nashville Coal Co., 365 U.S. 320, 327 (1961)) (emphasis omitted); *see also* United States v. Phillipsburg Nat'l Bank & Trust, 399 U.S. 350, 364-65 (1970); Standard Oil Co. v. United States, 337 U.S. 293, 299 n.5 (1949); Heerwagen v. Clear Channel Commc'ns, 435 F.3d 219, 227 (2d Cir. 2006) (defining geographic market as "how far consumers will go to obtain the product or its substitute in response to a given price increase and how likely it is that a price increase for the product in a particular location will induce outside suppliers to . . . increase supply-side competition in that location"); United States v. Eastman Kodak Co., 63 F.3d 95, 104-105 (2d Cir. 1995); Morgenstern v. Wilson, 29 F.3d 1291, 1296 (8th Cir. 1994) (defining geographic market as "the geographic area to which consumers can practically turn for alternative sources of the product and in which the antitrust defendants face competition"); A.A. Poultry Farms v. Rose Acre Farms, 881 F.2d 1396, 1403 (7th Cir. 1989) (defining geographic market as "the set of sellers to which a set of buyers can turn for supplies at existing or slightly higher prices") (quoting FTC v. Elders Grain, 868 F.2d 901, 907 (7th Cir. 1989)); Am. Key Corp. v. Cole Nat'l Corp., 762 F.2d 1569, 1580 (11th Cir. 1985); Pa. Dental Ass'n v. Med. Serv. Ass'n, 745 F.2d 248, 260 (3d Cir. 1984) (defining geographic market as the area in which "a potential buyer may rationally look for . . . goods and services"); Cal. *ex rel.* Lockyer v. Mirant Corp., 266 F. Supp. 2d 1046, 1055-56 (N.D. Cal. 2003) (same), *aff'd sub nom.* Cal. *ex rel.* Lockyer v. Dynegy, Inc., 375 F.3d 831 (9th Cir. 2004); Blanchard & Co. v. Barrick

relevant product markets, the "area of effective competition" in a particular case depends upon the cross-elasticity of demand and, in some instances, also of supply.[38] In *Brown Shoe Co. v. United States*,[39] the Supreme Court explained:

> The criteria to be used in determining the appropriate geographic market are essentially similar to those used to determine the relevant product market. . . . Congress prescribed a pragmatic, factual approach to the definition of the relevant market and not a formal, legalistic one. The geographic market selected must, therefore, both "correspond to the commercial realities" of the industry and be economically significant. Thus, although the geographic market in some instances may encompass the entire Nation, under other circumstances it may be as small as a single metropolitan area.[40]

Gold Corp., No. Civ.A-02-3721, 2003 WL 22071173, at *7 (E.D. La. 2003) (finding worldwide market for gold because change of price in London has direct and proportionate effect in Far East); City of Chanute v. Williams Natural Gas, 678 F. Supp. 1517, 1532 (D. Kan. 1988) (defining geographic market as area to which plaintiff could practicably turn for supplies, rather than all areas served by defendant); Laidlaw Acquisition Corp. v. Mayflower Group, 636 F. Supp. 1513, 1519 (S.D. Ind. 1986); United States v. First Nat'l State Bancorp., 499 F. Supp. 793, 801 (D.N.J. 1980) (analyzing where banks' customers may turn for services).

38. *See Heerwagen*, 435 F.3d at 227-34. The cross-elasticity of demand (supply) for a product between two different geographic areas measures the extent to which the quantity demanded (supplied) one area changes in response to a change in the price of the product in the other area.

39. 370 U.S. 294 (1962).

40. *Id.* at 336-37 (citations omitted); *see also* Apani Sw., Inc. v. Coca-Cola Enters., 300 F.3d 620, 626 (5th Cir. 2002) ("The geographic market must correspond to the commercial realities of the industry and be economically significant.") (quotations and citation omitted); 42nd Parallel N. v. E St. Denim Co., 286 F.3d 401, 406 (7th Cir. 2002) ("We also cannot close our eyes to the fact that 42nd's proposed geographic market is absurdly small . . . . By any sensible awareness of commercial reality, 42nd was swimming in a much larger competitive sea than the complaint lets on.") (citation omitted); Morgan, Strand, Wheeler & Biggs v. Radiology, Ltd., 924 F.2d 1484, 1490 (9th Cir. 1991) (finding submarket must be "sufficiently insulated from the larger market so that supply and demand are inelastic with the larger market"; rejecting submarket limited to Northwest Tucson) (citation omitted).

The Second Circuit addressed geographic market definition in *Heerwagen v. Clear Channel Communications.*[41] The court rejected an alleged national market for the sale of concert tickets to consumers because the evidence established a lack of cross-elasticity of demand for concerts in different geographic areas within the United States such that, for example, "a higher price [for a concert] in Boston will not lead Boston purchasers to buy tickets for the same concert held in New York."[42] Given the absence of significant cross-elasticity of demand between concerts taking place in different metropolitan areas of the United States, the relevant geographic markets were local, not national, in scope.[43]

Because direct measures of elasticities frequently are not available owing to a lack of sufficient data, courts and agencies have developed a number of criteria for determining whether a particular geographic area can be characterized as a relevant geographic market.

1. The Elzinga-Hogarty Test

Actual geographic sales patterns are often used to determine the extent of a relevant geographic market.[44] In areas in which the vast majority of sales to customers are made by suppliers located in that area, or the vast majority of customers of a firm or set of firms are located in a particular area, the relevant geographic market may be limited to that area.[45]

---

41. 435 F.3d 219 (2d Cir. 2006).
42. *Id.* at 228.
43. *Id.* at 228-30.
44. *See, e.g., id.* at 230-31 (finding local markets for concert tickets based on sales and practical alternatives); *see also* Tampa Elec. Co. v. Nashville Coal Co., 365 U.S. 320, 331-33 (1961) (finding relevant market comprised at least seven states from which coal is shipped); United States v. Eastman Kodak Co., 63 F.3d 95, 104 (2d Cir. 1995) (finding "film sellers operate on a world-wide scale"); United States v. Waste Mgmt., 743 F.2d 976, 980-81 (2d Cir. 1984) (finding haulers operated almost exclusively in their respective cities).
45. *See, e.g.,* United States v. Marine Bancorp., 418 U.S. 602, 619 (1974); United States v. Pabst Brewing Co., 384 U.S. 546, 559 (1966) (fact that 90 percent of beer sold in state came from brewers in Wisconsin or Minnesota supported limitation of geographic market to Wisconsin); Heerwagen v. Clear Channel Commc'ns, 435 F.3d 219, 228-30 (2d Cir. 2006) (finding geographic markets for live concerts are local because

The Elzinga-Hogarty test, which analyzes origin and destination patterns for the consumption and shipment of products, attempts to make use of these types of locational considerations in delineating geographic markets. [46] The Elzinga-Hogarty test computes two measures for a proposed market: LIFO ("little in from outside") and LOFI ("little out from inside"). LIFO is defined as the percentage of consumers outside the proposed market who do not travel into it, while LOFI is defined as the percentage of consumers in a proposed market who do not leave the market. Both LIFO and LOFI tests consider the source of production and

---

most concertgoers will not travel long distances to attend them); Houser v. Fox Theatres Mgmt., 845 F.2d 1225, 1230 & n.10 (3d Cir. 1988) (finding relevant market is Lebanon, Pennsylvania, because theater patrons in Lebanon primarily attend Lebanon theaters); *Waste Mgmt.*, 743 F.2d at 980 (market for solid waste hauling limited to portion of Dallas/Fort Worth metropolitan area in light of small overlap in service of each area and high cost of travel between the cities for daily waste hauling); Town of Concord v. Boston Edison Co., 721 F. Supp. 1456, 1459-60 (D. Mass. 1989) (finding relevant market is utility's service area because that was area in which utility competed for customers), *rev'd on other grounds*, 915 F.2d 17 (1st Cir. 1990); United States v. Rice Growers Ass'n, No. S-84-1066, 1986 WL 12562, at *7-8 (E.D. Cal. 1986) (in light of transportation costs and low level of purchases from or sales to other areas, California is a relevant geographic market for purchase of paddy rice for milling); United States v. Cent. State Bank, 621 F. Supp. 1276, 1293-94 (W.D. Mich. 1985) (market limited to two-county area where nearly 95 percent of total deposits of residents of two counties were held in banks within those two counties, *aff'd per curiam*, 817 F.2d 22 (6th Cir. 1987). *Cf.* Gordon v. Lewistown Hosp., 423 F.3d 184, 212 (3d Cir. 2005) (rejecting two-county market because more than 20 percent of patients came from outside the two counties); Republic Tobacco v. North Atl. Trading, 381 F.3d 717, 736-39 (7th Cir. 2004) (because customers were located throughout the United States, finding market could not be limited to nine-state area); California v. Sutter Health Sys., 130 F. Supp. 2d 1109, 1125 (N.D. Cal. 2001) ("Where a hospital outside of the proposed geographic market draws patients from the same region from which the merging hospitals draw their patients, the hospital located outside of the test market is considered a practical alternative . . . .") (citation omitted).

46. *See* Kenneth G. Elzinga & Thomas F. Hogarty, *The Problem of Geographic Market Delineation in Antimerger Suits*, 18 ANTITRUST BULL. 45 (1973); *see also* Kenneth G. Elzinga & Thomas F. Hogarty, *The Problem of Geographic Market Delineation Revisited: The Case of Coal*, 23 ANTITRUST BULL. 1 (1978).

impact of imports and exports. For example, if a significant number of consumers travel outside a specific geographic area to purchase a good or service, this may suggest that a broader relevant geographic market is warranted. However, if few consumers travel outside the proposed market to purchase the good in question, this may support the proposed market definition. Proponents of the test suggest that if these measures are sufficiently high in percentage terms, the proposed market is a relevant geographic market for antitrust purposes. Neither Professors Elzinga and Hogarty, nor courts, nor the agencies have determined how high these percentages must be in order for the test to delineate a relevant market, although Elzinga and Hogarty have suggested that 90 percent might indicate a "strong" market.[47]

Courts sometimes employ this test to identify relevant competitors of merging entities.[48] In *United States v. Oracle Corp.*,[49] the court applied the Elzinga-Hogarty test to enterprise resource planning software sales and found that the geographic market was global.[50] The court noted that the test is "an appropriate method of determining the 'area of effective competition,'" despite the presence of highly-developed relationships between vendors and customers in the market.[51]

---

47. *See* California v. Sutter Health Sys., 84 F. Supp. 2d 1057, 1069 (N.D. Cal. 2001), *aff'd*, 217 F.3d 846 (9th Cir. 2000); Adventist Health Sys., 117 F.T.C. 224, 293 (1994).

48. Elzinga & Hogarty, *The Problem of Geographic Market Delineation Revisited*, *supra* note 46, at 2; *see* Rome Ambulatory Surgical Ctr. v. Rome Mem'l Hosp., 349 F. Supp. 2d 389, 418-20 (N.D.N.Y. 2004) (using the Elzinga-Hogarty method to conclude that defendants were the sole providers in the relevant geographic market was sufficient to survive defendants' motion for summary judgment on plaintiff's attempted monopolization claim); United States v. Rockford Mem'l Corp., 717 F. Supp. 1251, 1266-75 (N.D. Ill. 1989) (applying this test to help define relevant geographic market), *aff'd*, 898 F.2d 1278 (7th Cir. 1990); *see also* United States v. Rockford Mem'l Corp., 898 F.2d 1278, 1285 (7th Cir. 1990) (Posner, J.) (characterizing lower court's market based on Elzinga-Hogarty methodology as "imperfect" but adopting it as the "less imperfect" alternative under the "clearly erroneous" review standard); *In re* Coca Cola Bottling, 118 F.T.C. 452, 581-82 (1994) (Elzinga-Hogarty test provides relevant information but is not dispositive.).

49. 331 F. Supp. 2d 1098 (N.D. Cal. 2004).

50. *Id.* at 1164-65.

51. *Id.* at 1165 (citing Tampa Elec. Co. v. Nashville Coal Co., 365 U.S. 320, 327 (1961)).

The Elzinga-Hogarty test has been criticized.[52] It measures only historic and current geographic patterns of behavior and does not consider how patterns would change if a firm were to attempt to exercise market power.[53] Courts have recognized that the relevant market might be broader than the existing pattern of commerce if customers could readily turn to more remote suppliers in response to a price increase by local suppliers.[54] Moreover, when the sales areas of firms in differing locations over a wide area have extensive overlaps, the relevant geographic market in which the prices for a particular group of customers is determined may be considerably larger than the combined area served by the firms that serve that group of customers.[55]

---

52. *See In re* Evanston Nw. Healthcare, No. 9315, 2005 FTC LEXIS 146, at *281 (F.T.C. 2005) (initial decision) (defining relevant geographic market for acute care hospital services as a portion of the North Shore area near Chicago encompassing seven hospitals and rejecting use of the Elzinga-Hogarty test, noting that Professor Elzinga testified at trial that the "Elzinga-Hogarty test is not appropriate for determining the relevant geographic market for hospital services").

53. *See* Minn. Ass'n of Nurse Anesthetists v. Unity Hosp., 208 F.3d 655, 662 (8th Cir. 2000); FTC v. Freeman Hosp., 69 F.3d 260, 269 (8th Cir. 1995); United States v. Mercy Health Servs., 902 F. Supp. 968, 978 (N.D. Iowa 1995), *vacated as moot*, 107 F.3d 632 (8th Cir. 1997).

54. The relevant geographic market also might be narrower than existing trade patterns if customers are currently forced to purchase from distant sources because of monopolistic prices charged by nearby sellers. *See generally* Santa Cruz Med. Clinic v. Dominican Santa Cruz Hosp., No. C93-20613, 1995 WL 853037, at *10 & n.10 (N.D. Cal. 1995).

55. *See, e.g.*, RSR Corp. v. FTC, 602 F.2d 1317, 1322-24 (9th Cir. 1979) (finding relevant geographic market to be national despite high cost of transport where shipping radius around plants served by firms accounted for a majority of national consumption and where regional prices were interrelated); Doc Magic, Inc. v. Ellie Mae, Inc., 2010 U.S. Dist. LEXIS 108628 (N.D. Cal. 2010) (holding that the existence of a local market does not preclude the possibility of the existence of a national market); Weeks Dredging & Contracting v. Am. Dredging Co., 451 F. Supp. 468, 491-92 (E.D. Pa. 1978) (finding fact that same leading companies tended to bid on projects in various harbors along East Coast supported finding that market consisted of entire East Coast and not each local harbor).

2. *Other Factors Considered by Courts*

The courts have considered a number of factors that may limit the size of geographic markets, including transportation costs—especially in relation to the price of the product[56]—and governmental barriers to movement of goods and services, such as licensing requirements,[57] tariffs, or quotas.[58] Courts also have cited industry practices such as separate distribution territories or pricing zones[59]; the existence of

---

56. *See, e.g.*, United States v. Gen. Dynamics Corp., 415 U.S. 486, 491 (1974) ("[A] realistic geographic market should be defined in terms of transportation arteries and freight charges that determine the cost of delivered coal. . . ."); Hornsby Oil v. Champion Spark Plug, 714 F.2d 1384, 1394 (5th Cir. 1983) (When "ascertaining the scope of a geographic market . . . transportation costs, delivery limitations and customer convenience . . . must be considered . . . ."); United States v. Dean Foods Co., 2010 U.S. Dist. LEXIS 34137 (E.D. Wis. 2010) (finding plaintiff's allegations created a plausible inference that targeted customers could not defeat a SSNIP by turning to more distant sellers because fluid milk has a limited shelf life and is costly to transport); Z-Tel Commc'ns v. SBC Commc'ns, 331 F. Supp. 2d 513, 523 (E.D. Tex. 2004) ("Where products are sold nationwide and transportation costs are insignificant, courts frequently define the geographic market as the entire nation.").

57. *See, e.g.*, United States v. Philadelphia Nat'l Bank, 374 U.S. 321, 367 & n.44 (1963) ("Entry [in the banking industry] is, of course, wholly a matter of governmental grace."); United States v. Marine Bancorp., 418 U.S. 602, 628 (1973) (same); *see also* United States v. Waste Mgmt., No. 03-CV-1409, 68 Fed. Reg. 47,930, 47,941-42 (2003) (noting that relevant geographic market for municipal solid waste disposal businesses is governed by strict laws and regulations). In *Delaware Health Care v. MCD Holding*, 957 F. Supp. 535, 543-44 (D. Del. 1997), *aff'd*, 141 F.3d 1153 (3d Cir. 1998), the court found that the plaintiff's alleged geographic market for hospital inpatient services, New Castle County, withstood summary judgment based in part on account licensure requirements.

58. *See, e.g.*, United States v. LTV Corp., No. 84-884, 1984 WL 21973, at *3 (D.D.C. 1984) (noting that DOJ had included in the relevant market all imports except those from Japan and the European Communities that were subject to quotas or voluntary limitations on shipments), *appeal dismissed*, 746 F.2d 51 (D.C. Cir. 1984).

59. *See, e.g.*, *In re* Coca-Cola Bottling, 118 F.T.C. 452, 583 (1994) (national and regional retailers viewed San Antonio as a separate retail market and

nationwide planning, nationwide contracts, or a national schedule of prices, rates, and terms[60]; industry recognition[61]; and the relationship among prices and price movements between two areas.[62] As with

---

accordingly ran localized advertising and marketing campaigns); Lynch Bus. Machs. v. A.B. Dick Co., 594 F. Supp. 59, 68 (N.D. Ohio 1984) (separate distribution territories); United States v. Hammermill Paper Co., 429 F. Supp. 1271, 1278 (W.D. Pa. 1977) ("no separate delivered pricing zone"). *But see* Bearing Distribs. v. Rockwell Automation, No. 06-cv-831, 2006 WL 2709779, at *9 (N.D. Ohio 2006) (mere existence of regional and local distributors did not mean that relevant market was not national in scope).

60. *See, e.g.*, United States v. Grinnell Corp., 384 U.S. 563, 575-76 (1966); Republic Tobacco v. North Atl. Trading, 381 F.3d 717 (7th Cir. 2004) (finding national market because suppliers sold to national wholesalers). *Compare* Kaiser Aluminum & Chem., 93 F.T.C. 764, 814-15 (1979) (national market), *vacated & remanded on other grounds*, 652 F.2d 1324, 1329 (7th Cir. 1981), *and* United States v. Mrs. Smith's Pie Co., 440 F. Supp. 220, 230 (E.D. Pa. 1976) (national market), *with* Jim Walter Corp. v. FTC, 625 F.2d 676, 682-83 (5th Cir. 1980) (evidence insufficient to establish national market).

61. *See, e.g.*, United States v. Phillipsburg Nat'l Bank & Trust, 399 U.S. 350, 364-65 (1970); Morgenstern v. Wilson, 29 F.3d 1291, 1297 (8th Cir. 1994); F. & M. Schaefer Corp. v. C. Schmidt & Sons, 597 F.2d 814, 817 (2d Cir. 1979) (per curiam); Tasty Baking v. Ralston Purina, Inc., 653 F. Supp. 1250, 1262 (E.D. Pa. 1987) (noting that the companies generally perceived "markets defined by metropolitan areas").

62. The courts have stated that "if a change in price in one area has an effect on price in another area both areas may be included in one geographic market." United States v. Bethlehem Steel Corp., 168 F. Supp. 576, 599-600 (S.D.N.Y. 1958); *see also* Heerwagen v. Clear Channel Commc'ns, 435 F.3d 219, 228-30 (2d Cir. 2006); United States v. Eastman Kodak Co., 63 F.3d 95, 108 (2d Cir. 1995) (finding worldwide market where "the difference in price [in the United States] between Kodak film and that of its competitors is small and declining"); Rothery Storage & Van Co. v. Atlas Van Lines, Inc., 792 F.2d 210, 219-21 (D.C. Cir. 1986) (finding absence of evidence that prices in two areas move independently undercuts claim that there are separate geographic markets); RSR Corp. v. FTC, 602 F.2d 1317, 1323 n.3 (9th Cir. 1979) ("[W]hen one region discounts the price of secondary lead, the price is eventually affected nationwide"); Horst v. Laidlaw Waste Sys., 917 F. Supp. 739, 744 (D. Colo. 1996) ("[F]our landfills were sensitive to price changes charged by one another, a signal that they are part of the same geographic market."); *Tasty Baking*, 653 F. Supp. at 1260-61 (finding pricing policies reflect

defining the relevant product market, however, evidence of parallel price movements can be difficult to interpret because similar price trends in different locations may result from common economic or marketing conditions rather than product substitutability.

3. Frequently Observed Outcomes

While geographic market issues are highly fact-specific, and generalizations are therefore subject to many exceptions, markets for manufactured goods frequently are regional, [63] national, [64] or international,[65] whereas many service markets (e.g., retailing) are local, particularly when individual customers must travel to the sellers to make purchases.[66] Markets may also be local for goods with a high ratio of

---

awareness of localized competitive conditions in distinct urban and regional markets); Monfort v. Cargill, Inc., 591 F. Supp. 683, 700 (D. Colo. 1983) (price differentials in fed cattle), *aff'd*, 761 F.2d 570 (10th Cir. 1985), *rev'd on other grounds*, 479 U.S. 104 (1986); Marathon Oil v. Mobil Corp., 530 F. Supp. 315, 321-22 (N.D. Ohio) (price differentials in petroleum industry), *aff'd*, 669 F.2d 378 (6th Cir. 1981); United States v. Healthco, Inc., 387 F. Supp. 258 (S.D.N.Y. 1975); *Coca-Cola*, 118 F.T.C. at 582-83 (finding parallel price movements suggest areas are in the same market, but only weak evidence in this case).

63.   *See, e.g.*, Bacchus Indus. v. Arvin Indus., 939 F.2d 887, 893 (10th Cir. 1991) (finding market for evaporative coolers is "the twelve western states").

64.   *See, e.g.*, United States v. E.I. duPont de Nemours & Co., 351 U.S. 377, 395 (1956) (market for flexible packaging material is nationwide); Murrow Furniture Galleries v. Thomasville Furniture Indus., 889 F.2d 524, 529 (4th Cir. 1989) (furniture market is nationwide).

65.   *See, e.g.*, *Eastman Kodak Co.*, 63 F.3d at 104 (film market is worldwide); *see also* Lockheed Martin Corp. v. Boeing Co., 314 F. Supp. 2d 1198, 1226-29 (M.D. Fla. 2004) (rejecting claim that the geographic market should be narrowed to the United States based on the characteristics of the purchaser, which in this case was the U.S. government, and instead finding a worldwide market for the service of designing and developing expendable satellite launch vehicles because those services were equally marketable to both the U.S. government and commercial purchasers).

66.   *See, e.g.*, United States v. Philadelphia Nat'l Bank, 374 U.S. 321, 358 (1963) ("In banking, as in most service industries, convenience of location is essential to effective competition" and localizes banking competition.); United States v. Phillipsburg Nat'l Bank & Trust, 399 U.S. 350, 362-63 (1970) (same); Heerwagen v. Clear Channel Commc'ns, 435

transportation cost to value. [67] And, in some unique circumstances, geographic markets might be closely intertwined with the geographic component of the product being sold. For example, in *United States v. AMR Corp.*,[68] the court considered competitive practices in the airline industry, and specifically the hub-and-spoke system of American Airlines. The court defined the relevant market as four city-pair airline routes, all connected to American's hub at Dallas/Fort Worth International Airport. [69] This is because for time-sensitive business travelers, air travel to other destinations is not a substitute for travel between two particular cities.

D. *Merger Guidelines* Approach

The purpose of market delineation is to identify the other products and sellers that constrain the price of a particular product sold by a particular supplier. In delineating relevant markets, the *Merger Guidelines* focus on the extent to which buyers of a particular product from a particular seller will substitute to the same product or other products from other sellers in response to an increase in the price of the initial product from the initial seller.[70] The *Merger Guidelines* provide

---

F.3d 219, 230-31 (2d Cir. 2006) (finding a local market for concert tickets based on sales and practical alternatives); United States v. Cent. State Bank, 621 F. Supp. 1276, 1293 (W.D. Mich. 1985) (single city market for banking services), *aff'd per curiam*, 817 F.2d 22 (6th Cir. 1987). *But see* Total Benefit Servs. v. Group Ins. Admin., 875 F. Supp. 1228, 1237 (E.D. La. 1995) (noting that evidence indicated that insurance "customers looked to suppliers from all over the country"); Adventist Health Sys., 117 F.T.C. 224, 297 (1994) (finding complaint failed to carry burden of proof that Ukiah-Willits-Lakeport or Ukiah-Willits constituted a relevant geographic market for the provision of inpatient acute care hospital services).

67. *See also* Tasty Baking v. Ralston Purina, Inc., 653 F. Supp. 1250, 1260-62 (E.D. Pa. 1987) (four cities and two regions are each separate geographic markets for snack cakes and pies); *In re* Coca-Cola Bottling, 118 F.T.C. 452, 584 (1994) (relevant geographic market for branded carbonated soft drinks was ten-county area centered around San Antonio, Texas).

68. 335 F.3d 1109 (10th Cir. 2003).

69. *Id.* at 1111; *accord* Spirit Airlines v. Northwest Airlines, 431 F.3d 917 (6th Cir. 2006) (identifying relevant geographic markets as two city pairs).

70. MERGER GUIDELINES, *supra* note 1, § 4. The merger guidelines issued by the National Association of Attorneys General (NAAG) apply a

that "[m]arket definition focuses solely on demand substitution factors, i.e., on customers' ability and willingness to substitute away from one product to another in response to a price increase or a corresponding non-price change such as a reduction in product quality or service."[71]

While the approach to defining markets in the 2010 *Merger Guidelines* is largely the same as the approach promulgated in earlier versions, the current *Guidelines* focus more attention on the relative importance of market definition in the merger review process. For example, the Guidelines include caveats about situations in which more than one market could reasonably be defined, and what inferences to draw from that definition. In particular, the *Merger Guidelines* note that market definition plays two roles: (i) specifying the lines of commerce and sections of the country in which competitive concerns may arise; and (ii) facilitating the identification of market participants and the measurement of shares and concentration.[72] In a departure from prior versions of the *Guidelines* (though not from agency practice), the 2010 *Merger Guidelines* further indicate that the agencies will not necessarily begin their analyses with market definition and that a number of analytical tools available to the agencies do not rely upon market definition but concentrate on the effects of the proposed merger.[73] Nonetheless, a necessary part of any merger analysis is the evaluation of

---

consumer perception test, defining the product market to include the products sold by the merging firms together with those comparably priced goods that customers accounting for 75 percent of the purchases from the merging firms consider to be "suitable substitutes." NAT'L ASS'N OF ATTORNEYS GENERAL, HORIZONTAL MERGER GUIDELINES § 3.1 (1993), *reprinted in* 4 Trade Reg. Rep. (CCH) ¶ 13,406.

71.   MERGER GUIDELINES, *supra* note 1, § 4.

72.   *Id.*

73.   *Id.* In contrast, the 1992 *Merger Guidelines* explicitly listed market definition and the analysis of shares and concentration as the first step in the merger review process. U.S. DEP'T OF JUSTICE & FED. TRADE COMM'N, HORIZONTAL MERGER GUIDELINES § 0.2 (1992), *available at* http://www.justice.gov/atr/public/guidelines/hmg.htm [hereinafter 1992 MERGER GUIDELINES]. Regardless of the explicit approach laid out in the 1992 *Merger Guidelines*, it is not clear that actual merger review necessarily strictly followed this process. *See* U.S. DEP'T OF JUSTICE & FED. TRADE COMM'N, COMMENTARY ON THE HORIZONTAL MERGER GUIDELINES 2 (Mar. 2006), *available at* http://www.justice/gov/-atr/public/guidelines/215247.htm.

competitive alternatives available to customers that constrain the price(s) of the product(s) under consideration.[74]

Although not binding on the courts,[75] courts have often relied upon the approach to market definition under the old version of the *Guidelines* in defining product markets.[76]

1. Product Market

Under the *Guidelines*, the agencies define an antitrust market for each product that may compete with a product of the other merging firm. In doing so, the agencies seek to identify the products (and their producers) that could make it unprofitable for the first merging firm to raise the price of that product absent the merger (i.e., that constitute the relevant market). If a product from the second merging firm is included in the market for a product from the first merging firm, a competitive overlap exists.

In order to identify the products that make it unprofitable for the first merging firm to raise the price of a product (i.e., that are in the relevant market), the agencies identify a small number of products that are the closest substitutes for the customers that are buying the product in question from the first merging firm. (If virtually identical products are sold by other firms, then the group of virtually identical products would

---

74. MERGER GUIDELINES, *supra* note 1, § 4.
75. *See, e.g.*, Olin Corp. v. FTC, 986 F.2d 1295, 1302-03 (9th Cir. 1993) (refusing to be bound by the *Merger Guidelines*).
76. *See* FTC v. Whole Foods Mkt., 548 F.3d 1028, 1037-38 (D.C. Cir. 2008) (citing *Merger Guidelines* in analyzing relevant product market); United States v. UPM-Kymmene Oyj, No. 03-C-2528, 2003 WL 21781902, at *8 (N.D. Ill. 2003) (finding that "the product-market methodology set out in the Horizontal Merger Guidelines is legally sound"); United States v. Sungard Data Sys., 172 F. Supp. 2d 172, 182 (D.D.C. 2001) (citing *Merger Guidelines* in defining legal standard to determine product market); United States v. Visa U.S.A., Inc., 163 F. Supp. 2d 322, 335 (S.D.N.Y. 2001) (citing *Merger Guidelines* to analyze relevant product market), *aff'd*, 344 F.3d 229 (2d Cir. 2003); California v. Sutter Health Sys., 130 F. Supp. 2d 1109, 1119 (N.D. Cal. 2001) (citing *Merger Guidelines* to analyze relevant product market); FTC v. Swedish Match, 131 F. Supp. 2d 151, 160 (D.D.C. 2000) (same); FTC v. Staples, Inc., 970 F. Supp. 1066, 1076 & n.8 (D.D.C. 1997) (citing "analytical framework set forth in the *Merger Guidelines*" in discussion of relevant product market).

normally constitute the initial set of closest substitutes.) The agencies then ask whether a hypothetical monopolist of these sources of supply would profitably impose "at least a small but significant and non-transitory increase in price" (SSNIP) for the product in question, or a set of products including that product. For the purpose of their analyses, the agencies generally use a SSNIP of 5 percent.[77] This hypothetical price increase is intended to approximate "the effects of price changes commensurate with those that might result from a significant lessening of competition caused by the merger."[78] But the agencies recognize that a 5 percent SSNIP is not appropriate in all circumstances. The size of the SSNIP to be analyzed "depends upon the nature of the industry and the merging firms' positions in it, and the agencies may accordingly use a price increase that is larger or smaller than five percent."[79]

If such a price increase would cause enough buyers to shift to other products not in the initial set so that the price increase would be unprofitable for the hypothetical monopolist, the agencies expand the candidate product market to include additional substitutes for the initial product and repeat the hypothetical monopolist analysis until a set of products is identified for which the price increase would be profitable.[80] This set of products is then a relevant product market in which to analyze the competitive effects of the merger on the price of the product in question.

Whether a candidate market satisfies the hypothetical monopolist test ultimately depends on two characteristics of the market: (i) the own-price elasticity of demand for the candidate product(s), which measures the rate at which sales are lost when price is increased, and (ii) the premerger margin between the price and the variable or incremental costs (defined over the relevant range of output), which measures the loss in profits per unit of sales lost as a result of the price increase.[81]

Economic data of sufficient quality to estimate demand elasticities often are not available, and econometric estimates of demand elasticities frequently have serious shortcomings that may make them unreliable.[82]

---

77.   MERGER GUIDELINES, *supra* note 1, § 4.1.2.

78.   *Id.*

79.   *Id.*

80.   *Id.* § 4.1.1.

81.   *See generally* MERGER GUIDELINES, *supra* note 1, § 4.1.3.

82.   *See, e.g.*, FTC v. Swedish Match, 131 F. Supp. 2d 151, 161 (D.D.C. 2000) (rejecting econometric analyses offered by both plaintiff's and defendant's experts after detailed review of underlying data and

Whether or not econometric estimates of demand elasticities are available, the agencies analyze documentary evidence and seek the views of market participants, including both sellers and their customers, regarding the substitutability of products in response to small changes in relative prices.[83] The *Guidelines* provide:

> In considering customers' likely responses to higher prices, the Agencies take into account any reasonably available and reliable evidence, including, but not limited to:
> - how customers have shifted purchases in the past in response to relative changes in price or other terms and conditions;
> - information from buyers, including surveys, concerning how they would respond to price changes;
> - the conduct of industry participants, notably sellers' business decisions or business documents indicating sellers' informed beliefs concerning how customers would substitute among products in response to relative changes in price, and industry participants' behavior in tracking and responding to price changes by some or all rivals;
> - objective information about product characteristics and the costs and delays of switching products, especially switching from products in the candidate market to products outside the candidate market;
> - the percentage of sales lost by one product in the candidate market, when its price alone rises, that is recaptured by other products in the candidate market, with a higher recapture percentage making a price increase more profitable for the hypothetical monopolist;
> - evidence from other industry participants, such as sellers of complementary products;
> - legal or regulatory requirements; and

assumptions); New York v. Kraft Gen. Foods, 926 F. Supp. 321, 358, 361 (S.D.N.Y. 1995) (describing criticisms of plaintiff's computations); *In re* B.A.T. Indus., 104 F.T.C. 852, 931 (1984) (rejecting cross-elasticity study). For additional discussion of econometric calculations relating to market definition, see *supra* ch. III.

83. *See, e.g.*, United States v. Oracle Corp., 331 F. Supp. 2d 1098, 1125-33, 1136-45 (N.D. Cal. 2004); FTC v. Arch Coal, Inc., 329 F. Supp. 2d 109, 120-24 (D.D.C. 2004); *In re* Owens-Illinois, Inc., 115 F.T.C. 179, 301 (1992); *In re* Weyerhauser Co., 106 F.T.C. 172, 275 (1985).

- the influence of downstream competition faced by customers in their output markets.[84]

The *Guidelines* do not look to cross-elasticity of supply—that is, supply substitution factors—as a determinant of the relevant product market. Instead, they consider cross-elasticity of supply separately, in the course of identifying the firms that currently participate in or could enter the relevant product market.[85]

In cases in which a hypothetical monopolist could profitably increase prices to a subset of customers, the agencies may define price discrimination markets.[86] The *Merger Guidelines* set out two conditions that must be met in order for price discrimination to occur: (i) suppliers must price differently to targeted customers; and (ii) targeted customers must not be able to engage in arbitrage in order to defeat targeted price increases.[87] Price discrimination may occur most often in markets for intermediate goods, where prices are frequently negotiated individually. In such cases, suppliers may obtain information about customers that can be used to target certain subsets of customers. Once the agencies identify sets of customers that meet the conditions described above, they apply the standard hypothetical monopolist test to define markets for targeted customers.

---

84. MERGER GUIDELINES, *supra* note 1, § 4.1.3. The agencies consider the documented views of the merging firms as expressed in their ordinary course of business documents. When firms routinely concentrate on some presumptively competitive products and ignore others, they may be providing a practical assessment of the products that are inside or outside the relevant product market. *See, e.g.*, Cmty. Publishers v. Donrey Corp., 892 F. Supp. 1146, 1153-54 (W.D. Ark. 1995), *aff'd sub nom.* Cmty. Publishers v. DR Partners, 139 F.3d 1180 (8th Cir. 1998).
85. MERGER GUIDELINES, *supra* note 1, § 5.1. The *Guidelines* consider as market participants those producers that do not currently operate in the relevant market but that would provide rapid supply responses to a SSNIP. Entry or product repositioning that occurs over a longer period of time or that requires significant sunk costs is considered separately. *Id.* § 9. Earlier versions of the *Guidelines* state that generally only entry that is likely within two years will be considered, *see* 1992 MERGER GUIDELINES, *supra* note 73, § 3.2, but this timeframe has been dropped from the current *Guidelines*. *See* MERGER GUIDELINES, *supra* note 1, § 9.
86. *Id.* § 4.1.4.
87. *Id.* § 3.

2. *Geographic Market*

The agencies undertake geographic market definition in order to define the geographic scope of competition. The agencies may define geographic markets based on the location of either suppliers or customers.[88] In most cases, the agencies focus on the location of the suppliers to which buyers would turn in response to a price increase by the suppliers from which they are purchasing. However, when price discrimination is feasible, the agencies may instead focus on the location of customers that may be targeted with a price increase.[89] In such cases, suppliers located outside the market may be included as participants in the market.

Geographic market definition follows the same principles and considers similar types of evidence as product market definition. In particular, the agencies apply the hypothetical monopolist test to determine whether a hypothetical monopolist in a particular region could impose a SSNIP on at least some customers in that region.

The agencies consider: (i) historical patterns of purchases across geographic locations; (ii) the cost of transporting the product; (iii) the importance of proximity between suppliers and customers; (iv) evidence on whether suppliers base business decisions on geographic location; (v) the costs of switching suppliers; and (vi) the influence of downstream competition.[90]

3. *"Critical Loss" Analysis*

If the appropriate data are available, the agencies and merging parties may conduct "critical loss" analyses in order to assist in delineating markets or to "corroborate" the definition of markets.[91] Critical loss analysis proceeds by computing the amount of lost sales that would be required to render a SSNIP on one or more products in a candidate market unprofitable; this number is the "critical loss." The "critical loss"

---

88. *Id.* § 4.2.
89. *Id.*
90. *Id.* § 4.2.1. As with defining the relevant product market, however, evidence of parallel price movements can be difficult to interpret because similar price trends in different locations might result from common economic or marketing conditions unrelated to substitutability across products from suppliers in different locations.
91. MERGER GUIDELINES, *supra* note 1, § 4.1.3.

can then be compared to evidence on the number of sales that would actually be lost in the event of a SSNIP. If the critical loss exceeds the predicted actual loss, then the hypothetical monopolist would increase its profits by imposing the SSNIP in question. Essentially, the comparison of the critical loss with the predicted actual loss is an effort to determine whether the hypothetical monopolist would find the SSNIP profitable. Critical loss analyses have become a frequently used tool before the agencies in the merger context[92] and have also been used by courts.[93]

Calculation of the critical loss requires data on premerger margins (defined over the relevant range of output) as well as a decision on the size of the SSNIP. With reliable data to estimate variable margins (the estimation can be complex because of multiple producers and products), the critical loss can be estimated. The *Guidelines* caution, however, that "high pre-merger margins normally indicate that each firm's product individually faces demand that is not highly sensitive to price."[94] As a

---

92.   *See* Barry C. Harris & Joseph J. Simons, *Focusing Market Definition: How Much Substitution Is Necessary?*, 12 RES. L. & ECON. 207 (1989); Frederick I. Johnson, *Market Definition Under the* Merger Guidelines*: Critical Demand Elasticities*, 12 RES. L. & ECON. 239 (1989); John R. Morris & Gale R. Mosteller, *Defining Markets for Merger Analysis*, 36 ANTITRUST BULL. 599 (1991); James Langenfeld & Wenging Li, *Critical Loss Analysis in Evaluating Mergers*, 46 ANTITRUST BULL. 299 (2001); Daniel P. O'Brien & Abraham L. Wickelgren, *A Critical Analysis of Critical Loss Analysis*, 71 ANTITRUST L.J. 161 (2003); Carl Shapiro, *The 2010* Horizontal Merger Guidelines*: From Hedgehog to Fox in Forty Years*, 77 ANTITRUST L.J. 701 (2010).

93.   *See, e.g.*, California v. Sutter Health Sys., 130 F. Supp. 2d 1109, 1128 (N.D. Cal. 2001) (citing the critical loss test as an analytical tool for addressing the question of whether the geographic market has been properly defined by analyzing the number of consumers that must leave the market, if faced with price increases, before a hypothetical monopolist would abandon such increases); FTC v. Swedish Match, 131 F. Supp. 2d 151, 160-61 (D.D.C. 2000) (discussing use of "critical loss" test to determine if hypothetical monopolist's 5 percent price increase for products in proposed market would be profitable; court commented that test requires proper analysis of both profit margins and demand elasticities because both volume of switching to substitutes and impact on profits need to be considered).

94.   MERGER GUIDELINES, *supra* note 1, § 4.1.3. This follows directly from the Lerner Index, which relates margins (at the profit-maximizing price) to the inverse of the elasticity of demand facing the firm. Comments on the *Guidelines* prior to their final release noted that industries

result, high premerger margins indicate that both the critical loss *and* the predicted actual loss are likely to be small.

The difficult task is to develop data and analyses that bear on predicted actual loss. It is often not possible to develop reliable estimates of actual loss from, for example, econometric analyses of demand. Therefore, the typical approach is to analyze various sources of information and data bearing on customer responses to changes in relative prices, including customer interviews, customer surveys, and documents dealing with the reasons for and effects of price changes.[95]

In practice, the agencies often use evidence of competitive effects to delineate relevant markets or to corroborate definitions. For example, evidence may show that the number—or changes in the number—of competitors in a candidate market, such as the number of national retailers in a geographic region, has a significant effect on price. Evidence also may show that the number—or changes in the number—of other types of sellers, such as the number of local sellers, does not have a significant effect on price in the candidate market. These two types of evidence, taken together, support a conclusion that the candidate market is in fact a relevant market for purposes of analyzing competition.[96]

4. *The Upward Pricing Pressure (UPP) Test*

A notable change in the 2010 *Merger Guidelines* is the suggestion that unilateral effects may be shown without defining a relevant market. The *Guidelines* explain that "[i]n some cases, where sufficient information is available," the competitive effect of a merger in a market involving differentiated products can be determined by consideration of the value of diverted sales, "which can serve as an indicator of the upward pricing pressure on the first product resulting from the merger."[97]

---

characterized by significant dynamic competition may still have high short-run margins. *See* Dennis W. Carlton, Comment on Department of Justice and Federal Trade Commission's Proposed Horizontal Merger Guidelines (Jun. 4, 2010), *available at* http://www.ftc.gov/os/comments/-hmgrevisedguides/548050-00034.pdf.

95.   MERGER GUIDELINES, *supra* note 1, § 4.1.3.
96.   Evidence of this type was used in *FTC v. Staples, Inc.,* 970 F. Supp. 1066, 1081-86 (D.D.C. 1997).
97.   MERGER GUIDELINES, *supra* note 1, § 6.1; *see also* Joseph Farrell & Carl Shapiro, *Antitrust Evaluation of Horizontal Mergers: An Economic Alternative to Market Definition,* 10 B.E. J. THEORETICAL ECON. art. 9, at

Some of the sales lost due to the price rise will merely be diverted to the product of the merger partner and, depending on relative margins, capturing such sales loss through merger may make the price increase profitable even though it would not have been profitable prior to the merger.[98]

If the value of diverted sales is large, the agencies may be able to conclude that the merger may result in significant postmerger price effects without "rely[ing] on market definition or the calculation of market shares and concentration."[99] Although the *Guidelines* state that the agencies will rely on the value of diverted sales to determine likely postmerger effects in markets with differentiated products, [100] the application of this test, both in agency practice[101] and in court, [102] is unclear.

---

1 (2010) (discussing the economic foundations of the upward pricing pressure (UPP) test).

98.   *Id.* § 6.1. The 1992 *Merger Guidelines* contained many of the same basic economic principles. 1992 MERGER GUIDELINES, *supra* note 73, § 2. However, the 2010 *Merger Guidelines* update and extend the analysis.

99.   MERGER GUIDELINES, *supra* note 1, § 6.1.

100. *Id.*

101. *See, e.g.,* Statement of Commissioner J. Thomas Rosch on the Release of the 2010 *Horizontal Merger Guidelines* (Aug. 19, 2010), *available at* http://www.ftc.gov/os/2010/08/100819hmgrosch.pdf (noting the "overemphasis on economic formulae," including "economic models relying largely on margins" like the UPP model in the 2010 *Guidelines*).

102. *See* City of New York v. Group Health, No. 06 Civ. 13122, 2010 WL 2132246, at *3 (S.D.N.Y. 2010) (rejecting city's attempt to define the relevant market as "the low-cost municipal health benefits market" based on the cost differential between providers in that alleged market and other providers because participation in the alleged market was characterized by a bidding competition, and the participants were chosen by the city itself).

CHAPTER V

MEASURING MARKET POWER: SHARES AND OTHER TECHNIQUES

An important part of antitrust analysis is to try to identify whether a firm or group of firms has or could obtain market power once a relevant market has been defined. Market share and concentration statistics are frequently a useful starting point in an assessment of whether a firm or group of firms have sufficient control over the supply in a market to exercise market power, but too much attention to share and concentration statistics can obscure the market characteristics that underlie those statistics and that determine the actual market power of the firm or group of firms.[1] Market share does not equal market power but rather can be an initial indication as to whether market power might exist. Identification of low market shares or concentration can be used as a screen to suggest that the existence of individual or joint market power is unlikely to exist. High market shares, however, need not imply the existence of market power. For example, a high market share may not indicate significant market power if entry barriers are low, if expansion could be readily accomplished by incumbent firms, if competitors are well positioned to expand, or if historical sales are not indicative of a firm's ability to compete for future sales.[2]

---

1. *See* U.S. DEP'T OF JUSTICE & FED. TRADE COMM'N, HORIZONTAL MERGER GUIDELINES § 4 (2010) ("The measurement of market shares and market concentration is not an end in itself, but is useful to the extent it illuminates the merger's likely competitive effects."), *available at* http://www.justice.gov/atr/-public/guidelines/hmg-2010.html [hereinafter MERGER GUIDELINES]; *id.* § 5 ("The Agencies evaluate market shares and concentration in conjunction with other reasonably available and reliable evidence for the ultimate purpose of determining whether a merger may substantially lessen competition.").

2. *See, e.g.,* United States v. Gen. Dynamics Corp., 415 U.S. 486, 493-94 (1974) (explaining that General Dynamics' share at the time of the inquiry overstated its power in the coal market because its share was expected to decline due to its limited reserves); *see also* The Boeing Co. and McDonnell/Douglas Corp., No. 971-0051 (F.T.C. 1997) (explaining that although Boeing had nearly 60 percent of the current large

This Chapter first explains the traditional methods of calculating market shares and concentration levels, and identifies numerous issues to consider in applying these methods. The Chapter then discusses issues related to the interpretation of market shares and concentration and the range of characteristics that may make it more or less likely that market power exists individually or jointly for a given level of concentration or market share. Because market shares and concentration are generally at most an initial indicator of the potential for market power to exist, the final part of this Chapter discusses other empirical methods for measuring market power directly.

A. Fundamentals of Market Share and Concentration Data Calculation

The definition of the relevant market will affect substantially the calculations of market shares and, as a result, is often the biggest source of dispute in market share calculations.[3] As the definition of the relevant market broadens, the market shares of the firm or firms in question often decline as a broader market definition may result in the addition of more firms in the relevant market. For example, a superpremium ice cream manufacturer with a 50 percent market share of the superpremium segment may have a much lower share if the relevant market is defined as all ice cream (including superpremium, premium, and store brand products), which would include many more manufacturers.[4] On the other hand, a broader market definition may imply a higher rather than lower market share for the firm or firms in question.[5] Thus, market definition is a necessary and crucial first step in the measurement of market shares.

---

      commercial aircraft market, McDonnell Douglas no longer constituted a meaningful competitive force in the commercial aircraft market).

3.   See *supra* ch. IV for discussion of market definition.

4.   This example is adapted from Analysis of Proposed Consent Order to Aid Public Comment, *In re* Nestle Holdings, Inc., *available at* http://www.ftc.gov/-os/2003/06/dryeranalysis.htm.

5.   For example, in a debate about whether HMO and PPO insurance plans are in the same market, whether a firm's share increases or decreases under the broader market definition will depend on the firm's relative share of HMO and PPO lives.

1. Market Share Calculation

Once a relevant market is properly defined, the calculation of market shares may appear relatively straightforward; however, a number of factors impact the reliability and usefulness of any statistics, including the metrics, data sources, and time period used. Calculation of market shares must also consider any relationships among the competitors.

a. Choice of Metric

The choice of metric used to calculate market share can be influential.[6] Sales are often seen as the de facto measure of a firm's market share. However, market share can also be calculated based on production, capacity, or volume of reserves. The *Merger Guidelines* explain:

> In most contexts, the Agencies measure each firm's market share based on its actual or projected revenues in the relevant market .... In cases where one unit of a low-priced product can substitute for one unit of a higher-priced product, unit sales may measure competitive significance better than revenues ....
>
> In markets for homogeneous products, a firm's competitive significance may derive principally from its ability and incentive to rapidly expand production in the relevant market in response to a price increase or output reduction by others in that market .... In such markets, capacities or reserves may better reflect the future competitive significance of suppliers than revenues, and the Agencies may calculate market shares using those measures.[7]

In theory, if products and associated services are truly homogeneous, it should not matter whether dollars or units are used, since prices will be the same across firms or brands. More often, however, products are either physically differentiated or sold with different services (e.g., different amounts of product support, including presale and postsale service and warranties) resulting in disparate pricing.[8] When products are

---

6.   *See* Gregory J. Werden, *Assigning Market Shares,* 70 ANTITRUST L.J. 67, 73-78 (2002).

7.   MERGER GUIDELINES, *supra* note 1, § 5.2.

8.   *See* Werden, *supra* note 6, at 74-75 (explaining the difficulty of finding a "common denominator" across products, using bread as an example of a

differentiated or manufacturers have very different supply capabilities, the metric must adjust for these differences. For example, if products differ with respect to their intensity of usage (e.g., a customer has to buy two of competitor A's products to substitute for one of competitor B's products), those differences ought to be reflected in measures of market share or market concentration.[9]

Dollar sales are often used when computing market shares because dollar sales "tend to be the best measure of attractiveness to customers, since they reflect the real-world ability of firms to surmount all of the obstacles necessary to offer products on terms and conditions that are attractive to customers."[10]

Economists have also recommended using dollar sales to compute market shares on the grounds that sales figures reflect a firm's actual presence in the market. The use of dollar sales may give a better initial screen for market power because firms with market power are likely to charge higher prices and therefore would have greater market share.[11]

However, the use of dollar sales as a market share metric may be difficult or inappropriate for practical reasons. For example, adjusting for freight costs and taxes may be difficult and may cause prices to vary in ways that have nothing to do with a firm's future ability to compete. Controlling for fluctuations in exchange rates may also prove difficult.[12]

In addition, some caution is warranted when computing market shares based on dollar sales information. For example, higher-priced products may or may not have attributes that make them better than average substitutes for lower-priced products in the market, but a dollar sales-based measure of market shares makes the assumption that higher-

---

product commonly sold in various package sizes, with various numbers of slices of differing thickness).

9. In many cases this can be done by changing the units of measurement. For example, consider two fertilizer products: If using one product requires 10 pounds per acre and another requires 20 pounds per acre, a market share calculated based on pounds sold would not take this difference into account, while market share calculated based on the number of acres fertilized would.

10. MERGER GUIDELINES, *supra* note 1, § 5.2.

11. Janusz A. Ordover & Robert D. Willig, *The 1982 Department of Justice Merger Guidelines: An Economic Assessment*, 71 CAL. L. REV. 535, 560 (1983).

12. *See* MERGER GUIDELINES, *supra* note 1, § 4.2

priced products are better than average substitutes.[13] Using dollar sales when a market includes both branded and private label products may overstate the appropriate market shares of the branded firms because of the price difference between branded and unbranded products.[14]

Whether and how dollar sales data are used when computing market shares also will be affected by the degree to which firms in the industry are vertically integrated. For vertically-integrated firms, no market-based price may be available so that a dollar-based analysis would require a complex analysis of intra-company pricing.[15] If a firm's sales of a product are mostly sold to a downstream subsidiary (because, for example, the product is used as an input to other products), analyzing data reflecting the firm's sales to outside customers probably will not reflect that firm's competitive importance in the marketplace. Sales figures that do not include sales to downstream subsidiaries may understate the firm's competitive presence. However, shares based on total sales may overstate the amount of supply that would be available for purchase by nonvertically-integrated customers unless vertically-integrated firms could and would divert capacity to nonintegrated customers.[16]

---

13. *See id.* § 5.2 ("In cases where one unit of a low-priced product can substitute for one unit of a higher-priced product, unit sales may measure competitive significance better than revenues.").

14. *See* Werden, *supra* note 6, at 76.

15. This point was discussed in the 1992 *Merger Guidelines. See* U.S. DEP'T OF JUSTICE & FED. TRADE COMM'N, HORIZONTAL MERGER GUIDELINES § 1.14 n.15 (1992), *available at* http://www.justice.gov/atr/public/guidelines/hmg.pdf [hereinafter 1992 MERGER GUIDELINES]. The use of an output measure may be appropriate for vertically integrated firms, since it avoids the need to establish appropriate transfer prices. PHILLIP E. AREEDA & HERBERT HOVENKAMP, 2B ANTITRUST LAW: AN ANALYSIS OF ANTITRUST PRINCIPLES AND THEIR APPLICATION ¶ 535e, at 281 (3d ed. 2007).

16. Although the current *Merger Guidelines* do not address captive consumption within a vertically-integrated entity (i.e., consumption of the upstream entity's product by the downstream entity), they do indicate that all firms that currently produce products in the relevant market should be considered market participants, including vertically-integrated firms "to the extent that their inclusion accurately reflects their competitive significance." MERGER GUIDELINES, *supra* note 1, § 5.1. The 1984 *Merger Guidelines* dealt more directly with the issue, but it is unclear whether this earlier approach embodies current agency doctrine:

Another metric that can be used to calculate market shares is the amount of capacity that is available to produce the relevant product. For many homogeneous product markets, the comparative capacities of competing firms may be more indicative of a firm's share than current sales or production.[17] For example, market shares based on capacity typically are used in the electric power industry and other industries in which equipment determines the ability to produce.[18] If a firm easily can supply more output at or below its current costs, its competitive significance (assuming homogeneous demand) may be better represented by its capacity to supply additional units than by its actual sales or output. For example, firms with small market shares based on current output may nonetheless be competitively significant if they can quickly and easily increase output in response to an increase in price.[19]

Capacity-based shares, however, must be used and interpreted with care. A firm's total capacity may overstate its competitive importance for a number of reasons. It may be difficult to interpret capacity data in

---

> Captive production and consumption of the relevant product by vertically integrated firms are part of the overall market supply and demand. Such firms may respond to an increase in the price of the relevant product in either of two ways. They may begin selling the relevant product, or alternatively, they may continue to consume all of their production but increase their production of both the relevant product and products in which the relevant product is embodied. Either kind of supply response could frustrate collusion by firms currently selling the relevant product. If a firm would be likely to respond either way to a "small but significant and non-transitory" increase in price, the Department will include that firm in the market.

U.S. DEP'T OF JUSTICE & FED. TRADE COMM'N, HORIZONTAL MERGER GUIDELINES § 2.23 (1984), *available at* http://www.justice.gov/atr/hmerger/11249.pdf [hereinafter 1984 MERGER GUIDELINES].

17. The *Merger Guidelines* explain that "[i]n markets for homogeneous products, a firm's competitive significance may derive principally from its ability and incentive to rapidly expand production in the relevant market in response to a price increase or output reduction by others in that market" rather than from its current market share. MERGER GUIDELINES, *supra* note 1, § 5.2; *see also* Werden, *supra* note 6, at 83-85.

18. Werden, *supra* note 6, at 83-85.

19. *Id.* at 81-82.

situations in which costs increase with the use of additional capacity (e.g., overtime payments and additional maintenance costs). It may be appropriate to ignore high-cost capacity in determining market share in industries with sufficient modern, low-cost capacity to satisfy the entire anticipated demand, even in the event of an exercise of market power.[20] In such cases, the competitive significance of different portions of a firm's capacity varies with market demand. Similarly, one firm's technology may be more costly to employ than that of another firm, a difference that may not be accounted for in an analysis based purely on capacity data.[21]

Further, consideration of market shares based on capacity must account for the ability to deploy that capacity. Not all capacity may be available in a sufficiently timely fashion. In addition, a firm may not have control over its capacity because it has sold its capacity rights to others. When this is the case, it may be appropriate to attribute a firm's capacity to the owners of the capacity rights, particularly when those owners have long-term contracts and when the owners can resell either the rights or the output resulting from these rights.[22] Thus, in some circumstances, shares based on uncommitted or available capacity may be appropriate.[23]

Finally, capacity is only one element of a firm's competitive presence. To be competitive, a firm may also need a sales and distribution system, an installed base of customers, a service team, and/or time to develop a good reputation among customers. A firm may have

---

20. *Id.* at 83-85. For example, only the efficient capacity associated with larger plants was considered when assigning shares in *Monfort of Colorado Inc. v. Cargill, Inc.*, 591 F. Supp. 683, 706 (D. Colo. 1983), *aff'd*, 761 F.2d 570 (10th Cir. 1985), *judgment rev'd*, 479 U.S. 104 (1986).

21. AREEDA & HOVENKAMP, *supra* note 15, § 535c2, at 277-79; *see* Ordover & Willig, *supra* note 11, at 561.

22. *See, e.g.*, Analysis of the Proposed Consent Order and Draft Complaint to Aid Public Comment, *In re* BP Amoco p.l.c., *available at* http://www.ftc.gov/os/2000/04/bpamocoana.htm (Apr. 13, 2000) (assigning market shares by percentage ownership in the Trans-Alaska Pipeline System).

23. *See* MERGER GUIDELINES, *supra* note 1, § 5.2; *see also* Consol. Gold Fields, PLC v. Anglo Am. Corp. of S. Africa Ltd., 698 F. Supp. 487, 501 (S.D.N.Y. 1988), *aff'd in part, rev'd in part*, 871 F.2d 252 (2d Cir. 1989) (pointing out the exclusion of sales to private investors and communist governments because they had not increased in response to increased prices); Werden, *supra* note 6, at 99-101.

sufficient productive capacity but lack a product that is considered a close substitute for other market products. Capacity data typically do not take these other considerations into account.

In natural resource industries, a firm's reserves are often indicative of the firm's long-term ability to supply a market or to frustrate monopolistic price increases initiated by others and, therefore, may be an appropriate metric with which to calculate market shares.[24] However, as is the case for capacity measures, the analysis must consider whether the firm has access to other resources that it would need to increase its sales, including equipment and a distribution network. In addition, long-term contracts giving others the right to exploit reserves may make it more appropriate to allocate the reserves to the firm that has the long-term contract rather than to the owner of the remaining rights. Practical problems such as a lack of reliable data with respect to the universe of reserves that should be included in the market may also hinder a proper market share analysis.[25]

b. Data Sources

For some markets, data that can be used to measure market shares are available through industry or government reports. Data may also be gathered from individual firms in the industry, and may be collected by the FTC or DOJ via interviews or compulsory processes such as civil investigative demands. In other cases, however, data are not readily available and economists and courts must rely on estimates of total market size and of the shares of individual firms.

One tool used to estimate market size is a survey of consumer purchases. When relying on survey samples, however, it is important to ensure that the estimates are accurate.

Common questions that should be asked about the estimates include:

---

24. *See* FTC v. Arch Coal, Inc. 329 F. Supp. 2d 109, 127 (D.D.C. 2004) ("[U]ncommitted reserves . . . are particularly relevant to assessing future competitiveness."); United States v. Amax, Inc., 402 F. Supp. 956, 968, 971 (D. Conn. 1975); FED. TRADE COMM'N, BUREAU OF ECONOMICS, THE PETROLEUM INDUSTRY: MERGERS, STRUCTURAL CHANGE, AND ANTITRUST ENFORCEMENT 132 (2004), *available at* http://www.ftc.gov/os/2004/08/040813mergersinpetrolberpt.pdf.

25. *See* Werden, *supra* note 6, at 83.

- Are any firms omitted from the survey?[26]
- If a sample is used, is the sample statistically valid?[27]
- For each firm, are all of its relevant sales reflected?[28]
- Do firms use comparable methodologies in determining their sales?[29]

Regardless of the data source, the analysis must guard against double counting of sales and/or capacity. In some industries, products are resold to other manufacturers. Both market shares and concentration level statistics will be misleading if these re-sales are not taken into account and double-counting is not avoided.

c. Choice of the Appropriate Time Period

Market share calculation requires the use of some standard time period.[30] A year is generally chosen in order to smooth out seasonal variations in sales and eliminate fluctuations due to unusual factors such

---

26. For example, are foreign firms and vertically-integrated firms included? If the survey is performed by a trade association, are nonmembers' sales included?

27. For example, if the survey is based on a particular geographic area, are the firms' shares in that area representative of the firms' shares in the whole relevant geographic market? If one or more of the firms has a particularly large presence in the geographic area chosen as a sample, the shares will not represent the firms' shares in the broader relevant geographic market.

28. For example, in markets in which it is appropriate to include a firm's captive consumption as part of its sales, is this captive consumption reflected in the market shares? Is the relevant portion of the sales of vertically-integrated firms included?

29. For example, sales data across firms may not be comparable due to differences in the measurement of transportation costs, agent fees, frequent purchaser discounts, taxes, or allowances returns. One firm may measure sales based on retail prices and another may use wholesale prices.

30. The argument over the appropriate time period often relates to a more fundamental argument regarding whether a market share in a given time period truly evinces market power. *See* Telecor Communications v. Sw. Bell Tel. Co., 305 F.3d 1124, 1142 (10th Cir. 2002) (rejecting argument that contracts were temporary and therefore not evidence of market power).

as temporary shortages, transitory marketing effects (e.g., advertising blitzes, specials, or sales), or other short-term factors. [31] In some circumstances, however, a year is too short a period. The *Merger Guidelines* provide that in markets with sporadic individual sales, the antitrust enforcement agencies may use a period of time longer than one year.[32] On the other hand, using historically distant data when calculating market shares may reflect demand and supply conditions significantly different from those that exist at the time of the inquiry.[33]

In addition, even if market shares are measured appropriately on a yearly basis, it can be helpful to measure market shares at various times during the year, as well as across years. Seasonal analysis is helpful when the competitive positions of firms vary during the year. For example, certain competitors may dedicate their capacity to other markets during some seasons of the year so that they do not compete in the relevant market during those seasons. Analyzing a firm's market share over time may also reveal trends that suggest that its current market share overstates (or understates) its long-term competitive significance.

d.   Independent v. Controlled Competitors

Each market share analysis should reflect the reality of the relationships between competing firms. Control relationships are often easily determined by considering corporate ownership and structure. For example, the shares of different subsidiaries under the same ownership are conventionally summed to obtain a firm's market share.

Relationships among competitors, however, sometimes can be difficult to interpret, as when a firm holds minority interests in another firm that may or may not give it control over the other firm's business decisions,[34] or when foreign producers work together to coordinate their

---

31.   Capacity is frequently averaged over a year in order to account for maintenance, changeovers in production, and other factors that affect the realistic ability of a firm to produce a given output, even when the units are "production per week" or "production per day."

32.   MERGER GUIDELINES, *supra* note 1, § 5.2.

33.   *See* Werden, *supra* note 6, at 92-93.

34.   *See generally* Timothy F. Bresnahan & Steven C. Salop, *Quantifying the Competitive Effects of Production Joint Ventures*, 4 INT'L J. INDUS. ORG. 155, 174 (1986); Daniel P. O'Brien & Steven C. Salop, *Competitive Effects of Partial Ownership: Financial Interest and Corporate Control*, 67 ANTITRUST L.J. 559, 569-71 (2000); Robert J. Reynolds & Bruce R.

U.S. sales. When evidence of control and/or an agreement between or among firms to coordinate sales in the relevant market exists, appointing those shares to a single market participant may be appropriate.[35]

Analysis of significant but not controlling interests is more complex. Although aggregation is not appropriate without control, firm incentives may be affected by ownership linkages. Similarly, joint ventures can present special challenges to assessing and assigning market shares. How a joint venture is treated should depend on the nature of the venture and whether the entity acts as an independent participant or is controlled by one or more of its owners. If a joint venture is truly independent in its decision making, it should be given a separate market share. If its operations are controlled by other firms, however, its share should be allocated to those firms.[36]

2. Market Concentration Calculation

The most frequently employed method of measuring concentration levels in a given market is the Herfindahl-Hirschman Index (HHI). The HHI for a given market is calculated by adding together the squares of the individual market shares of all the firms included in the relevant market.[37] In a very unconcentrated market, the HHI would be close to zero, since the square of each firm's market share would be close to zero. At the other extreme, in a single-firm market, the HHI would equal 10,000.[38]

Snapp, *The Competitive Effects of Partial Equity Interests and Joint Ventures,* 4 INT'L J. INDUS. ORG. 141 (1986).

35.   *See* Werden, *supra* note 6, at 101-03.

36.   *See id.* at 103.

37.   For example, a market that has five firms with market shares of 40 percent, 30 percent, 15 percent, 10 percent, and 5 percent would have an HHI of 2850 (2850 = 1600 + 900 + 225 + 100 + 25). *See* MERGER GUIDELINES, *supra* note 1, § 5.3. For discussion of the HHI, see generally Albert O. Hirschman, *The Paternity of an Index,* 54 AM. ECON. REV. 761 (1964); John E. Kwoka, Jr., *The Herfindahl Index in Theory and Practice,* 30 ANTITRUST BULL. 915 (1985); Richard A. Miller, *The Herfindahl-Hirschman Index as a Market Structure Variable: An Exposition for Antitrust Practitioners,* 27 ANTITRUST BULL. 593 (1982).

38.   In the past, economists and courts also used a concentration measure known as the four-firm concentration ratio. The four-firm concentration ratio is calculated by adding the market shares of the four largest firms

B. Interpretation of Market Share and Concentration Statistics

Although market shares and concentration levels are almost always calculated in antitrust cases, they represent only a starting point in an assessment of market power—providing an initial screen as to the potential for the existence of market power. Interpretation of these results is the necessary second step and can be very difficult. While firms with low market share may be considered unlikely to have market power while market power may be more likely (depending on market characteristics) for firms with very high market shares—there is no magic level to distinguish between low and high market shares. Similarly, no concentration level in and of itself will likely condemn a merger or suggest that there is a risk of collusion or otherwise anticompetitive behavior. Rather, as with market shares, low concentration is less likely to raise market power concerns while high concentration is more likely to raise such concerns. As then-Judge Clarence Thomas stated in *United States v. Baker Hughes, Inc.,*[39] "[t]he Herfindahl-Hirschman Index cannot guarantee litigation victories."[40]

---

that compete in the relevant market. It ranges from close to zero (when there are a very large number of firms with very small shares of the market) to 100 percent (when four or fewer firms share the entire market). For example, a market that has five firms with market shares of 40 percent, 30 percent, 15 percent, 10 percent, and 5 percent would have a four-firm concentration ratio of 95 percent. Although the four-firm ratio is often closely correlated with the HHI, the HHI is more commonly employed and is considered a much more useful measure of market concentration. For a comparison of HHIs and four-firm concentration ratios, see generally Paul A. Pautler, *A Guide to the Herfindahl Index for Antitrust Attorneys,* 5 RES. L. & ECON. 167 (1983). Results using the two measures diverge at higher levels of concentration. The 1984 *Merger Guidelines* explain the DOJ's preference for the HHI over the four-firm ratios. The 1984 *Merger Guidelines* note that "the HHI reflects . . . the composition of the market outside the top four firms . . . [and] gives proportionately greater weight to the market shares of the larger firms, which probably accords with their relative importance in any collusive interaction." 1984 MERGER GUIDELINES, *supra* note 16, § 3.1.

39.   908 F.2d 981 (D.C. Cir. 1990).

40.   *Id.* at 992; *see also* Ball Mem'l. Hosp. v. Mut. Hosp. Ins., 784 F.2d 1325, 1336 (7th Cir. 1986) ("Market share is just a way of estimating market power, which is the ultimate consideration. When there are better ways to estimate market power, the court should use them.").

Instead, how one interprets market share and concentration statistics will depend on market characteristics. Indeed, any assessment of market share and concentration must take a variety of aspects of the market into consideration, including whether there are any trends or other evidence of changes in the shares or concentration levels suggesting that market conditions are in flux, whether the nature of the firms competing in the market (either buyers or sellers) make the market more (or less) competitive, and/or whether the market has special characteristics that affect how shares should be interpreted.

1. Market Share as a Predictor of Market Power

Although several economic models of firm behavior predict that larger market shares are associated with higher economic profits, the relationship has been difficult to detect empirically.[41] This may be because economic profits are very difficult to measure. In addition, it is likely that the relationship between market shares and measures of market performance (e.g., profitability) is industry-specific.[42] Moreover, high market shares and large economic profits do not necessarily imply that prices will increase. Accordingly, no agreed upon "critical" market share exists that provides an initial indication that a firm with a market share greater than that level may have significant unilateral market power.

In *United States v. Aluminum Co. of America*,[43] Judge Hand wrote that a market share of 90 percent "is enough to constitute monopoly; it is doubtful whether sixty or sixty-four percent would be enough; and certainly thirty-three percent is not."[44] Judge Hand's proposition may be interpreted as, from a legal perspective, that high market shares are prima facie evidence of a high degree of market power, moderately sized

---

41.   DENNIS W. CARLTON & JEFFREY M. PERLOFF, MODERN INDUSTRIAL ORGANIZATION ch. 8 (4th ed. 2005).

42.   "[E]conomic studies make it clear that other industry-specific and market-specific factors beyond concentration (such as the elasticity of market demand, the ability of firms to solve cartel problems, and the ease of entry and rival repositioning) are also important in determining price and the competitive effects of mergers." ANDREW I. GAVIL, WILLIAM E. KOVACIC & JONATHAN B. BAKER, ANTITRUST LAW IN PERSPECTIVE: CASES, CONCEPTS AND PROBLEMS IN COMPETITION POLICY 506 (2d ed. 2008).

43.   148 F.2d 416 (2d Cir. 1945).

44.   *Id.* at 424.

market shares might be evidence of market power, and low market share are presumptively not indicative of market power.

In practice, there is no consensus among the courts on a market share threshold above which prima facie evidence of monopoly power or a high degree of market power is considered to exist, or below which there is considered a lack of evidence of market power. Courts have frequently considered market shares of 70 percent or higher as prima facie evidence of monopoly power.[45] At the other end of the spectrum, very low market shares have frequently been considered insufficient to give a firm market power. For example, in *Rothery Storage & Van Co. v. Atlas Van Lines, Inc.*,[46] the defendant had a 6 percent share of the market.[47] Judge Bork noted that a monopolist may increase its revenues by lowering output to raise its product's market price, but he explained that a firm has power to do this only if it has a high market share:

> If a group of Atlas' size reduced its output of services, there would be no effect upon market price because firms making up the other 94% of the market would simply take over the abandoned business. The only effect would be a loss of revenues to Atlas. Indeed, so impotent to raise prices is a firm with a market share of 5 or 6% that any attempt by it to engage in a monopolistic restriction of output would be little short of suicidal.[48]

There is no consensus as to the specific market share level below which significant market power is considered unlikely to exist—antitrust agencies and scholars have indicated that market power is unlikely at market shares below levels ranging from 25 percent in some instances to

---

45.   *See, e.g.*, United States v. Dentsply Int'l, 399 F.3d 181, 188 (3d Cir. 2005) (stating that a market share between 75 percent and 80 percent of sales is "more than adequate to establish a prima facie case of power"); Morgenstern v. Wilson, 29 F.3d 1291, 1296 n.3 (8th Cir. 1994) ("An eighty percent market share is within the permissible range from which an inference of monopoly power can be drawn."); R.J. Reynolds Tobacco Co. v. Philip Morris Inc., 199 F. Supp. 2d 362, 394 (M.D.N.C. 2002) (51 percent market share was "far below the generally accepted 70% to 75% minimum share necessary to support a finding of monopoly power").

46.   792 F.2d 210 (D.C. Cir. 1986).

47.   *Id.* at 217.

48.   *Id.*

30 to 50 percent in others.[49] Judicial findings of no market power have been based on a range of market share levels falling below 35 percent.[50]

---

49.   The 1992 *Merger Guidelines* included an express reference to a 35 percent safe harbor. *See* 1992 MERGER GUIDELINES, *supra* note 16, § 2.211. This express safe harbor was omitted from the current version of the *Guidelines*. Some scholars have suggested a slightly higher standard of around 40 percent for identifying a "dominant position" of a single firm. "Smaller rivals are as sensitive to the interests of dominant firms as mice around an elephant." F.M. SCHERER & DAVID R. ROSS, INDUSTRIAL MARKET STRUCTURE AND ECONOMIC PERFORMANCE 221 (3d ed. 1990). On the other hand, other scholars disagree: "If the defendant's own share is modest, the existence of a large number of even smaller competitors will restrain its power very effectively, even if entry barriers are high. The contrary assertion by an expert is presumptively incredible." AREEDA & HOVENKAMP, *supra* note 15, ¶ 532c, at 250. "[M]any economists regard a share in the range of 30 to 50 percent as too low to indicate significant market power in an industry with a competitive fringe comprising the remainder of the market." CARLTON & PERLOFF, *supra* note 41, at 644.

50.   *See, e.g.,* Brokerage Concepts, Inc. v. U.S. Healthcare, 140 F.3d 494, 516-17 (3d Cir. 1998) (finding that 25 percent market share was insufficient to impose per se liability); Valley Products Co. v. Landmark, 128 F.3d 398, 402 n.3 (6th Cir. 1997) (noting that "courts have repeatedly held that a 30 percent market share is insufficient to confer the market power without which a tie cannot be illegal *per se* . . . ."); United States v. Eastman Kodak Co., 63 F.3d 95, 100, 110 (2d Cir. 1995) (affirming the district court's holding that a 30 percent share was "too small to give rise to an inference of market power"); Breaux Bros. Farms v. Teche Sugar Co., 21 F.3d 83, 87 (5th Cir. 1994) (9.4 percent to 17.5 percent market share is insufficient for a per se violation); Hardy v. City Optical Inc., 39 F.3d 765, 767 (7th Cir. 1994) (30 percent is the "minimum market share from which the market power required . . . can be inferred"); Virtual Maint. v. Prime Computer, 11 F.3d 660, 664 (6th Cir. 1993) (11 percent share insufficient as a matter of law to support inference of market power); Capital Imaging Associates, P.C. v. Mohawk Valley Med. Associates, 996 F.2d 537, 547 (2d Cir. 1993) (market shares ranging from 1.15 percent to 6.75 percent are insufficient to survive summary judgment); A.I. Root Co. v. Computer/Dynamics, Inc., 806 F.2d 673, 675-78 (6th Cir. 1986) (granting summary judgment based on a 4 percent market share); Assam Drug Co. v. Miller Brewing Co., 798 F.2d 311, 318-19 (8th Cir. 1986) (granting summary judgment on the premise that a 19.1 percent market share does not constitute market power); Woman's Clinic v. St. John's Health Sys., 252 F. Supp. 2d 857, 867-68 (W.D. Mo.

The Department of Justice, in its now-withdrawn report on Section 2 of the Sherman Act, found that courts have typically required at least a majority market share (i.e., above 50 percent) to infer monopoly power:

> The Department is not aware, however, of any court that has found that a defendant possessed monopoly power when its market share was less than fifty percent. Thus, as a practical matter, a market share of greater than fifty percent has been necessary for courts to find the existence of monopoly power.[51]

Similarly, some courts have expressly stated that a 50 percent share is below the level at which monopoly power may be presumed.[52] However,

---

2002) (granting summary judgment and finding a 35 percent market share insufficient market power); *Morgenstern*, 29 F.3d at 1296 n.3 (30 percent market share insufficient); United Air Lines v. Austin Travel Corp., 867 F.2d 737, 742 (2d Cir. 1989) (31 percent market share insufficient); Grappone, Inc. v. Subaru of New England, Inc., 858 F.2d 792, 797 (1st Cir. 1988) (finding anything below a 30 percent share makes proving market power difficult); Domed Stadium Hotel, Inc. v. Holiday Inns, Inc., 732 F.2d 480, 490 (5th Cir. 1984) (4 percent does not denote market power); Phillips v. Crown Cent. Petroleum Corp., 602 F.2d 616, 628-29 (4th Cir. 1979) (4 percent share is insufficient to establish market power); Gen. Cigar Holdings v. Altadis, S.A., 205 F. Supp. 2d 1335, 1349-51 (S.D. Fla. 2002) (39 percent market share insufficient).

51.   U.S. DEP'T OF JUSTICE, COMPETITION AND MONOPOLY: SINGLE-FIRM CONDUCT UNDER SECTION 2 OF THE SHERMAN ACT 22 (2008), *available at* http://www.justice.gov/atr/public/reports/236681.pdf (report withdrawn May 11, 2009). *Cf.* U.S. Anchor Mfg. v. Rule Indus., 7 F.3d 986, 1000 (11th Cir. 1993) ("[W]e have discovered no cases in which a court found the existence of actual monopoly established by a bare majority share of the market.").

52.   *See* Blue Cross & Blue Shield United of Wisc. v. Marshfield Clinic, 65 F.3d 1406, 1411 (7th Cir. 1995) ("Fifty percent is below any accepted benchmark for inferring monopoly power from market share.") (internal citations omitted); Fineman v. Armstrong World Indus., Inc., 980 F.2d 171, 201-02 (3d Cir. 1992) (55 percent market share is insufficient to prove monopoly power); R.J. Reynolds Tobacco Co. v. Philip Morris Inc., 199 F. Supp. 2d 362, 394 (M.D.N.C. 2002) (51 percent market share was "far below the generally accepted 70% to 75% minimum share necessary to support a finding of monopoly power").

some courts have held that market shares below 50 percent might nevertheless support a finding of monopoly power.[53]

Recognizing that market shares are an imperfect indicator of market power, some courts have eschewed thresholds, and have determined that market share statistics must be considered in the context of the conditions of the specific market.[54]

An instance in which a smaller market share may be evidence of the exercise of market power is in markets in which sellers can price discriminate. With price discrimination, a firm with a low share in a broad market may still be able to charge higher prices to a set of customers who are less likely to switch to other products. This requires the firm to be able to price discriminate on customer characteristics and will result in a price discrimination market that is separately defined.[55]

Additionally, smaller shares may be associated with market power in oligopolistic arrangements. For example, in *Brooke Group v. Brown & Williamson Tobacco Corp.*, [56] the Supreme Court found it conceivable

---

53. *See* Reazin v. Blue Cross & Blue Shield of Kan., Inc., 899 F.2d 951, 966-72 (10th Cir. 1990) (finding a market share between 45 percent and 62 percent was sufficient to support a jury's finding of monopolization in light of special characteristics of market and specific evidence of power over price and competition); Hayden Publ'g Co. v. Cox Broad. Corp., 730 F.2d 64, 69 n.7 (2d Cir. 1984) (depending on other market factors, a firm may have market power even with a market share of less than 50 percent); Broadway Delivery Corp. v. United Parcel Serv. of Am., 651 F.2d 122, 129 (2d Cir. 1981) (finding a share less than 50 percent, "[b]ut when the evidence presents a fair jury issue of monopoly power, the jury should not be told that it must find monopoly power lacking below a specified share . . . .").

54. *See* Am. Council of Certified Podiatric Physicians & Surgeons v. Am. Bd. of Podiatric Surgery, 185 F.3d 606, 623 (6th Cir. 1999) (instructing that "market share is only a starting point for determining whether monopoly power exists, and the inference of monopoly power does not automatically follow from the possession of a commanding market share"); Tops Mkts. v. Quality Mkts., 142 F.3d 90, 98 (2d Cir. 1998) (holding that a "court will draw an inference of monopoly power only after full consideration of the relationship between market share and other relevant market characteristics"); *see also* CARLTON & PERLOFF, *supra* note 41, at 644 ("Market shares are imperfect indicators of market power, so additional analysis of the economic conditions is necessary before one can reach a conclusion about market power.").

55. *See* MERGER GUIDELINES, *supra* note 1, § 4.1.4.

56. 509 U.S. 209 (1993).

that a firm with a 12 percent market share could lead efforts in an oligopolistic market to engage in predatory pricing.[57]

2. *Concentration Level as a Predictor of Noncompetitive Markets*

There is no single "critical concentration" level above which concerns might be raised as to whether a market might begin to behave anticompetitively through the joint exercise of market power.[58] As a general matter, the higher the concentration level, the greater the strength and probability of rivals' response to changes in competitive conditions, which can enhance the likelihood of tacit or express collusion, everything else held equal.[59] With fewer firms, it may be easier for firms to agree and enforce an anticompetitive collusive arrangement, and, therefore, market concentration can be seen as a measure of cartel stability. Similarly, the greater the concentration level, the lower the likelihood that competition may include an aggressive competitor or "maverick." Case law, enforcement agency practice, and scholarly research, however, indicate that different markets can tolerate different levels of concentration before a significant threat of anticompetitive pricing emerges.

In case of a merger between two firms, the extent that prices are likely to increase postmerger may depend, in part, on whether customers view the two firms' products as their first and second choices. When customers who purchase from one of the merging firms views the other merging firm's product as the next-best alternative, the merged firm will find it more profitable to raise prices, all else equal, than it would have if the two firms' products had not been close substitutes. This is because customers who would have been lost to the rival premerger will now be diverted to the other product the firm now sells. Given that market shares reflect the fraction of customers who select the product as their first

---

57.   *Id.* at 228-29. Thorough analysis of this type of situation requires information on several firms' market shares and market-wide concentration levels.

58.   With respect to the link between concentration levels and market power, "the empirical research does not reliably identify any particular concentration level common across industries at which price increases kick in or raise particular competitive concerns." GAVIL, KOVACIC & BAKER, *supra* note 42, at 506.

59.   *See* MERGER GUIDELINES, *supra* note 1, § 7.

choice, a convenient assumption for second choices is that they are also distributed in the same proportion as the observed market shares. Under such an assumption, higher concentration levels generally will reflect the extent to which a merger will raise prices.[60]

The *Merger Guidelines* set out three levels of concentration depending on the postmerger HHI level: "unconcentrated" markets are markets with HHIs below 1500, "moderately concentrated" markets have HHIs between 1500 and 2500, and "highly concentrated" markets have HHIs over 2500.[61] Most transactions challenged (and even investigated) by the federal antitrust agencies fall squarely into the "highly concentrated" category. [62] As with market shares, however, a high concentration level is not necessarily anticompetitive. For example, the agencies have emphasized that they do not view a merger as anticompetitive simply because it is in a market with a high concentration level.[63]

---

60. *See* Jonathan B. Baker, *Market Concentration in the Antitrust Analysis of Horizontal Mergers*, *in* ANTITRUST LAW AND ECONOMICS 234, 246-47 (Keith Hylton ed., 2010). The *Merger Guidelines* also focus more on the closeness of competition between merging firms (and diversion ratios) and less on measures of marketwide concentration than did prior versions of the *Guidelines*. *See* MERGER GUIDELINES, *supra* note 1, § 6.1.

61. MERGER GUIDELINES, *supra* note 1, § 5.3.

62. *See, e.g.*, FTC v. Libbey, Inc., 211 F. Supp. 2d 34, 39-40, 47, 50-51 (D.D.C. 2002) (finding deal would result in a postmerger HHI of 6241, and Anchor, despite its small market share (7 percent), was Libbey's most aggressive competitor). Among the markets in which the FTC conducted enforcement actions in horizontal mergers from 1996-2007, 94 percent of them fell in the "highly concentrated" category. *See* FED. TRADE COMM'N, HORIZONTAL MERGER INVESTIGATION DATA, FISCAL YEARS 1996-2007 tbl. 3.1 (2008). For the DOJ and FTC from 1999-2003, 95 percent of the challenged horizontal mergers fell in the "highly concentrated" category. *See* FED. TRADE COMM'N & U.S. DEP'T OF JUSTICE, MERGER CHALLENGES DATA, FISCAL YEARS 1999-2003, at 10, tbl. 1 (2003), *available at* http://www.ftc.gov/os/2008/12/081201hsrmergerdata.pdf.

63. *See* Timothy J. Muris, Chairman, Fed. Trade Comm'n, Prepared Remarks at the Workshop on *Horizontal Merger Guidelines* (Feb. 17, 2004), *available at* http://www.ftc.gov/speeches/muris/040217hmgwksp.shtm; The *Commentary on the Horizontal Merger Guidelines* states:

> Indeed, the Agencies do not make enforcement decisions solely on the basis of market shares and concentration, but both measures nevertheless play an important role in the analysis . . .

3. Market Share Trends, Unstable Concentration Levels, and Changes in Market Conditions

Since *United States v. General Dynamics Corp.*, [64] courts and scholars have recognized that the purpose of analyzing market shares is to reflect each firm's future competitive significance. The *Merger Guidelines* state that market shares are "based on the best available indicator of firms' future competitive significance in the relevant market."[65] As a result, both trends in market shares and future market conditions are often taken into account in interpreting market shares and the resulting concentration levels.[66]

Trends in shares may indicate a market or a competitor in flux.[67] A declining share may indicate that a firm has less competitive significance than its current share would otherwise suggest. Similarly, an increasing

---

> Application of the Guidelines as an integrated whole to case-specific facts—not undue emphasis on market share and concentration statistics—determines whether the Agency will challenge a particular merger.

U.S. Dep't of Justice & Fed. Trade Comm'n, Commentary on the Horizontal Merger Guidelines § 1 (2006), *available at* http://www.justice.gov/atr/public/guidelines/215247/htm#20.

64. 415 U.S. 486 (1974).
65. Merger Guidelines, *supra* note 1, § 5.2.
66. However, this is not to say that the market shares themselves should be directly adjusted to reflect the trend.

> Extrapolating market share trends into the future also is generally unwarranted. Unless the cause of a market share trend is both self-evident and immutable, the current output share of a product is most likely to be the best predictor of the output share of that product in the near future. Market share trends may be sufficiently clear and irreversible . . . [b]ut even in such cases, the best course may be to account for misleading impressions from current shares through informed interpretation of the observed shares rather than directly adjust the shares themselves.

Werden, *supra* note 6, at 94.
67. For a discussion of the problems presented by markets undergoing significant change, or dynamic markets, see *infra* pt. B.5.a.

share could indicate that the affected firm has greater competitive significance than evidenced by its current share.[68]

The *Merger Guidelines* consider "rapid entrants" as participants in the relevant market.[69] Rapid entrants are "[f]irms that are not current producers in a relevant market, but that would very likely provide rapid supply responses with direct competitive impact in the event of a SSNIP [small but significant non-transitory increase in price], without incurring significant costs."[70] Rapid entrants also include firms that could easily shift sales into the relevant geographic market(s) or to targeted customers or shift production capacity to the relevant product(s).[71]

Predictable future events and regulatory conditions must also be taken into consideration in analyzing market shares and concentration levels. Regulatory restrictions may impact a firm's ability to compete. For example, noise restrictions on aircraft have a greater impact on carriers with aging aircraft than they do on air carriers using newer aircraft with quieter engines. Removal of tariffs that previously protected a firm from competition will likely lead to lower market shares for domestic firms. An expiration of a patent can have a significant effect on market share as new competitors are allowed to introduce competitive

---

68.   An examination of pricing may also be instructive in connection with trends in shares. For example, if market shares have shifted dramatically over time, the extent to which prices have changed, including the timing of those changes, may be important.

69.   MERGER GUIDELINES, *supra* note 1, § 5.1.

70.   *Id.*

71.   *Id.* This concept is related to the notion of barriers to entry, which are explored in depth in ch. VII, *infra*. For a more detailed discussion of uncommitted entrants, see Janusz A. Ordover & Robert D. Willig, *Economics and the 1992* Merger Guidelines: *A Brief Survey*, 8 REV. INDUS. ORG. 139, 141-44 (1993); *see also* Carter Hawley Hale Stores v. The Limited, Inc., 587 F. Supp. 246, 253 (C.D. Cal. 1984); Heublein, Inc., 96 F.T.C. 385, 576 (1980); *In re* Coca-Cola Bottling Co., 93 F.T.C. 110, 204-05 (1979); *In re* RSR Corp., 88 F.T.C. 800, 876-77 (1976), *aff'd*, 602 F.2d 1317 (9th Cir. 1979); *In re* Liggett & Myers Inc., 87 F.T.C 1074, 1148, 1158-59 (1976), *aff'd*, 567 F.2d 1273 (4th Cir. 1977); *In re* The Budd Co., 86 F.T.C. 518, 572 (1975). Some courts, however, have refused to include producers in a market simply on the basis of their ability to switch facilities. *See, e.g.*, Kaiser Aluminum & Chem. v. FTC, 652 F.2d 1324, 1330 (7th Cir. 1981); Reynolds Metals Co. v. FTC, 309 F.2d 223, 227 (D.C. Cir. 1962); United States v. Black & Decker Mfg. Co., 430 F. Supp. 729, 735, 737-38, 773-76 (D. Md. 1976).

products. To the extent that regulatory changes are anticipated in a particular market, they must be taken into consideration when interpreting market shares.

Further, unstable concentration levels and market shares over time may suggest the measurements are misleading. If a market's concentration level and underlying market shares are generally unstable over time (and there is reason to believe that the instability will continue), the current level of concentration may not fairly characterize the market's future concentration.

A number of factors may cause instability in a market. When individual shares vary from year to year, the presence of a high concentration ratio may simply reflect the fact that during a given year there can be only a few winners of key pieces of business.[72] Moreover, firms' shares may fluctuate widely from year to year when a market is characterized by few sales in a year.[73]

4. Customer and Competitor Attributes and Strategies

Measures of market share or concentration levels may not accurately measure market power if the analysis does not take into consideration the nature of the market's customers and competitors. Both may engage in strategies that enhance competition and counteract the likelihood of anticompetitive activity. Buyers with market power are sometimes able to offset market power on the seller side or obtain prices below those that would exist in a competitive market by using purchasing strategies to reduce prices.[74] Moreover, in some markets, buyers can preclude

---

72. For example, consider a market in which only two major contracts were awarded in a given year, and assume that a large number of firms compete for those contracts each year. In this market, an annual sales-based market share would be very high even though there is substantial competition each year for the contracts. *See* United States v. Baker Hughes Inc., 908 F.2d 981, 986 (D.C. Cir. 1990) (noting that the trial judge found the number of units sold varied from 22 to 42 to 38 over a three-year period and thus "at any given point in time an individual seller's future competitive strength may not be accurately reflected") (internal quotations omitted); *see also infra* pt. B.5.c.

73. *See* SCHERER & ROSS, *supra* note 49, at 306-08.

74. *See, e.g., In re* Brand Name Prescription Drugs Antitrust Litig., 123 F.3d 599, 606 (7th Cir. 1997) ("The bigger a buyer is, the more likely it is to be able to obtain a discount from a member of a cartel, since the volume of its purchases may compensate the member for endangering the

collusion among competitors by limiting the flow of information among sellers, selecting a favored supplier, or entering into the market in collaboration with a seller. Buyers may construct auctions designed to pressure bidders to lower their prices.[75] If suppliers must incur customer-specific sunk costs so that buyers commit to a seller for a period of time, a seller might have short-run market power.[76] In any of these cases, market shares and concentration levels might be misleading.

---

cartel by granting a discount."); Hosp. Corp. of Am. v. FTC, 807 F.2d 1381, 1391 (7th Cir. 1986) ("The bigger a buyer is, the more easily and lucratively a member of the cartel can cheat on his fellows; for with a single transaction, he may be able to increase his sales and hence profits dramatically. But with all the members thus vying for the large orders of big buyers, the cartel will erode.") (internal citations omitted); United States v. Archer-Daniels-Midland Co., 781 F. Supp. 1400, 1416 (S.D. Iowa 1991) (finding large power buyers that accounted for 60 percent of the relevant market's purchases would preclude merging defendants from raising prices); United States v. Country Lake Foods, 754 F. Supp. 669, 674 (D. Minn. 1990) (permitting merger in market in which three large customers accounted for 90 percent of purchases).

75.   The possibility that outcomes in auction markets might differ from those observed in other markets is supported to some extent by the experimental economics literature which indicates that when the rules of exchange and the amount of information vary from one market setting to another, so does market performance. *See, e.g.*, Charissa P. Wellford, *Antitrust: Results from the Laboratory* 11-19 (Fed. Trade Comm'n, Bureau of Economics, Working Paper No. 202, 1993). This is especially true when the number of buyers and sellers is small. For example, when there is only one seller, markets following the rules of exchange of large organized stock exchanges (double auctions) still converge to and stabilize at the perfectly-competitive equilibrium. *See* Vernon L. Smith & Arlington W. Williams, *The Boundaries of Competitive Price Theory: Convergence, Expectations, and Transaction Costs, reprinted in* VERNON L. SMITH, BARGAINING AND MARKET BEHAVIOR: ESSAYS IN EXPERIMENTAL ECONOMICS ch. 14 (2000). In contrast, if only one seller exists in a market that seems closer to traditional retailing (in which the sellers post a "take-it-or-leave-it" price), the market more often achieves a price that is above the competitive level. This result may imply that auction markets are less conducive to the exercise of market power than are other market formats. For a recent discussion on the implication of bidding markets to antitrust analysis, see Paul Klemperer, *Bidding Markets*, 3 J. COMP. L. & ECON. 1 (2007).

76.   *See* David T. Scheffman & Pablo T. Spiller, *Buyers' Strategies, Entry Barriers, and Competition,* 30 ECON. INQUIRY 418, 419 (1992).

Just as the nature of customers affects competition, so does the character of the competitors. The competitive strategies of firms in a particular market may have sufficient variation that a firm individually might be able to affect the market outcome and place a significant constraint on the prices and output strategies of rivals even if the firm does not have a substantial market share. For example, if a firm is unusually aggressive in pursuing sales, the remaining firms in the industry may find it difficult to attain or maintain a cooperative equilibrium, which may lead to lower prices than might be expected if all firms had less aggressive strategies. This effect will not be revealed in concentration or market share statistics, but is nonetheless an important consideration in a market power analysis.

Firms that use aggressive pricing strategies that differ significantly from those of competitors are usually called "mavericks."[77] The factors that might lead a firm to act as a maverick include: particularly low costs; a differing technology that allows the firm to take better advantage of scale economies; atypically large excess capacity; differentiated products that can be substitutes for rivals' offerings but that cause the firm to face a demand that differs from that of its rivals; differing costs of punishing a defector to an agreement; differing probabilities of being detected as a defector; and differing levels of vertical integration.[78]

5. Market Characteristics

Market characteristics describe the nature of competition within the relevant market. The market characteristics discussed in this Part must be

---

77. The *Merger Guidelines* define a maverick as "a firm that plays a disruptive role in the market to the benefit of consumers." MERGER GUIDELINES, *supra* note 1, § 2.1.5; *see also* United States v. H&R Block, Inc., 2011 U.S. Dist. LEXIS 130219, at *112-13 (D.D.C. 2011) ("In the context of antitrust law, a maverick has been defined as a particularly aggressive competitor that 'plays a disruptive role in the market to the benefit of consumers.'") (citations omitted).
78. Many of the items in this list were identified in Jonathan B. Baker, *Two Sherman Act Section 1 Dilemmas: Parallel Pricing, the Oligopoly Problem, and Contemporary Economic Theory*, 38 ANTITRUST BULL. 143, 202 (1993) (arguing that economic theory provides clues to detecting maverick firms in an industry and that such detection is a key to merger analysis); *see also* Jonathan B. Baker, *Mavericks, Mergers, and Exclusion: Proving Coordinated Competitive Effects Under the Antitrust Laws*, 77 N.Y.U. L. REV. 135, 175-77 (2002).

taken into account in an analysis of market shares and concentrations to determine whether the data appropriately reflect the level of competition in the relevant market.

a.   Dynamic Markets

As discussed above, markets that exhibit unstable or changing market shares require analysis to assess the future strength of market participants. In some markets, however, the instability is so significant that the market is described as "dynamic." Dynamic markets are markets that are undergoing technological or other forms of change. Because they are in flux, they may not lend themselves to collusive or coordinated pricing, even when they are relatively concentrated.

When a firm's cost structure changes, its profit-maximizing price is also likely to change. As a result, continual changes in costs can make it difficult for firms to collude on prices.[79] Moreover, when technologies are changing rapidly, firms may fear that a failure to market their products aggressively today may hurt their competitive position tomorrow (i.e., it may make it more difficult for them to build sales to be able to exploit economies of scale).[80] Together, these effects make tacit collusion more difficult. Accordingly, a high concentration level is not necessarily troubling in a dynamic market.

b.   Innovation Markets[81]

Innovation markets, also known as research and development markets, consist of the research and development directed to particular new or improved goods or processes and the close substitutes for that research and development. [82] When assessing the competitive

---

79.   *See, e.g.*, FTC v. Tenet Health Care, 186 F.3d 1045 (8th Cir. 1999) (considering possible anticompetitive effects in health care market).

80.   For a discussion of a number of case studies in which technological change is believed to have disrupted pricing, see SCHERER & ROSS, *supra* note 49, at 285-94.

81.   For additional discussion of market power analysis in innovation markets, see *infra* ch. VI.

82.   *See* U.S. DEP'T OF JUSTICE & FED. TRADE COMM'N, ANTITRUST GUIDELINES FOR THE LICENSING OF INTELLECTUAL PROPERTY § 3.2.3 (1995), *available at* http://www.justice.gov/atr/public/guidelines/-0558.htm#t323 [hereinafter ANTITRUST GUIDELINES FOR THE LICENSING OF INTELLECTUAL PROPERTY]. Close substitutes are "research and

significance of current and likely potential participants in an innovation market, which the FTC advises to approach conservatively, [83] the agencies will take all relevant evidence into account, including market share data to the extent they are available and accurately reflect the competitive significance of market participants. If the data are unavailable or do not accurately portray competitive significance in the marketplace, market shares may be assigned based on shares of identifiable assets, expenditures, or shares of a related product. If participants are deemed to have comparable capabilities and incentives for research and development, agencies may assign equal market shares. [84]

Consideration of market shares may not adequately measure competition if firms compete for the market and not within the market. That is often the case in innovation markets, in which the introduction of a superior product frequently leads (through network efforts, economies of scale, or superiority) to dominance in the market. Rivalry may result in the introduction of an improved product and the innovator's achieving a dominant position. Therefore, future market shares cannot be inferred from historical market shares as competition may be characterized by a succession of dominant firms that capture all or most of the market.

c.   Bidding Markets

Markets in which the buyer of goods or services solicits bids for its business present special challenges for market analysis, especially in markets in which orders are infrequent or "lumpy." Assigning equal shares to all firms may be appropriate in markets in which each firm has, on a forward-looking basis, an equal likelihood of securing sales. [85]

---

development efforts, technologies, and goods that significantly constrain the exercise of market power with respect to the relevant research and development, for example by limiting the ability and incentive of a hypothetical monopolist to retard the pace of research and development."
Id.

83.   FED. TRADE COMM'N, ANTICIPATING THE 21ST CENTURY: COMPETITION POLICY IN THE NEW HIGH-TECH, GLOBAL MARKETPLACE 33 (1996), *available at* http://www.ftc.gov/opp/global/report/gc_v1.pdf.

84.   ANTITRUST GUIDELINES FOR THE LICENSING OF INTELLECTUAL PROPERTY, *supra* note 82, § 3.2.3.

85.   The 1992 *Merger Guidelines* expressly recognized this possibility. *See* 1992 MERGER GUIDELINES, *supra* note 15, § 1.41 n.15. Curiously, the

Models that assign firms equal market shares are often termed "bidding models" because each firm that submits a bid may be equally well positioned to win a competition. If each of the major firms has similar costs and has substantial excess capacity or has the ability to expand its capacity quickly in response to increased orders, it may be appropriate to assign each firm a proportional share.[86]

More specifically, consider a defense contractor that makes no sales of a product in a given year because it did not win the last government contract that was awarded in its market. If the contractor retains the ability to bid competitively on the next contract, it does not make sense to assign the losing contractor a market share of zero percent and the winning contractor a market share of 100 percent, since both contractors will have a competitive influence on the next bid. On the other hand, if the contractor that wins the first bid has an advantage in future bids, that advantage should be taken into account in the economic analysis.[87]

In some markets, customers find it profitable to invite only some of the possible competitors to submit bids. This type of behavior is most likely to be observed when significant transaction costs are associated with submitting and evaluating a bid. In these situations, it may or may not be appropriate to limit the market to the firms asked to participate in bidding depending on the institutional structure of the market and the competitive issue that is to be addressed. The homogeneity of the participating firms (or lack thereof) is an important consideration. If the firms selected to bid are more like each other than the other firms in the market, then it may make more sense to allocate market share on a proportional basis to the selected firms.

2010 *Merger Guidelines* did not specifically address this possibility. *See* 2010 MERGER GUIDELINES, *supra* note 1, § 5.2.

86.   *See* Grumman Corp. v. LTV Corp., 665 F.2d 10, 12, 14 (2d Cir. 1981) (noting that although the Navy might have a sole supplier of carrier-based fighter aircraft at any point in time, other firms could bid competitively on the next contract).

87.   For simplicity, the discussion assumes there is no competitive fringe. However, a modified bidding model may apply when the market has a group of firms that are large enough to supply a large share of the market but also a number of additional fringe firms. While the impact of the fringe competitors on market pricing must be considered, the presence of a competitive fringe does not alter the economic fact that the larger competitors are similarly situated and, as a result, may deserve equal market shares even though they may have different levels of sales or capacity.

On the other hand, when firms are not homogeneous, either because they produce differentiated products or because they differ in their pricing strategy, the selection of the firms to bid makes a significant difference in the analysis. If some firms are members of a bid-rigging cartel, the inclusion of a nonmember could result in more competitive bidding than if that member is excluded. The comparative aggressiveness of the bidder compared to its other competitors is also a factor, even if the aggressive pricer's final output is similar to that of the other firms.

Similarly, if two merging firms that participate in bidding markets are very close substitutes for each other and if relatively few other firms are close substitutes to the merging firms, then customers with both firms on their bid lists will find that the merger reduced the number of close substitutes by one, which may (depending on other market characteristics) mean that the merger has had an anticompetitive effect. On the other hand, if the firms are not close substitutes (as might be evidenced by the fact that the firms rarely seriously compete for the same accounts), it might overstate the anticompetitive effect of the merger to assign each firm an equal proportional market share.

The frequency of orders in a bidding market has an important impact on the likelihood of collusion and other anticompetitive behavior. In particular, in a market with frequent orders, it may be possible for colluders to reward one another by allocating bids and allowing each participant in a collusive scheme to win a number of rigged bids in a given year. But, even a single order awarded to a nonparticipant will eliminate the effectiveness of an agreed-upon price increase. When business is lumpy (and subcontracting does not occur on a regular basis), it may be harder to allocate bids and/or to arrange for side-payments. A market with very few orders will give competitors limited opportunities to learn about each other's pricing strategies and signal one another. In addition, because there are so few opportunities for business, competitors may have a strong incentive to bid aggressively for that business.[88]

d. Two-Sided Markets

Two-sided markets (or, more generally, multi-sided markets) serve two (or multiple) distinct groups of end-users which benefit from

---

88.   For a discussion of a number of case studies where lumpy orders are believed to have disrupted pricing, see SCHERER & ROSS, *supra* note 49, at 306-08.

interacting through one or several common platforms. [89] Examples include credit card payment systems which must attract merchants as well as cardholders, and videogame consoles such as Sony PlayStation and Microsoft Xbox which bring together game developers and players.

To date, academic and legal sources provide little discussion regarding market share calculation in two-sided markets, as market definition has been the dominant topic of interest. Much of the literature addresses the adaptation of standard market power assessment techniques, such as the hypothetical monopolist test, to two-sided market contexts. [90] Two-sided markets present many challenges for market definition and thus the calculation of market shares; courts and practitioners have not yet reached consensus on how to treat the two-sided characteristics of industries such as electronic payment networks. For instance, when applying a hypothetical monopolist test to the merchant side of a payment network, it is not clear how to account for the potential responses of card issuers. [91]

C. Alternative Measures of Market Power

An alternative to measuring market shares as an indicator of market power is to attempt to measure market power directly with an analysis of industry profits.

In economics, efforts to measure industry profits as an indicator of market power began in the 1940s and 1950s with the structure-conduct-performance paradigm (SCPP). The SCPP posits that market structure

---

89.   Jean-Charles Rochet & Jean Tirole, *Two Sided Markets: A Progress Report*, 37 RAND J. ECON. 645, 645 (2006).

90.   *See, e.g.*, David S. Evans, *The Antitrust Economics of Multi-Sided Platform Markets*, 20 YALE J. REG. 325 (2003); Renata B. Hesse, *Two-Sided Platform Markets and the Application of the Traditional Antitrust Analytical Framework*, 3 COMPETITION POLICY INT'L 191 (2007).

91.   Renata B. Hesse & Joshua H. Soven, *Defining Relevant Product Markets in Electronic Payment Network Antitrust Cases*, 73 ANTITRUST L.J. 709, 716 (2006). In *United States v. Visa U.S.A., Inc.*, 344 F.3d 229 (2d Cir. 2003), the court applied a hypothetical monopolist test when the DOJ challenged network exclusivity rules which banned Visa and Mastercard issuers from issuing credit cards on some competitors' networks. It examined the effects of a price increase on card issuers as well as merchant customers, but did not discuss how, if at all, the interplay between the two sides contributed to market definition analysis or the likely impact on market shares.

(e.g., market concentration) determines market conduct (i.e., how the firms in the market compete), which leads to market performance (usually taken to be the profitability of the industry).[92] In the 1970s and 1980s, new techniques, which can generally be put under the heading of New Empirical Industrial Organization (NEIO), were developed to measure market power. [93] This Part discusses the problems with measuring profits, and more recent NEIO approaches to measuring market power.

1. *Profits and Market Power*

A typical approach to analyzing profits as an indicator of market power is to calculate profit as rate of return by taking a measure of net income (revenue minus costs) as a percentage of a measure of asset value, and compare it to a benchmark rate of return that is believed to be consistent with the rate of return in a competitive industry. Two main critiques have been leveled against this approach: one related to how profits are measured, and another related to the relationship between profits and market power.

The first critique is that the economic concept of profit, which is relevant to an assessment of market power, is often unrelated to the accounting concept of profit, and the two are very difficult to reconcile.[94]

---

92.   The approach has a long history in economics dating back to the 1940s and 1950s with the work of Joe Bain. *See, e.g.*, Joe S. Bain, *The Profit Rate as a Measure of Monopoly Power*, 55 Q.J. ECON. 271 (1941).

93.   *See, e.g.*, Timothy F. Bresnahan, *Empirical Methods of Industries with Market Power, in* II HANDBOOK OF INDUSTRIAL ORGANIZATION ch. 17, at 1012-13 (R. Schmalensee & R.D. Willig eds., 1989).

94.   Economic profits represent the excess of revenue over all of the costs necessary for the production of the products and services in question, including a return on the capital already invested and opportunity costs. Economic profits are not the same as accounting profits, which equal revenues minus accounting costs. A principal difference between economic profits and accounting profits is that the two treat capital costs (such as plants and equipment) differently. For true economic profits, capital costs equal the replacement costs of the capital assets that are "used up" in a given year. For accounting profits, capital costs are measured using standard accounting rules of depreciation. Using these standard rules, the amount "charged" for depreciation often has little to do with the amount of the capital that is used up. Accounting depreciation also fails to consider replacement costs. For a discussion of economic

Franklin Fisher was prominent in developing this critique,[95] and he reached the conclusion that the economic rate of return is unknowable from available accounting data:

> [T]here is no way in which one can look at accounting rates of return and infer anything about . . . the presence or absence of monopoly profits. . . . Economists (and others) who believe that analysis of accounting rates of return will tell them much (if they can only overcome the various definitional problems which separate economists and accountants) are deluding themselves.[96]

An alternative measure of profit that is often used is the price-cost margin, which as a measure of market power is known as the Lerner Index. The Lerner Index is the difference between the price of a product and its marginal cost, expressed as a percentage of the product's price.[97] In economic theory, for a single firm, it is equal to the inverse of the elasticity of demand facing the firm.[98] While this measure of profit is also difficult to observe from accounting data,[99] it is still commonly used in merger analysis to perform critical loss analyses to define relevant markets or evaluate the potential for the postmerger exercise of market

---

profits, see FRANKLIN M. FISHER ET AL., FOLDED, SPINDLED, AND MUTILATED: ECONOMIC ANALYSIS AND *U.S. V. IBM* ch. 7 (1983).

95. *See* Franklin M. Fisher & John J. McGowan, *On the Misuse of Accounting Rates of Return to Infer Monopoly Profits*, *reprinted in* INDUSTRIAL ORGANIZATION, ECONOMICS AND THE LAW: COLLECTED PAPERS OF FRANKLIN M. FISHER ch. 4 (John Monz ed., 1991) [hereinafter Fisher & McGowan I]; Franklin M. Fisher, *On the Misuse of Accounting Rates of Return: Reply*, *reprinted in* INDUSTRIAL ORGANIZATION, ECONOMICS AND THE LAW: COLLECTED PAPERS OF FRANKLIN M. FISHER, *supra*, ch. 5; Franklin M. Fisher, *On the Misuse of the Profits-Sales Ratio to Infer Monopoly Power*, *reprinted in* INDUSTRIAL ORGANIZATION, ECONOMICS AND THE LAW: COLLECTED PAPERS OF FRANKLIN M. FISHER, *supra*, ch. 6.

96. Fisher & McGowan I, *supra* note 95, at 91.

97. *See supra* ch. III.

98. *See* CARLTON & PERLOFF, *supra* note 41, at 93.

99. *See, e.g.*, Timothy F. Bresnahan, *Empirical Methods of Industries with Market Power*, *in* II HANDBOOK OF INDUSTRIAL ORGANIZATION ch. 17, at 1012 (R. Schmalensee & R.D. Willig eds., 1989) ("Firms' price-cost margins are not taken to be observables; economic marginal cost (MC) cannot be directly or straightforwardly observed.").

power.[100] There has also been a modest resurgence in the use of price-cost margins with the introduction of the concept of upward pricing pressure in the new *Merger Guidelines*.[101]

The second critique related to the relationship between profits and market power observes that profits, however measured, may reflect either higher prices (market power), or lower costs (efficiency), or both.[102] Research demonstrated that the empirical relationships observed in the economics literature between industry profits and concentration were more consistent with an efficiencies explanation than a market power explanation.[103] The rationale for this outcome is that efficient

---

100.   As discussed above, critical loss analysis evaluates whether a price increase would be profitable by estimating what the loss in sales would be in response to the price increase. It is used in market definition analysis to evaluate whether a price increase by a hypothetical monopolist would be profitable, and in merger analysis to evaluate whether the merged entity would have the incentive to raise price postmerger. Some recent papers on critical loss include Jonathan B. Baker, *Market Definition: An Analytical Overview*, 74 ANTITRUST L.J. 129, 154-57 (2007) (cautioning that critical loss analysis may lead to misleading results); Joseph Farrell & Carl Shapiro, *Improving Critical Loss Analysis*, ANTITRUST SOURCE, Feb. 2008; Daniel P. O'Brien & Abraham L. Wickelgren, *A Critical Analysis of Critical Loss Analysis*, 71 ANTITRUST L.J. 161 (2003); Michael L. Katz & Carl Shapiro, *Critical Loss: Let's Tell the Whole Story*, ANTITRUST, Spring 2003, at 49; David T. Sheffman and Joseph J. Simons, *The State of Critical Loss Analysis: Let's Make Sure We Understand the Whole Story*, ANTITRUST SOURCE, Nov. 2003, *available at* *http://www.americanbar.org/content/dam/aba/publishingantitrust_-source/03/11/scheffman.authcheckdam.pdf.*

101.   *See* MERGER GUIDELINES, *supra* note 1, § 6.1; *see also* Carl Shapiro, *The 2010 Horizontal Merger Guidelines: From Hedgehog to Fox in Forty Years*, 77 ANTITRUST L.J. 49 (2010).

102.   This critique was developed by Harold Demsetz. *See* Harold Demsetz, *Industry Structure, Market Rivalry, and Public Policy*, 16 J.L. & ECON. 1, (1973); Harold Demsetz, *Two Systems of Belief About Monopoly*, *in* INDUSTRIAL CONCENTRATION: THE NEW LEARNING 164 (Harvey J. Goldschmid et al. eds., 1974). This issue became known as the "endogeneity problem" because concentration itself is endogenous: that is, concentration is not an exogenous or independent factor but is determined by the cost structures of firms in the industry.

103.   *See, e.g.*, Sam Peltzman, *The Gains and Losses from Industrial Concentration*, 20 J.L. & ECON. 229 (1977); Michael Smirlock et al.,

firms grow to become large firms, which leads to a concentrated industry. This may be similarly stated as: economies of scale lead to concentrated industries.

2. New Empirical Analyses of Market Power

In response to the criticisms of the SCPP approach and the problem of measuring profits, new approaches were developed to measure market power more directly. These new approaches generally fall under the heading of NEIO and may be defined as approaches that involve an econometric model of an industry in which market power is measured explicitly.[104] They can be broadly categorized into one of two types of analysis: a *structural* analysis or a *reduced-form* analysis. Both approaches essentially attempt to test whether the outcome observed for an industry (e.g., the prices and quantities) are consistent with firms behaving competitively or exercising market power.

In a structural analysis, market power typically is measured using an econometric model of prices, quantities, and other relevant variables (e.g., seasonality adjustments) over time, and by making specific assumptions about the shapes of the industry demand and supply curves.[105] Many structural models include parameters that measure directly how firms interact competitively with each other.[106] Other structural models take a *menu approach* in which the data are fitted to different models of competition (e.g., collusion, Bertrand, Cournot)[107] to see which model provides the best fit to the data. The main drawbacks of the structural approach are that it typically requires significant data, and the results depend on the specific assumptions made in the model.

Reduced-form analysis generally requires less data and fewer assumptions but is less powerful in explaining and measuring the degree of market power. The underlying competitive behavior modeled in a structural analysis is "buried" in the reduced-form model. Typically, reduced-form models test the hypotheses of competitive or collusive

---

Tobin's q and the Structure-Performance Relationship, 74 AM. ECON. REV. 1051 (1984).

104. *See* Bresnahan, *supra* note 99, ch. 17.

105. *See* CARLTON & PERLOFF, *supra* note 41, ch. 8.

106. An alternative interpretation is that these parameters provide a measure of the average "collusiveness" of conduct. *See* Bresnahan, *supra* note 99, at 1029.

107. *See supra* ch. III.

behavior without obtaining a measure of market power for intermediate outcomes in which these two extreme hypotheses are rejected.

Regardless of whether structural or reduced-form models are used, a central feature of such models is that they rely on variation in exogenous variables (i.e., variables, such as price or quantity, that the model is not used to estimate) to identify market power. This Part provides a summary of the main NEIO methods, organized according to the general strategy used to infer market power from the data.[108]

a. Natural Experiments Involving a Rotation or Shift in the Demand Curve

This approach focuses on how firms adjust prices in response to exogenous shocks that affect the slope (or elasticity) of the demand curve facing the industry.[109] Suppose that an exogenous event occurred that rotated the demand curve around the industry equilibrium point making it steeper (i.e., less elastic) or flatter (i.e., more elastic) at that point, such that future price increases would lead to smaller or greater quantity losses, respectively, than was previously the case. If the market is operating competitively, such a change in demand should not lead to a change in price. On the other hand, oligopoly or monopoly theory implies that such a change in demand elasticity will shift the marginal revenue of firms, which will change their pricing decisions and shift the resulting equilibrium price and quantity. Under this method, the degree of market power is inferred from the industry price response to a change in the market demand elasticity.

Finding events that rotate a demand curve is often difficult, but they can be caused, for example, by changes in the prices of competing products, changes in national income, changes in ad valorem taxes, or

---

108. Although the methods described in this Part are grouped according to the principal way the data identify market power, many studies use a combination of identifying strategies. Similar classifications of NEIO methods are provided by JEFFREY M. PERLOFF ET AL., ESTIMATING MARKET POWER AND STRATEGIES (2007); Bresnahan, *supra* note 99, at 1031-32; Vrinda Kadiyali et al., *Structural Analysis of Competitive Behavior: New Empirical Industrial Organization Methods in Marketing,* 18 INT'L J. RES. IN MKTG. 161 (2001).

109. *See* Bresnahan, *supra* note 99, at 1033.

changes in technology. Fringe firms can also rotate the demand curve when they enter an oligopolistic market.[110]

In a more general version of this approach, a shift in the demand curve in response to an exogenous shock is used. However, the inference on market power in this instance depends on the assumption made regarding the shape of the supply curve. If the cost of production does not depend on the scale of production (i.e., the industry marginal cost curve is flat), a shift in demand that causes a shift in the scale of production will not lead to a change in price if the industry is competitive. Under oligopoly or monopoly, though, theory implies that the shift in the marginal revenue of the firms will change their pricing decisions and shift the resulting equilibrium price.

This approach becomes complicated if marginal costs change with scale of production, which will often depend on the technology used to make the product. In these instances, an exogenous shift in demand can cause both price and quantity to change even if the industry is competitive. This makes it possible to confuse market power with shifts in marginal costs.[111]

b. Natural Experiments Involving Shifts in Costs

A similar natural experiment can be conducted by analyzing revenue changes in response to exogenous cost changes. Economic theory shows that, in the case of a monopolist, revenues will always fall when marginal costs increase; otherwise, the monopolist would have increased prices before the change in costs. Thus, comparing the change in revenues in response to movements in costs can reveal whether a firm has market power. Suppose, for example, that the costs of all the inputs of a firm increase by 1 percent, which must cause an increase of 1 percent in the firm's marginal costs. If the industry is not competitive, the firm's revenues will increase by less than 1 percent.

Another variation of this approach analyzes costs and revenues across markets for the same industry. It assumes that each local market is at the long-run competitive equilibrium. Then, for each firm, revenues should shift proportionately to costs, while, at the market level, revenues

---

110. *See* CARLTON & PERLOFF, *supra* note 41, at 147-49.
111. *See* Jonathan B. Baker & Timothy F. Bresnahan, *Empirical Methods of Identifying and Measuring Market Power*, 61 ANTITRUST L.J. 3, 12 (1992) (noting that "[t]his phenomenon makes it easy to confuse market power and high marginal cost explanations for price rises").

will expand less than proportionately to costs—because the price increase will reduce the quantity demanded. This variation has been used for local media markets, the cigarette industry, and airport pairs originating in Atlanta.[112]

The main advantage of this approach is that it estimates a single equation and requires relatively little data, namely, revenues and cost shifters. However, the test is not very powerful in detecting market power and the results depend on the critical assumption that the industry is in the long-run equilibrium (even when the test typically relies on short-term adjustments to variations in factor prices). In addition, the method does not provide a measure of market power; it only tests for the existence of market power.[113] More recent studies use structural models of demand and supply to assess changes in market power made possible by changes in the industry environment that create exogenous changes in costs.[114]

---

112. *See* John C. Panzar & James N. Rosse, *Testing for "Monopoly" Equilibrium*, 35 J. INDUS. ECON. 443 (1987); Daniel Sullivan, *Testing Hypotheses About Firm Behavior in the Cigarette Industry*, 93 J. POL. ECON. 586 (1985); Thorsten Fischer & David R. Kamerschen, *Measuring Competition in the U.S. Airline Industry Using the Rosse-Panzar Test and Cross-Sectional Regression Analyses*, 6 J. APPLIED ECON. 73 (2003).

113. For some specifications of the cost function, the Rosse and Panzar test is powerless, as it cannot discriminate between market structures. *See* Charles E. Hyde & Jeffrey M. Perloff, *Can Market Power Be Estimated?*, 10 REV. INDUS. ORG. 465, 468-69 (1995). It is also noteworthy from the Fischer and Kamerschen results that the Rosse-Panzar statistic can be very far from the proportional price increase in which a 1 percent change in marginal costs leads to a price increase in the vicinity of 1 percent. This casts doubt on the ability of the reduced-form equation to capture the idiosyncrasies of a particular market without imposing more structure on the underlying model.

114. *See, e.g.*, Robert N. Rubinovitz, *Marker Power and Price Increases for Basic Cable Service Since Deregulation*, 24 RAND J. ECON. 1 (1993); Lars-Hendrik Röller & Frode Steen, *On the Workings of a Cartel: Evidence from the Norwegian Cement Industry*, 96 AM. ECON. REV. 321 (2006).

c.   Competitive Reaction to Exogenous Shocks (And New Entrants)

In oligopolies, the main obstacle to collusion (in the absence of entry) is cheating (e.g., secret price cutting) on the collusive agreement.[115] Since detecting cheating can be difficult, to police a collusive agreement oligopolists will often establish a trigger at which they abandon the collusive agreement and compete. For example, if a firm fails to retain its historical number of customers, it may conclude that one of its competitors cheated, and retaliate by cutting prices. After a period of competition, the oligopolists may re-establish the collusive agreement. Thus, collusive industries can go through periods of collusion and competition.[116] This approach, therefore, seeks to identify whether firms have market power by analyzing the pattern of prices and output in an industry over time.[117] Another set of studies analyzes the competitive industry reaction by incumbents to new entrants.[118]

---

115.   George J. Stigler, *A Theory of Oligopoly*, 72 J. POL. ECON. 44 (1964).

116.   There is a substantial academic literature on the economic factors relevant to whether an explicit cartel is likely to be formed, and to its stability and effectiveness. For recent surveys, see, for example, Margaret C. Levenstein & Valerie Y. Suslow, *What Determines Cartel Success?*, 44 J. ECON. LIT. 43 (2006).

117.   *See* Edward J. Green & Robert H. Porter, *Noncooperative Collusion Under Imperfect Price Information*, 52 ECONOMETRICA 87 (1984); Julio J. Rotemberg & Garth Saloner, *A Supergame-Theoretic Model of Price Wars During Booms*, 76 AM. ECON. REV. 390 (1986). The model assumes that the punishment for cheating on the collusion agreement (i.e., a price war) is less affected by the current demand because the price war occurs in the future when demand tends to revert to normal levels. *See also* Robert H. Porter, *A Study of Cartel Stability: The Joint Executive Committee, 1880-1886*, 14 BELL J. ECON. 301 (1983).

118.   *See* Timothy F. Bresnahan & Peter C. Reiss, *Entry and Competition in Concentrated Markets*, 99 J. POL. ECON. 977 (1991). For similar types of analysis, see also Steven T. Berry, *Estimation of a Model of Entry in the Airline Industry*, 60 ECONOMETRICA 889 (1992); Vrinda Kadiyali, *Entry, Its Deterrence, and Its Accommodation: A Study of the U.S. Photographic Film Industry*, 27 RAND J. ECON. 452 (1996); Pablo T. Spiller & Edgardo Favaro, *The Effects of Entry Regulation on Oligopolistic Interaction: The Uruguayan Banking Sector*, 15 RAND J. ECON. 244 (1984).

d. Econometric Estimation of Marginal Costs

An alternative approach to relying on accounting records to measure price-cost margins, which the NEIO literature takes as being unreliable, is to try to estimate costs using econometric techniques. The approach uses data on input prices and quantities to estimate the firms' incremental costs when they change their output. Accounting data may be used to cross-check the results of the econometric models.

A pioneering study by Robert Hall analyzed aggregate changes in labor expenditure and changes in total output to estimate incremental costs.[119] This method can be thought of as a natural experiment in which discrete changes in output lead to changes in inputs. Holding everything else constant, the resulting average incremental cost is taken as an estimate of marginal costs. For many industries, Hall finds that when output rises, firms sell the output for considerably more than they pay for the incremental inputs, suggesting a large gap between price and marginal cost. As with other reduced-form approaches, a problem with this method is that it does not provide a direct measure of market power. A benefit, however, is that it requires less data and fewer assumptions than structural models.

Other analysts have used structural models of demand and supply with a third equation that estimates marginal costs directly from the inputs used in the production process.[120] These models can add precision to the marginal cost estimation and test different hypotheses with respect to firms' competitive interaction. In general, they have been applied to aggregate industry data on factor inputs and total output (typically labor, capital, materials, and energy inputs are used). An alternative approach to measuring marginal costs is to derive them from demand parameters and an assumption regarding the nature of the competitive conduct.[121]

119. Robert E. Hall, *The Relationship Between Price and Marginal Cost in U.S. Industry*, 96 J. POL. ECON. 921 (1988).
120. Early studies in this area include Elie Appelbaum, *The Estimation of the Degree of Oligopoly Power*, 19 J. ECONOMETRICS 287 (1982); Elie Appelbaum, *Testing Price Taking Behavior*, 9 J. ECONOMETRICS 283 (1979); Frank M. Gollop & Mark J. Roberts, *Firm Interdependence in Oligopolistic Markets*, 10 J. ECONOMETRICS 313 (1979).
121. *See, e.g.*, Aviv Nevo, *Measuring Market Power in the Ready-to-Eat Cereal Industry*, 69 ECONOMETRICA 307, 308 (2001).

e. Econometric Estimation of Oligopolies' "Strategic Interaction" Parameters

As noted above, many NEIO models include parameters that measure directly the competitiveness of oligopoly conduct. These conduct parameters provide a measure of the average "collusiveness" of conduct in the industry by measuring each firm's expectation of its rivals' reaction to a change in price or output—i.e., the oligopoly *strategic interaction.*[122]

An early study from Spiller and Favaro derives a supply equation for the Uruguayan banking industry that includes a term with conduct parameters.[123] The results show that large firms expect each other to behave as in a cartel; meanwhile, small firms expected little or no reaction from both the large and the small firms. Furthermore, the study shows a change in the conduct parameters after entry restrictions to the industry were relaxed. Large firms did not react to each other so forcefully as before deregulation.[124]

f. Residual Demand Estimation

Residual demand analysis offers a tool for analyzing the pricing behavior of a dominant firm (although, it can be extended to other models of competitive interaction). Dominant firms set prices taking into account the supply response of all other sellers in the marketplace. The demand for the dominant firm's product is often called the firm's "residual" demand because in the extreme case where the firm's rivals simply sell as much as they can at a given price, the dominant firm's demand is the residual or remaining demand in the marketplace. The dominant firm prices its product based on its residual demand and its marginal cost. In a perfectly-competitive market, a firm's residual demand curve is flat, while the residual demand of a monopolist is the

---

122. These studies use different econometric strategies to estimate market conduct parameters, including those discussed in the previous sections.
123. *See* Spiller & Favaro, *supra* note 118.
124. Other studies that estimate market conduct parameters include James A. Brander & Anming Zhang, *Market Conduct in the Airline Industry: An Empirical Investigation*, 21 RAND J. ECON. 567 (1990); Peter C. Reiss & Pablo T. Spiller, *Competition and Entry in Small Airline Markets*, 32 J.L. & ECON S.179 (1989); K. Sudhir, *Competitive Pricing Behavior in the Auto Market: A Structural Analysis*, 20 MKTG. SCI. 42 (2001).

same as the industry demand curve. For oligopolies, the less elastic the residual demand curve, the greater the firm's market power.

Although residual demand estimation takes into account both demand and cost factors, the basic empirical strategy is similar to the comparative statistics on costs described above, but it is applied to an alleged dominant firm, rather than to the industry. The empirical analysis attempts to explain the prices received by the dominant firm in terms of factors that affect only its costs, as well as factors that affect its costs *and* the costs of its competitors. In particular, if cost changes that only affect the dominant firm are an important determinant of its price, then the firm possesses market power. This conclusion follows because the firm would not change its price in response to changes in its costs if it were fully constrained by the actions of rival firms. Similarly, if variations in a firm's price can be explained *solely* by factors that affect the costs of other firms in the market, then the firm probably lacks unilateral market power.

This theoretical construct is helpful because it provides a basis for determining whether a particular firm faces a relatively inelastic demand curve, which would give it the ability to raise price profitably. It also examines the degree to which changes in costs are passed through to customers. This method requires estimating the residual demand elasticity, which can be used as a summary statistic of market power.[125]

---

125.   *See* Jonathan B. Baker & Timothy F. Bresnahan, *Estimating the Residual Demand Curve Facing a Single Firm*, 6 INT'L J. INDUS. ORG. 283 (1988) (studying whether U.S. brewing firms can profitably pass through cost increases to customer when those cost increases do not affect its rivals); *see also* Simran K. Kahai et al., *Is the "Dominant Firm" Dominant? An Empirical Analysis of AT&T's Market Power*, 39 J.L. & ECON. 499 (1996) (estimating AT&T's residual demand elasticity in the interstate long-distance telephony market as a function of the industry demand elasticity adjusted by the supply elasticity of the fringe firms). Residual demand analysis has been applied to estimate market power in a variety of industries. *See, e.g.*, Phillip A. Beutel & Mark E. McBride, *Market Power and the Northwest-Republic Airline Merger: A Residual Demand Approach*, 58 S. ECON. J. 709 (1992); Lawrence E. Haller & Ronald W. Cotterill, *Evaluating Traditional Share—Price and Residual Demand Measures of Market Power in the Catsup Industry*, 11 REV. INDUS. ORG. 293 (1996).

3. Demand Estimation for Differentiated Products

With the exception of residual demand studies, most of the methods discussed so far have been developed to assess market power for firms that sell a homogeneous product. When firms sell differentiated products, the approach is conceptually similar, but the econometric model needs to identify more parameters, and typically requires more data and stronger assumptions regarding the functional form of demand. The advantage is that models that account for product differentiation can better analyze the role it plays in allowing firms to exercise market power.

To attempt to predict market power with differentiated products, economists have concentrated on estimating full systems of demand equations. With additional assumptions on marginal costs, the estimated demand systems allow for inferences on market power. However, without reliable measures of marginal cost, these models have the same limitations and have to rely on the same econometric methods described in the previous Part in which "natural" experiments are used to identify market power in the data. In the last two decades, with advances in computing power and access to large datasets (for example, from retailers' scanner data), economists have developed powerful models that can estimate demand parameters for multiple products and examine the sources of market power. These models also allow for simulations to examine the likely effect on prices and quantities of changes in the industry, most notably, proposed mergers.

D. Conclusion

While market shares and concentration statistics are not perfect proxies for market power, they are used in the courts and before the agencies for an initial assessment of market power and the likely performance of a market. However, market shares and concentration statistics must be calculated appropriately and interpreted with care. Market share does not equal market power, and a single number is never a substitute for careful analysis and interpretation of the competitive interaction among market participants.

The empirical analysis of market power remains a core issue, and the relevance of the analysis to antitrust law and litigation continues to evolve. A vast amount of research has been conducted over the last 20 years in an attempt to identify and to quantify market power. In this regard, economic analysis hopefully will continue to inform the antitrust laws.

CHAPTER VI

MARKET POWER ANALYSIS: EXTENSIONS AND COMPLEXITIES

Many industries present special challenges for market definition and market power analysis. This Chapter discusses four types of markets that present special difficulties: differentiated product markets, which involve products that are substitutes for one another but have distinct characteristics; cluster markets, which include firms that compete based on their ability to provide a range of products rather than a single product; innovation markets, where firms compete to develop new products; and markets with networks, in which the value of a product depends in part on the number and nature of the other consumers.

A. Differentiated Product Markets

Antitrust issues often involve differentiated products, products that can be distinguished from one another by price, physical differences or brand name. [1] Differentiated products may be contrasted with homogeneous products, products that have similar physical and subjective attributes and thus are virtually perfect substitutes. Among the differentiated products that have raised antitrust issues are superpremium ice cream, ready to eat cereal, white bread, intense mints, ski resorts, and cruise line services.[2]

The factors that distinguish differentiated products may not prevent them from participating in the same market for antitrust purposes.[3] It may be difficult, however, to determine whether purchasers' willingness

---

1. For a discussion of how products may be differentiated, see Richard E. Caves & Peter J. Williamson, *What Is Product Differentiation, Really?*, 34 J. INDUS. ECON. 113 (1985).

2. The textual examples are taken from Caves & Williamson, *supra* note 1, and also from U.S. DEP'T OF JUSTICE & FED. TRADE COMM'N, COMMENTARY ON THE HORIZONTAL MERGER GUIDELINES 27-31 (2006), *available at* http://www.justice.gov/atr/public/guidelines/215247.htm [hereinafter MERGER GUIDELINES COMMENTARY].

3. *See* United States v. E.I. du Pont de Nemours & Co., 351 U.S. 377, 394 (1956) ('The Sherman Act does not "require that products be fungible to be considered in the relevant market.").

and ability to substitute between two differentiated products is significant enough to warrant including them in the same market, and the extent to which competition from one differentiated product will affect the conduct of a seller of another differentiated product. Thus, addressing issues of market definition and market power in the case of differentiated products often raises a number of difficult issues.

1. *Market Definition*

Defining markets in the case of differentiated products generally is a matter of drawing a line between products in a chain of potential substitutes. For example, ice cream includes superpremium ice creams like Ben & Jerry's and Starbucks, premium ice creams like Edy's and Dreyer's, and lower-priced store brand ice creams.[4] Moreover, ice cream may also compete with frozen yogurt and other desserts. Economists have often suggested that this line drawing is essentially an arbitrary procedure, particularly when the differences between the various products may not appear significant. [5] Some argue that in such circumstances, defining markets and measuring shares will tell an analyst little about potential market power,[6] and instead suggest using alternative methods, such as estimation of diversion ratios and merger simulation to understand market power.[7] These alternatives to market definition, which are given increased emphasis in the *Merger Guidelines*[8] issued by the FTC and DOJ, are briefly discussed below.

---

4.   *See* Analysis of Proposed Consent Order to Aid Public Comment, *In re* Nestle Holdings, Inc., *available at* http://www.ftc.gov/os/2003/06/-dreyeranalysis.htm; *see also* MERGER GUIDELINES COMMENTARY, *supra* note 2, at 6.

5.   *See, e.g.*, Jonathan B. Baker, *Market Definition: An Analytical Overview*, 74 ANTITRUST L.J. 129, 131 (2007); James A. Keyte, *Market Definition and Differentiated Products: The Need for a Workable Standard*, 63 ANTITRUST L.J. 697 (1995); Gregory J. Werden & George A. Rozanski, *The Market Delineation Dilemma*, ANTITRUST, Summer 1994, at 40.

6.   *See* Franco Mariuzzo et al., *Firm Size and Market Power in Carbonated Soft Drinks*, 23 REV. INDUS. ORG. 283, 283 (2003).

7.   *See infra* pt. A.2.

8.   "The Agencies' analysis need not start with market definition. Some of the analytical tools used by the Agencies to assess competitive effects do not rely on market definition . . . ." U.S. DEP'T OF JUSTICE & FED. TRADE COMM'N, HORIZONTAL MERGER GUIDELINES § 4 (2010), *available at*

Nonetheless, market definition continues to be an important element in antitrust cases involving differentiated products. These markets generally are defined by asking whether, if one firm was the only seller of a product or group of products, could that firm profitably raise prices above competitive levels (also referred to as the "hypothetical monopolist test" or "SSNIP test").[9] Antitrust analysts addressing the issue of market definition for differentiated products have considered several issues relating to potential supermarkets, including: Should submarkets be defined? What is the significance of branded products? Can a retail channel be a separate market? Should used or recycled products be included in the market?

a.   Submarkets

The notion of submarkets has been criticized by some courts and commentators as both "superfluous" and "confusing."[10] The *Merger Guidelines* do not use the term submarkets. The 1992 *Guidelines* included the "smallest market principle," which says that the smallest group of products that satisfies the hypothetical monopolist test will be taken as the relevant market, and thus seems to preclude the use of submarkets.[11] The most recent version of the *Guidelines* states that the hypothetical monopolist test might lead to more than one relevant market and that a merger may be evaluated in any relevant market that satisfies

http://www.justice.gov/atr/public/guidelines/hmg-2010.html   [hereinafter MERGER GUIDELINES].

9.   *Id.* § 4.1.1.
10. *See* Allen-Myland, Inc. v. IBM, 33 F.3d 194, 208 n.16 (3d Cir. 1994) ("The use of the term 'submarket' is somewhat confusing, and tends to obscure the true inquiry."); *In re* Air Passenger Computer Reservation Sys. Antitrust Litig., 694 F. Supp. 1443, 1458 n.9 (C.D. Cal. 1988) ("[T]he prefix 'sub' merely creates confusion and is superfluous."), *aff'd sub nom.* Alaska Airlines v. United Airlines, 948 F.2d 536 (9th Cir. 1991); Pepsico, Inc. v. Coca-Cola Co., No. 98-Civ.-3282, 1998 WL 547088, at *5 (S.D.N.Y. 1998) ("[S]peaking of submarkets is both superfluous and confusing in an antitrust case," and "nothing would be lost by deleting the word 'submarket' from the antitrust lexicon.") (citing IIA PHILLIP AREEDA, ANTITRUST LAW ¶ 533c, at 170, 173 (1995)).
11. U.S. DEP'T OF JUSTICE & FED. TRADE COMM'N, HORIZONTAL MERGER GUIDELINES § 1.1 (1992), *available at* http://www.justice.gov/atr/public/-guidelines/hmg.htm [hereinafter 1992 MERGER GUIDELINES].

that test.[12] Thus, any collection of products that might meaningfully have been called a submarket would be a market under the *Guidelines*.

Nonetheless, courts have turned to the concept of submarkets to explain markets with highly differentiated product segments. In *Brown Shoe Co. v. United States*,[13] the Supreme Court recognized that, within a broad market, "well-defined submarkets may exist which, in themselves, constitute product markets for antitrust purposes."[14] The concept of submarkets has been considered in numerous antitrust cases. Courts have evaluated elasticities and analyzed whether market characteristics insulate firms within the submarket from those that are outside of it.[15] In addition, submarkets have been used to take into consideration pockets

---

12. MERGER GUIDELINES, *supra* note 8, § 4.1.1. The *Guidelines* also state that "when the Agencies rely on market shares and concentration, they usually do so in the smallest relevant market satisfying the hypothetical monopolist test." *Id.*

13. 370 U.S. 294 (1962).

14. *Id.* at 325. In particular, the Court set out a number of "practical indicia" of submarkets. Those indicia are: "industry or public recognition of the submarket as a separate economic entity, the product's peculiar characteristics and uses, unique production facilities, distinct customers, distinct prices, sensitivity to price changes, and specialized vendors." *Id.*

15. *See, e.g.*, FTC v. Whole Foods Mkt., 533 F.3d 869, 878 (D.C. Cir. 2008) ("A broad market may also contain relevant submarkets . . . ."); Bogan v. Hodgkins, 166 F.3d 509, 516 (2d Cir. 1999) ("While a submarket may function as the relevant market for antitrust purposes, more is required than a showing that a product differs from others. Submarkets do exist, notwithstanding the empirical difficulty of demonstrating them, but the plaintiffs have not even made an effort to do so."); Olin Corp. v. FTC, 986 F.2d 1295, 1304 (9th Cir. 1993) (holding that even if a relevant market comprises all pool sanitizers, that would not preclude identifying a relevant submarket comprising only dry sanitizers); Rothery Storage & Van Co. v. Atlas Van Lines, Inc. 792 F.2d 210, 218 n.4 (D.C. Cir. 1986) ("The 'industry or public recognition of the submarket as a separate economic' unit matters because we assume that economic actors usually have accurate perceptions of economic realities."); *see also* Final Judgment, United States v. Rockwell Int'l, No. 80-1401, 1980 WL 2000 (W.D. Pa. 1980) (consent decree resolving alleged anticompetitive effects of acquisition in the lubricated plug valve market and the lubricated tapered plug valve submarket); Xidex Corp., 102 F.T.C. 1 (1983) (consent decree resolving challenge to an acquisition based on an anticompetitive effect in the non-silver duplicate microfilm and a submarket consisting of a certain type of such microfilm).

of competition among sellers of differentiated products.[16] One analysis suggests that submarkets may be useful for two purposes.[17] First, they may provide a way to address unilateral anticompetitive effects when two firms that are each other's closest competitors propose a merger. Second, they may provide a way to address price-discrimination markets.[18]

b.   Branded Products

Often in differentiated consumer goods markets, products that carry certain major brand names consistently sell for a premium above the price of products with other brands, such as a store-owned brand or private label, even though the differences between those products might not be readily apparent if the labeling is removed. The existence of those price differentials raises the question of whether the branded products constitute a separate market. That is, could a firm that controlled the premium-priced brands raise prices profitably, even though the prices of the same products sold under other brands did not increase?

As analyzed by courts, whether certain branded products are in a different relevant market from other identical or similar products depends on the facts of each specific industry. Agencies and courts have found branded products to be in separate relevant markets in a number of cases. For example, the FTC found that a stand-alone market for branded soft drinks exists distinct from unbranded soft drinks because of the great degree of product differentiation between the two kinds of soft drinks.[19] The FTC claimed that a price premium of 80-90 percent was necessary before significant numbers of consumers would switch from one of the major brands to a store brand or a private label soft drink.[20] In another matter, the FTC similarly found that "superpremium" ice cream was in a separate market from other types of ice cream.[21] In pharmaceuticals,

---

16.   *See* FTC v. Staples, Inc., 970 F. Supp. 1066, 1075-80 (D.D.C. 1997); Jonathan B. Baker, *Stepping Out in an Old* Brown Shoe*: In Qualified Praise of Submarkets,* 68 ANTITRUST L.J. 203, 214 (2000).

17.   Baker, *supra* note 5, at 150.

18.   For discussion of price-discrimination markets, see *supra* ch. IV.

19.   *See In re* Coca-Cola Co., 117 F.T.C. 795 (1994).

20.   *Id.*

21.   Analysis of Proposed Consent Order to Aid Public Comment, *In re* Nestle Holdings, Inc., *available at* http://www.ftc.gov/os/2003/06/-dreyeranalysis.htm.

however, courts on several occasions have rejected market definitions based solely on generic drugs, and found that generic and brand name drugs are in a single market.[22]

c.   Retail Channels

The channels by which products reach consumers are often themselves differentiated, and courts and agencies, at times, have identified specific channels of distribution as relevant markets.[23] The channel of distribution has been included in the market definition in cases involving mergers of manufacturers who sold to a specific type of channel and in mergers of retailers or wholesalers that participate in those channels directly. For example, the FTC objected to a merger of manufacturers of drycast concrete hardscapes because it would reduce competition in a market for the sale of that product to "national home centers."[24] Smaller competitors did not provide these centers with the geographic coverage that the merging parties offered, nor did they have the scale necessary to offer the wide variety of services that the merging parties provided those centers. Thus, these smaller competitors could not replace the competition provided by merging parties for the national home center business.[25]

In *FTC v. Whole Foods Market,*[26] the FTC alleged a market consisting of "premium natural and organic supermarkets" separate from "conventional" supermarkets.[27] The district court believed that there was sufficient evidence that a monopolist over such stores could raise prices

---

22.   *See* Geneva Pharms. Tech. Corp. v. Barr Labs., 201 F. Supp. 2d 236, 268-69 (S.D.N.Y. 2002) (rejecting submarket for a generic drug that would have excluded branded versions). For a discussion of market definition in the pharmaceutical context, see Howard Morse, *Product Market Definition in the Pharmaceutical Industry*, 71 ANTITRUST L.J. 633, 667-70 (2003). In one case, however, the court found that markets for generic lorazepam tablets and generic clorazepate tablets were "sufficient to survive a motion to dismiss." FTC v. Mylan Labs., 62 F. Supp. 2d 25, 54 (D.D.C. 1999).

23.   In some cases, retail channels have been called cluster markets, a concept that is discussed, *infra*, in part B of this Chapter.

24.   *See* Administrative Complaint, CRH plc, No. 9335, at 4 (Jan. 14, 2009), *available at* www.ftc.gov/os/adjpro/d9335/index.shtm.

25.   *Id.*

26.   548 F.3d 1028 (D.C. Cir. 2008).

27.   *Id.* at 1032.

to their "core customers," but because such stores competed with other types of supermarkets for their "marginal customers," the market would be at least as large as all supermarkets.[28] The circuit court, however, found that the district court's focus on marginal customers was mistaken and that core customers could "be worthy of antitrust protection."[29]

Courts also found specific retail channels to be relevant markets in a number of earlier cases. In *FTC v. Staples, Inc.*,[30] the district court found that non-superstore sellers of office supplies are not able to constrain superstore prices effectively.[31] This finding was based largely on price evidence (e.g., comparisons of prices in areas where more than one superstore competed to prices in areas where Staples was the only superstore) and documents describing the merging firms' pricing practices.[32] However, the court also considered other "practical indicia," including the format of the stores.[33] Similarly, in *FTC v. Cardinal Health*,[34] the court concluded that the wholesale distribution channel for prescription drugs was a "distinct submarket within the larger market of drug delivery."[35] Relying heavily on the special services provided by the defendant wholesalers, the court concluded that the "[b]usiness and economic realities of this industry demonstrate that the other forms of distribution lack the practical availability to be included within the relevant product market."[36] In short, although customers theoretically could purchase directly from manufacturers, the economic realities of the marketplace made that impractical.[37] In *California v. American Stores*

---

28.   FTC v. Whole Foods Mkt., 502 F. Supp. 2d 1, 35-36 (D.D.C. 2007).
29.   *Whole Foods*, 548 F.3d 1028. This opinion is a holding, not a decision of the court, as one judge of the three judge panel wrote the opinion, one judge dissented, and one judge filed a concurring opinion. The concurring opinion found "a great deal of credible evidence" in favor of the FTC's market definition. *Id.* at 1043.
30.   970 F. Supp. 1066 (D.D.C. 1997).
31.   *Id.* at 1077.
32.   *Id.*
33.   *Id.* at 1078.
34.   12 F. Supp. 2d 34 (D.D.C. 1998).
35.   *Id.* at 47.
36.   *Id.* at 49. The court also relied on wholesaler documents indicating that the wholesalers did not consider "the other forms of distribution to be viable competitors or substitutes." *Id.*
37.   *Id.* at 48-49.

Co. ,[38] the court found that supermarkets (i.e., full-line grocery stores with more than 10,000 square feet) are a relevant market.[39] In *Bon-Ton Stores v. May Department Stores Co.*,[40] the court found that the relevant product market was traditional department stores, despite the defendant's claim that the market was broader.[41] Some years later, however, in its review of the Federated/May merger, the FTC concluded that the product market could not be limited to "conventional department stores,"[42] due to changes in the retail landscape.

In other cases, however, courts have rejected the concept of a submarket with only one class of stores. For example, in *Thurman Industries v. Pay 'N Pak Stores*,[43] the court rejected the plaintiff's argument that the relevant product market should include only home centers.[44] As with all market definition issues, whether a retail channel defines a market will depend on the facts of the specific case.[45]

---

38. 697 F. Supp. 1125, 1129 (C.D. Cal. 1988), *aff'd in part and rev'd in part on other grounds*, 872 F.2d 837 (9th Cir. 1989), *rev'd on other grounds*, 495 U.S. 271 (1990).

39. *Id.* at 1129. On appeal, the Ninth Circuit indicated that, while it did not evaluate the relevant market, it might have reached a different conclusion if it had. 872 F.2d at 841.

40. 881 F. Supp. 860 (W.D.N.Y. 1994).

41. *Id.* at 870 (employing *Brown Shoe*'s consideration of "practical indicia").

42. Statement of the Commission Concerning Federated Department Stores, Inc./The May Department Stores Company, No. 051-0111 (Aug. 30, 2005), *available at* www.ftc.gov/os/caselist/0510001/050830stmt-0510001.pdf.

43. 875 F.2d 1369 (9th Cir. 1989).

44. *Id.* at 1380; *see also* PepsiCo, Inc. v. Coca-Cola Co., 315 F.3d 101, 108-09 (2d Cir. 2002) (rejecting argument that the form of distribution—independent food distributors—constituted a stand-alone relevant market); JBL Enters. v. Jhirmack Enters., 509 F. Supp. 357, 370-71 (N.D. Cal. 1981) (rejecting restriction of a market for shampoo and conditioner to sales made through salon and other professional outlets), *aff'd*, 698 F.2d 1011 (9th Cir. 1983).

45. *See* FTC v. Staples, Inc., 970 F. Supp. 1066, 1093 (D.D.C. 1997) ("For these reasons, the Court must emphasize that the ruling in this case is based strictly on the facts of this particular case, and should not be construed as this Court's recognition of general superstore relevant markets.").

d.   Used and Recycled Products

Certain products can be reused or recycled, which raises the question of whether used or recycled products should be included in the market with new products. Some economists have argued that used products place a significant competitive restraint on manufacturers of durable goods.[46] Others have shown, however, that the extent to which used goods restrain a durable goods manufacturer depends on the market context, in particular, on the ability of the supplier to pre-commit to particular production schedules,[47] and on the characteristics of the product that affect the viability of recycling.[48]

Courts have both included and excluded used and recycled products from the market. In *United States v. Aluminum Co. of America*,[49] the Second Circuit excluded recycled aluminum from the relevant market, giving Alcoa a 90 percent market share.[50] In *United States v. United Shoe Machinery*,[51] the court forced United Shoe Machinery to offer its equipment for sale (rather than for lease only) because the court believed that the resale of used equipment would help discipline the monopolist.[52] More recent cases have tended to follow *Alcoa* by excluding used products from the market. For example, in analyzing a merger of two gold producers, one district court tentatively rejected the inclusion of scrap because "scrap . . . respond[ed] sluggishly, if at all" to increased prices.[53] Similarly, in *United States v. Ivaco, Inc.*,[54] the court rejected the

---

46.   *See, e.g.*, Dennis W. Carlton & Robert H. Gertner, *Market Power and Mergers in Durable-Good Industries*, 32 J.L. & ECON. S203 (1989).

47.   *See, e.g.*, Luke Froeb, *Evaluating Mergers in Durable Goods Industries*, 34 ANTITRUST BULL. 99, 101 (1989).

48.   For a brief summary of the economics literature on this subject, see ANDREW I. GAVIL ET AL., ANTITRUST LAW IN PERSPECTIVE: CASES, CONCEPTS AND PROBLEMS IN COMPETITION POLICY 612-14 (2d ed. 2008).

49.   148 F.2d 416 (2d Cir. 1945).

50.   *Id.* at 424. A later economic study found that Alcoa did have substantial market power, largely because recycled aluminum was significantly different from primary aluminum. Valerie Y. Suslow, *Estimating Monopoly Behavior with Competitive Recycling: An Application to* Alcoa, 17 RAND J. ECON. 389 (1986).

51.   110 F. Supp. 295 (D. Mass. 1953).

52.   *Id.* at 350.

53.   Consol. Gold Fields, PLC v. Anglo Am. Corp. of S. Africa, Ltd., 698 F. Supp. 487, 501 (S.D.N.Y. 1988), *aff'd in part, rev'd in part*, 871 F.2d 252 (2d Cir. 1989).

argument that competition from used equipment could discipline a price increase given difficulties in obtaining replacement parts.[55] Nonetheless, if the availability of scrap, used, or recycled products restricts the ability of a seller of new products to raise prices above competitive levels, then those products should be considered part of the relevant market, and, as in *Alcoa*, the used materials should be included in the dominant firm's share of the market.[56]

2. Market Power

Measuring market power in differentiated product markets can be problematic. Firms in homogeneous product markets cannot increase prices over the level charged by their rivals for any significant length of time because they will lose all their sales. Their customers have no reason to pay them more than the price charged by other firms.[57] Firms in differentiated product markets, however, will lose only some sales if they increase prices; they will retain sales to the customers that most value the specific attributes of their product. Put another way, in a differentiated product market, each firm faces a downward sloping demand curve. For this reason, even in markets with large numbers of sellers and easy entry, a firm's price will not be driven to the level of its marginal costs if products are differentiated.

As a result, measuring market power when products are differentiated may be difficult. Market power is commonly defined as the ability profitably to "raise price, reduce output, diminish innovation, or otherwise harm customers" for a significant period of time.[58] But if the competitive level of prices is defined as a firm's marginal costs, then even a firm with many competitors and no protection from entry might be found to have market power. This problem may not be a significant issue in merger cases, where the competitive level of prices can be taken to be the price absent the merger, but it is more of an issue in monopolization cases in which the current level of prices might reflect

---

54.   704 F. Supp. 1409 (W.D. Mich. 1989).
55.   *Id.* at 1428.
56.   *Alcoa*, 148 F.2d at 424-25.
57.   An exception may exist if rivals are capacity constrained. Moreover, even if the product itself is homogenous, producers in a market may be able to differentiate themselves, for example, by offering better services, and thus charge premium prices.
58.   MERGER GUIDELINES, *supra* note 8, § 1.0.

significant market power and thus is not competitive. One alternative is to define the competitive level of prices as the level that allows a firm to earn a competitive rate of return on its investment, and no more. It may be very difficult, however, to determine if a firm is making more than a competitive rate of return.[59]

Moreover, firms in a differentiated product market have varying competitive importance to one another. For example, when two firms that compete in a differentiated product market merge, the ability of the merged firm unilaterally to impose a postmerger price increase will depend on whether the firms' products are close substitutes for each other. Top-of-the-line snow skis may belong in the same market with mid-range skis, but a merger between two top-of-the-line ski manufacturers might be viewed differently than the merger of a top-of-the-line manufacturer with a mid-range ski producer—even if each merger results in the same postmerger market share. Generally speaking, "[u]nilateral price effects are greater, the more the buyers of products sold by one merging firm consider products sold by the other merging firm to be their next choice."[60] For this reason, a simple calculation of market shares and concentration ratios may be a poor indicator of the likelihood that a merger will lead to unilateral anticompetitive effects.[61]

In the last few years, analysts have developed alternative methods for determining the likelihood of unilateral effects that take into account the differences in the substitutability of various firms' products. Agencies often use diversion ratios to measure the competitive relationships between merging parties.[62] When a firm selling a differentiated product raises its price, it loses sales as customers switch some of their purchases to competing products. The diversion ratio between two firms is the share of the quantity of sales lost when one firm raises its price that is captured by the other firm. For example, suppose when Firm A raises its price by 5 percent, its sales fall by 100 units, and Firm B's sales increase by 20 units. In this example, the diversion ratio of Firm A to Firm B is 20

---

59. For a detailed discussion of these issues, see Lawrence J. White, *Market Power and Market Definition in Monopolization Cases, in* ABA ANTITRUST SECTION, ISSUES IN COMPETITION LAW AND POLICY ch. 38 (2008) [hereinafter ISSUES IN COMPETITION LAW AND POLICY].

60. MERGER GUIDELINES, *supra* note 8, § 6.1.

61. *See* Franco Mariuzzo et al., *EU Merger Control in Differentiated Product Industries*, CESifo Working Paper No. 1312, (2004), *available at* http://www.cesifo-group.de/portal/pls/portal/docs/1/1189010.pdf.

62. MERGER GUIDELINES COMMENTARY, *supra* note 2, at 27.

percent. The agencies believe that unilateral anticompetitive effects generally are more likely the higher the diversion ratios between merging parties.[63]

Another method for determining the likelihood of unilateral anticompetitive effects is merger simulation.[64] Merger simulation is the use of mathematical models to make quantitative predictions of competitive effects. Merger simulations have the advantage of using a formal model, which forces analysts to clearly identify the underlying facts and assumptions that are crucial to supporting a conclusion concerning merger effects. Merger simulations, however, also have a number of disadvantages. They typically require a large amount of data, which has prevented their use in all but a small number of mergers. Moreover, there have been very few tests of the accuracy of these simulations' predictions and the tests that have been conducted have not produced encouraging results.[65] The FTC and DOJ do not treat merger simulation results as conclusive; rather "they place more weight on whether their merger simulations consistently predict substantial price increases than on the precise prediction of any single simulation."[66]

Merger analysis in differentiated product industries often focuses on unilateral anticompetitive effects because the FTC and DOJ believe that product differentiation may make collusion less likely, although certainly

63.   *Id.* at 27-28; *see also* MERGER GUIDELINES, *supra* note 8, § 6.1.
64.   For a discussion of merger simulation that includes a discussion of the use of simulation to address other competitive questions, see Gregory K. Leonard & J. Douglas Zona, *Simulation in Competitive Analysis, in* ISSUES IN COMPETITION LAW & POLICY, *supra* note 57, ch. 59; *see also* Oliver Budzinski & Isabel Ruhmer, *Merger Simulation in Competition Policy: A Survey,* 6(2) J. COMPETITION L. & ECON. 277 (2010); ABA ANTITRUST SECTION, ECONOMETRICS: LEGAL, PRACTICAL, AND TECHNICAL ISSUES ch. 11 (2005).
65.   *See* Budzinski & Ruhmer, *supra* note 63; Gregory J. Werden et al., *A Daubert Discipline for Merger Simulation* (Fed. Trade Comm'n, Working Paper, 2004), *available at* www.ftc.gov/be/daubertdiscipline.pdf. For attempts to test the accuracy of predictions from simulations, see Craig Peters, *Evaluating the Performance of Merger Simulation: Evidence from the U.S. Airline Industry,* 49 J.L. & ECON. 627 (2006) (suggesting that the simulation models tested do not predict postmerger price increases very well).
66.   *See* MERGER GUIDELINES, *supra* note 8, § 6.1.

not impossible.[67] When products are perfectly homogeneous, oligopolists need only coordinate on price or output. In contrast, when products are differentiated, firms compete in several dimensions, which complicates coordination. For example, products may be differentiated with respect to a variety of dimensions, including product quality, the distance between the consumer and the supplier, post-purchase service or maintenance, and the customization to meet specialized consumer needs. When products or the provided related services vary, firms comparing their prices with those of competitors must assess how consumers value quality differences, a task that is particularly difficult in a dynamic environment in which preferences differ across customers. Collusion, and particularly tacit collusion, can be complicated because it may be difficult for the firms to agree on a price structure that can also be used to identify cheating.

Nonetheless, product differentiation does not make collusion impossible. Firms may be able to adopt simple rules to overcome the difficulties involved in colluding. For example, they can agree to raise the prices of all their products by the same percentage. This agreement likely would benefit some firms more than others because of product differentiation, but it would be easy to implement and enforce if all prices are observable. Moreover, in one way, product differentiation may actually facilitate collusion. Product differentiation may reduce the sales that colluding firms within a market lose to those rivals that do not participate in the collusion. Firms may be able to ignore rivals that do not have close substitutes, reducing the number of industry members a conspiracy would have to include to be profitable. In line with this view, the antitrust agencies believe that in some cases, a merger in a differentiated product industry may make coordinated interaction more likely.[68]

---

67. "Although coordination may be less likely the greater the extent of product heterogeneity, mergers in markets with differentiated products nonetheless can facilitate coordination." MERGER GUIDELINES COMMENTARY, *supra* note 2, at 21. For a discussion of the relationship between product differentiation and coordination, *see* F.M. SCHERER & DAVID ROSS, INDUSTRIAL MARKET STRUCTURE AND ECONOMIC PERFORMANCE 279-84 (3d ed. 1990).

68. *See* MERGER GUIDELINES COMMENTARY, *supra* note 2, at 21.

B. Cluster Markets

Another approach to market definition defines a product market not with reference to a single product, but in terms of a "cluster" of products insulated from competition due to some element of cost advantage or consumer preference. The Supreme Court applied this concept in *United States v. Philadelphia National Bank*[69] in which it found that a variety of commercial banking products and services composed a distinct line of commerce.[70] In a later banking case, the Supreme Court elaborated on the concept, explaining that "[c]ommercial banks are the only financial institutions in which a wide variety of financial products and services—some unique to commercial banking and others not—are gathered together in one place."[71] The clustering of financial products and services in a single bank facilitates consumer access.[72] Consumers generally do not want to use multiple banks for their banking services because of the inconvenience involved. More generally, the Ninth Circuit has explained that "[a] cluster approach is appropriate where the product package is significantly different from, and appeals to buyers on a different basis from, the individual products considered separately."[73]

Although the Supreme Court's decision in *Philadelphia National Bank* does not articulate this reasoning, the economic rationale for a "cluster" of products or services is based on the relationship between the products or services included. In particular, a cluster market can be used if a set of products in the cluster are "transactional complements." Products are transactional complements if purchasing them from a single

---

69.　374 U.S. 321 (1963).

70.　*Id.* at 356-57.

71.　United States v. Phillipsburg Nat'l Bank & Trust Co., 399 U.S. 350, 360 (1970). These include loans and other types of credit, deposit accounts, checking services, and trust administration. This cluster of products and services was viewed as distinct from the services offered by savings and loans, finance companies, credit unions, and other financial institutions.

72.　*Id.*

73.　*See, e.g.*, United States v. Grinnell Corp., 384 U.S. 563, 572 (1966) (finding relevant market consisting of insurance company-accredited central station fire and burglary protective services); United States v. Connecticut Nat'l Bank, 418 U.S. 656, 664-66 (1974) (cluster of commercial banking services); JBL Enters. v. Jhirmack Enters., 698 F.2d 1011, 1016-17 (9th Cir. 1983) (finding lines of shampoos and conditioners sold to wholesalers were the relevant market because wholesalers purchase complete lines).

firm reduces customer transaction (or shopping) costs enough so that firms that only offer some of the products cannot constrain the prices charged for the cluster.[74] All of a market's competitors, however, need not offer the same range of products; some differentiation is possible among participating firms.[75]

Lower courts have extended the cluster market concept to several other industry settings, including traditional grocery supermarkets, premium, natural and organic supermarkets, department stores, pet products, fire protection services, and acute inpatient care hospital services.[76] On the other hand, cluster markets are not universally accepted. Courts have rejected the use of cluster markets relating to home remodeling supplies.[77] In addition, commentators and economists criticize the cluster approach as inconsistent with the demand-side focus of market definition.[78] Economists emphasize that the question of market

---

74. *See* Michael E. Vita et al., *Economic Analysis in Health Care Antitrust*, 7 J. CONTEMP. HEALTH L. & POL'Y 73, 80-85 (1991); Ian Ayres, Note, *Rationalizing Antitrust Cluster Markets*, 95 YALE L. J. 109, 119-25 (1985).

75. *See* United States v. Grinnell Corp., 384 U.S. 563, 572 (1966); Image Tech Servs. v. Eastman Kodak Co., 125 F.3d 1195 (9th Cir. 1997).

76. *See generally* ABA ANTITRUST SECTION, MERGERS AND ACQUISITIONS: UNDERSTANDING THE ANTITRUST ISSUES 54-57 (2000) (surveying cases in which cluster markets have been defined, and noting cases in which courts have declined to do so); *see also Grinnell Corp.*, 384 U.S. at 571-72 (finding relevant market to be a cluster of fire protection and burglar protective services); FTC v. Whole Foods Mkt., 548 F.3d 1028, 1032 (D.C. Cir. 2008) (defining submarket for "premium, natural and organic supermarkets"); Gen. Indus. Corp. v. Hartz Mountain Corp., 810 F.2d 795, 805 (8th Cir. 1987) (rejecting argument that each pet product constitutes a separate market); California v. Sutter Health Sys., 130 F. Supp. 2d 1109, 1119 (N.D. Cal. 2001) (affirming relevant market comprising all acute inpatient care services); FTC v. Alliant Techsystems Inc., 808 F. Supp. 9, 26, 29 (D.D.C. 1992) (applying "cluster" concept to ammunition).

77. *See* Thurman Indus. v. Pay 'N Pak Stores, 875 F.2d 1369, 1377 (9th Cir. 1989) .

78. Jonathan B. Baker, *The Antitrust Analysis of Hospital Mergers and the Transformation of the Hospital Industry*, 51 L. & CONTEMP. PROBS. 93, 125-26 (1988); *see also* Thomas L. Greaney, *Chicago's Procrustean Bed: Applying Antitrust Law in Health Care*, 71 ANTITRUST L.J. 857, 882-84 (2004).

definition turns on the attributes of buyer substitution.[79] Suppose, for example, that sellers supply a product both as part of a cluster (or bundle) as well as on a stand-alone basis, and the bundled product sells for less than the sum of the individual components. If enough buyers purchase only as a bundle, and would not substitute individual components if the bundle price rose, then it would be proper to define a cluster market. But if enough buyers would consider components as a reasonable substitute for the bundled product, then a cluster market approach could mislead by ignoring the competitive constraint imposed by component suppliers. Nonetheless, some critics acknowledge that cluster markets can be used for convenience when market participants, concentration, and entry conditions are similar across the product markets so that the competitive effects analysis for each market would likely be consistent.[80]

The pros and cons of the use of cluster markets can be illustrated by the decision of the Court of Appeals for the D.C. Circuit in *FTC v. Whole Foods Market.*[81] The Court of Appeals found support for the FTC's alleged "premium, natural, and organic supermarket" product market definition. This definition is essentially a cluster market concept where the "core" consumers are alleged to have a strong preference for high-end/organic meats and produce uniquely sold alongside other grocery items in the setting of a premium, natural, and organic supermarket.[82] These core customers who demand a package of products are alleged not to be protected from price increases by individual providers of various elements of the premium, natural, and organic supermarket package. For example, the FTC alleged that core customers of premium, natural, and organic supermarkets would not switch to natural and organic sections of conventional supermarkets in the event of a SSNIP. While the cluster market concept puts the focus squarely on the customers who strongly prefer to shop at premium, natural, and organic supermarkets, and around whom a market could potentially be defined, it also tends to obscure the key question in antitrust market definition in this context: Can marginal consumers who have a lesser preference for the package defeat a price

---

79. *See, e.g.*, Baker, *supra* note 5, at 132-38.
80. *See, e.g.*, Martin Frederic Evans & Kevin P. Lewis, *Bank Mergers and Acquisitions: Antitrust Considerations and Developments*, *in* BANK ACQUISITIONS AND TAKEOVERS 1988, CORPORATE LAW & PRACTICE COURSE HANDBOOK SERIES NO. 608, at 27, 59-60 (Robert C. Sheehan & H. Rodgin Cohen, Co-Chairmen 1988).
81. 548 F.3d 1028 (D.C. Cir. 2008).
82. *Id.* at 1038-40.

increase aimed at core customers? The defendants and their economic expert argued that, absent the ability to price discriminate against core customers, marginal customers could defeat such a price increase, so the market defined as premium, natural, and organic supermarkets would not pass the SSNIP test.[83] On appeal, the court held that in "some situations" core customers constitute a distinct market."[84] This case highlights the need for a cautious approach when defining cluster markets; care must be taken to define cluster markets in a manner consistent with proper application of the SSNIP test.

C. Innovation Markets

In some industries, the effect of firms' conduct goes beyond the prices and output for existing goods and services and has implications for the development of improved or new products. In these industries, antitrust analysis needs to account for welfare repercussions beyond conventional product and geographic markets. According to the *Antitrust Guidelines for the Licensing of Intellectual Property*, "[a]n innovation market consists of the research and development directed to particular new or improved goods or processes, and the close substitutes for that research and development." [85] In many industries, innovation is a significant determinant of welfare, and conduct that is detrimental to innovation is likely to reduce welfare. For example, pharmaceutical innovation has a direct effect on patient welfare. As new drugs are developed and marketed, consumers obtain a therapeutic benefit from this kind of innovation. Given the key role of innovation in these industries, antitrust policy aimed at maximizing welfare needs to assess the effect market structure and conduct have on innovation in addition to its effect on the prices and quantities of existing products.

Analyzing innovation markets is particularly difficult because no clear relationship exists between market structure and the optimal level of innovation.[86] In this context, the challenge is to determine how

---

83. *Id.* at 1038.

84. *Id.* at 1040.

85. U.S. DEP'T OF JUSTICE & FED. TRADE COMM'N, ANTITRUST GUIDELINES FOR THE LICENSING OF INTELLECTUAL PROPERTY § 3.2.3 (1995), *available at* http://www.usdoj.gov/atr/public/guidelines/0558.htm [hereinafter INTELLECTUAL PROPERTY GUIDELINES].

86. There are many models and predictions regarding market structure and innovation that vary with the specific characteristics of the market and the

antitrust policy can best promote innovation and thereby maximize welfare given that the market structure and conduct that yield the optimal rate of innovation are not known.[87] A tension arises between favoring lack of intervention (i.e., tolerating market power at the expense of static efficiency to preserve strong rewards to innovation and foster dynamic efficiency), and promoting antitrust oversight to improve static efficiency (by fostering entry but potentially reducing innovation).[88]

While the premises of antitrust analysis in innovative industries are different, antitrust policy still needs to distinguish anticompetitive conduct from conduct that increases welfare.[89] Whether the issue is the effect on prices or the effect on innovation, antitrust analysis still involves the definition of a relevant market and the assessment of market power and its effects.

In conventional markets, conduct aimed at raising prices may be curtailed by substitution opportunities. Accordingly, market definition is concerned with the set of substitutes that represent an alternative to consumers in the event of an attempt to raise prices (or restrict output). Analogously, in innovation markets, welfare is threatened by conduct that limits or delays R&D and subsequent innovation. In this context, market definition is concerned with alternative R&D efforts that may also yield the next generation of products (improved products or new products) and thereby constrain a hypothetical monopolist's incentives to

---

technology. Richard J. Gilbert, *Competition and Innovation*, 1 J. INDUS. ORG. ED. 1 (2006), *available at* http://www.bepress.com/ jioe/vol1/iss1/8. Generally, economic theory suggests that competition fosters innovation if "[c]ompetition in the old product is intense," "[t]he innovation is a major improvement," "[t]he innovation does not increase the ability of a monopolist to price discriminate among consumers," and "[m]arket conditions make preemption unlikely." *See* Richard J. Gilbert, *Competition and Innovation, in* ISSUES IN COMPETITION LAW AND POLICY, *supra* note 58, ch. 24.

87.   For a study of the effects of antitrust on innovative industries, *see* Ilya Segal & Michael D. Whinston, *Antitrust in Innovative Industries*, 97 AM. ECON. REV. 1703 (2007).

88.   This question was at the heart of *U.S. v. Microsoft.* For a discussion of the economics of this case, *see* Richard J. Gilbert & Michael L. Katz, *An Economist's Guide to* U.S. v. Microsoft, 15 J. ECON. PERSP. 25 (2001).

89.   Franklin Fisher argues that the same questions that are asked in traditional antitrust analysis should be asked to examine behavior in innovative industries. *See* Franklin M. Fisher, *Antitrust and Innovative Industries*, 68 ANTITRUST L.J. 559 (2001).

limit its own innovation effort. R&D alternatives stem from "specialized assets or characteristics of specific firms"[90] and are not necessarily offered by competitors in the existing product market; firms outside the market may dedicate assets to the next generation of products while innovation efforts by producers of substitute products may result in products that are not substitutable.[91] In practice, the universe of firms that can offer alternative R&D is easier to identify if very specific assets are needed to seek a particular type of innovation and the firms owning these assets can be identified.

Once a relevant market has been defined, antitrust analysis involves consideration of the level of competition and the effects of the challenged conduct. Consideration of market shares may not adequately measure competition if firms compete for the market and not within the market.[92] Analogously, historical information on profitability may not indicate a firm's expected returns from its innovation efforts. A better approach to assess whether a firm's efforts to reduce innovation would remain unchallenged (i.e., whether it has market power) is to assess its control over necessary R&D resources. As with market definition, this exercise is more straightforward if there is a well-defined universe of assets that can be dedicated to developing the next generation of products and their ownership is known.

As in other markets, the ability to limit R&D efforts does not necessarily translate into less innovation and less welfare. For example, merging firms that achieve market power may face downstream competition that preserves or creates strong incentives to innovate.[93] Further, conduct that restricts alternative R&D efforts may still be welfare maximizing, if the cost of the efforts would not exceed their benefits. As with antitrust analysis in general, welfare evaluation involves understanding the necessity of any restrictions and their overall effects on competition and welfare.

---

90. INTELLECTUAL PROPERTY GUIDELINES, *supra* note 85, § 3.2.3.
91. *See* David Encaoua & Abraham Hollander, *Competition Policy and Innovation*, 18 OXFORD REV. ECON. POL'Y 63 (2002).
92. For additional discussion of assessing market shares in innovation markets, see *supra* ch. V.
93. For a discussion of how innovation can be accounted for in merger analysis, *see* Richard J. Gilbert & Steven C. Sunshine, *Incorporating Dynamic Efficiency Concerns in Merger Analysis: The Use of Innovation Markets*, 63 ANTITRUST L.J. 569 (1995).

Consistent with this approach, the *Merger Guidelines* do not presume that a merger has negative effects on innovation.[94] Under the *Guidelines*, antitrust scrutiny of the effects of horizontal mergers on innovation focuses on assessing the likely effects of common ownership of R&D resources. If R&D resources of competing firms are complementary, a merger can enable innovation and have procompetitive effects. Antitrust enforcement may be concerned, however, with mergers that combine competing R&D resources. Specifically, one of the merging party's incentives to innovate may be reduced if a successful innovation results in a loss of revenues from the other merging party. In these circumstances, the *Merger Guidelines* indicate that if other market participants do not have similar innovation capabilities, a reduction in competition may lead to a reduction in innovation.[95]

D. Network Industries

Network industries exhibit a number of distinctive economic characteristics.[96] "In markets characterized by network effects, one

---

94.   *See* MERGER GUIDELINES, *supra* note 8, § 6.4.
95.   *Id.*
96.   *See, e.g.*, United States v. Visa U.S.A., Inc., 344 F.3d 229 (2d Cir. 2003); United States v. Microsoft Corp., 253 F.3d 34 (D.C. Cir. 2001); Money Station, Inc. v. Bd. of Governors, 81 F.3d 1128 (D.C. Cir.), *vacated*, 94 F.3d 658 (D.C. Cir. 1996); SCFC ILC, Inc. v. Visa U.S.A., 36 F.3d 958 (10th Cir. 1994) (concerning network-level competition between Discover/Novus and Visa); *In re* Payment Card Interchange Fee and Merchant Discount Antitrust Litig., 398 F. Supp. 2d 1356 (J.P.M.L. 2005) (concerning alleged price fixing in setting interchange fees in bank credit card networks); United States v. Microsoft, 87 F. Supp. 2d 30 (D.D.C. 2000) (concerning computer software and hardware networks); Complaint, United States. v. WorldCom, Inc., No. 00-01526 (D.D.C. June 26, 2000), *available at* http://www.justice.gov/atr/cases/-f5000/5051.htm (concerning long distance telephone networks and "backbone" networks that connect smaller networks to the internet); Money Station, Inc. v. Elec. Payment Servs., 1996-1 Trade Cas. (CCH) ¶ 71,426 (S.D. Ohio 1996) (concerning market power in the provision of ATM network services).
       Numerous articles have been written about network-based industries and network effects. *See, e.g.*, Donald I. Baker, *Compulsory Access to Network Joint Ventures Under the Sherman Act: Rules or Roulette?*, 1993 UTAH L. REV. 999 (1993); David A. Balto, *Access Demands to Payment Systems Joint Ventures*, 18 HARV. J. L. & PUB. POL'Y 623 (1995); Dennis

product or standard tends towards dominance, because 'the utility that a user derives from consumption of the good increases with the number of other agents consuming the good.'"[97] A network's value to any particular customer increases as more customers decide to use the network, an

---

W. Carlton & Alan S. Frankel, *The Antitrust Economics of Credit Card Networks*, 63 ANTITRUST L.J. 643 (1995) [hereinafter Carlton & Frankel I]; Dennis W. Carlton & Alan S. Frankel, *The Antitrust Economics of Credit Card Networks: Reply to Evans and Schmalensee Comment*, 63 ANTITRUST L.J. 903 (1995) [hereinafter Carlton & Frankel II]; Nicholas Economides, *Competition Policy in Network Industries: An Introduction*, *in* THE NEW ECONOMY AND BEYOND: PAST, PRESENT, AND FUTURE, 96 (Dennis Jansen ed., 2006); David S. Evans & Richard Schmalensee, *Economic Aspects of Payment Card Systems and Antitrust Policy Toward Joint Ventures*, 63 ANTITRUST L.J. 861 (1995) [hereinafter Evans & Schmalensee 1995]; David S. Evans & Richard Schmalensee, *A Guide to the Antitrust Economics of Networks*, ANTITRUST, Spring 1996, at 36 [hereinafter Evans & Schmalensee 1996]; Joseph Kattan, *Market Power in the Presence of an Installed Base*, 62 ANTITRUST L.J. 1 (1993); Michael L. Katz & Carl Shapiro, *System Competition and Network Effects*, 8 J. ECON. PERSP. 93 (1994); Mark A. Lemley & David McGowan, *Legal Implications of Network Economic Effects*, 86 CAL. L. REV. 479 (1998); Douglas Melamed, *Network Industries and Antitrust*, 23 HARV. J. L. & PUB. POL'Y 147 (1999); Howard A. Shelanski & J. Gregory Sidak, *Antitrust Divestiture in Network Industries*, 68 U. CHI L. REV. 1 (2001); Gregory J. Werden, *Network Effects and the Conditions of Entry: Lessons from the* Microsoft *Case*, 69 ANTITRUST L.J. 87 (2001); K. Craig Wildfang & Ryan W. Marth, *The Persistence of Antitrust Controversy and Litigation in Credit Card Networks*, 73 ANTITRUST L.J. 675 (2006).

97.   United States v. Microsoft, 253 F.3d 34, 49 (D.C. Cir. 2001) (quoting Michael L. Katz & Carl Shapiro, *Network Externalities, Competition, and Compatibility*, 75 AM. ECON. REV. 424, 424 (1985)); *see also* George L. Priest, *Rethinking Antitrust Law in an Age of Network Industries*, at 1 (Yale Law School John M. Olin Center for Studies in Law, Economics, and Public Policy, Research Paper No. 352, 2007), *available at* http://papers.ssrn.com/sol3/papers.cfm?abstract_id=1031166; Complaint ¶ 36, United States. v. WorldCom, Inc., No. 00-01526 (D.D.C. June 26, 2000), *available at* http://www.justice.gov/atr/cases/f5000/5051.htm ("As is true in network industries generally, the value of Internet access to end users becomes greater as more and more end users can easily be reached through the Internet. The benefit that one end user derives from being able to communicate effectively with additional users is known as a 'network externality.'").

effect known as "network externality." A telephone service becomes more valuable as additional customers are connected to it. A credit card becomes more attractive when greater numbers of consumers carry it and, as a result, more merchants are willing to accept it. An airline becomes more attractive when enough passengers begin flying a particular route to permit the carrier to offer more frequent service or to supply additional spokes from a hub. This link among consumers within a network may be "physical," as in a railroad track, electric power grid, or telephone line, or "virtual," as in a network of credit card users or users of software.

The market power of a network depends not only on the network effects, but also on (i) the degree of scale economies in production, (ii) the ability to differentiate the network from other products or networks, and (iii) the existence of alternatives to the network. Each of these factors is discussed below.

1. Scale Economies vs. Congestion

The optimal size of a network depends, in part, on the degree of both scale economies and network effects. Network externalities tend to produce markets dominated by one firm (particularly if production exhibits economies of scale) or a few firms (such as when there are increasing costs to production or the network can be differentiated). Lack of scale economies in production can mean that market power is more limited.

Network externalities influence the character of competition within network industries. A larger network is, all else equal, more attractive to customers than a smaller network. In addition to the network efficiencies in consumption, a network often enjoys economies of scale or scope in production. In some cases, however, congestion costs limit network size. For example, some new entrant air carriers have found it profitable to by-pass the network of a hub-and-spoke carrier and provide direct service. When the size of the network is limited by congestion costs, there is room for more than one network, which may reduce market power.

2. Network Differentiation

In some cases, more than one network can survive if networks offer differentiated services.

[N]etwork industries tend to have only a handful of competing networks. There is only one network of fax machines, all conforming to standards that enable them to communicate with each other. There is only one Internet. When network externalities are important, multiple networks can survive only if they are offering consumers somewhat different services.[98]

Airlines are a classic example of a network industry (subject to substantial congestion effects). DOJ has allowed airline mergers to proceed because, in part, passengers benefit from the network effects, which also offset potential anticompetitive harms. Congestion effects have limited whatever market power airlines might gain through growth because high demand can attract network and non-network competition.

3. Entry of Competitive Networks

In network industries, entry by another network may reduce an existing network's market power, in other cases the duplication of a network can be very costly. Furthermore, many markets may not be able to support multiple networks, or close substitutes may not be available. As a result, networks may be insulated by barriers to entry.[99]

On the other hand, superior technology and the intensity of network usage may facilitate entry into the network. For example, when a new network offers a clearly superior technology, the dominance of the established network may erode quickly. The ability of a new network to displace another is affected by whether customers have been "locked in" to the established technology by substantial sunk investments in such assets as complementary products and training.[100] An analysis of the ability of consumers to switch networks depends on the size of these sunk investments and the superiority of the new technology. Lock-in is not always a significant problem. The ability to overcome lock-in depends in part on the rate of growth of the industry. If new customers are available, a new firm can build a network based on industry growth, rather than conversion of existing customers.

Incumbents may also be displaced if users do not always use the entire network but rather rely on a limited portion of the network. A new network can form by beginning with core groups of consumers and then expanding. For example, cell phone users generally call only a small number of people regularly. Relying on this phenomenon, cell phone

---

98.   Evans & Schmalensee 1996, *supra* note 96, at 36.
99.   Barriers to entry are discussed in general in ch. VII, *infra*.
100.   *See* Kattan, *supra* note 96, at 6-7.

providers offer "friends and family" services to expand the network to new users. [101] This strategy may give a new network a toe-hold for possible entry. [102]

Antitrust agencies and academics have evaluated several methods to address market power issues in network industries. Based on the facts of the case, courts have agreed with some and rejected others. In cases in which the network is dominated by a single producer and in which a superior technology may have difficulty dislodging a dominant incumbent, some have called for structural remedies to ensure access to the network or to encourage and protect multiple networks. The use of a structural remedy was rejected in *United States v. Microsoft*,[103] when the appellate court stated: "[B]roader structural remedies present their own set of problems, including how a court goes about *restoring* competition to a dramatically changed, and constantly changing, marketplace."[104]

In some cases courts have used access regulation (regulating access to peripheral aspects of the network) to constrain some of the market power of a network. Examples of access regulations include the *Visa and MasterCard*[105] case and the *Microsoft*[106] case; Visa and MasterCard were required to permit member banks to offer multiple credit cards,[107] and Microsoft was required to allow access to source code for its operating

---

101. *See* Daniel Kearney, *Network Effects and the Emerging Doctrine of Cybertrespass,* 23 YALE L. & POL'Y REV. 313, 335-36 (2005) ("For example, the decision whether to use a Windows or Macintosh operating system may depend a great deal on what system is used by other members of one's family or firm and very little on what system is used by the firm or family across the street.").

102. *See* U.S. DEP'T OF JUSTICE, VOICE, VIDEO, AND BROADBAND: THE CHANGING COMPETITIVE LANDSCAPE AND ITS IMPACT ON CONSUMERS (Nov. 2008), *available at* http://www.usdoj.gov/atr/public/reports/-239284.pdf.

103. 253 F.3d 34 (D.C. Cir. 2001).

104. *Id.* at 49.

105. United States v. Visa U.S.A., Inc., 344 F.3d 229 (2d Cir. 2003).

106. Modified Final Judgment, United States v. Microsoft, No. 98-1232 (D.D.C. Sept. 7, 2006), *available at* http://www.usdoj.gov/atr/cases/-f218300/218339.htm.

107. *See* Visa U.S.A., Inc., 344 F.3d at 234 (requiring Visa and MasterCard to revoke their rule barring member banks from issuing American Express or Discover cards).

system.[108] In a number of cases networks are characterized as "essential facilities" if market entrants cannot operate effectively in isolation from the incumbent network.[109] In particular, if a firm cannot compete in a network industry unless it is allowed to join the dominant network, some argue good reason exists to grant the access request.[110]

Access regulation has not been universally accepted though. The Supreme Court has stated: "Compelling such firms to share the source of their advantage . . . may lessen the incentive for the monopolist, the rival, or both to invest in those economically beneficial facilities."[111] The Supreme Court went on to state: "Enforced sharing also requires antitrust courts to act as central planners, identifying the proper price, quantity, and other terms of dealing—a role for which they are ill suited."[112] Instead of simply regulating the price of a single network, access regulation requires regulation of the prices charged for individual components.[113] Furthermore, regulation of access to individual components often fails to take into account the effect of access on the overall configuration of the network.[114] As noted above, some networks are limited in the amount of service they can provide. Efficient pricing might require non-uniform pricing, such as substituting usage-based pricing for flat-rate pricing, which may lead to non-neutrality claims.

---

108. *See* Modified Final Judgment, United States v. Microsoft, No. 98-1232 (D.D.C. Sept. 7, 2006), *available at* http://www.usdoj.gov/atr/cases/-f218300/218339.htm.

109. *See, e.g.*, MCI v. AT&T, 708 F.2d 1081 (7th Cir. 1983).

110. A 1996 FTC report called for a "heightened degree of scrutiny" when a network refuses to admit a member who competes with its existing members. *See* FED. TRADE COMM'N, STAFF REPORT, ANTICIPATING 21ST CENTURY: COMPETITION POLICY IN THE NEW HIGH-TECH, GLOBAL MARKETPLACE ch. 9, at 8 (1996) (noting that if "intersystem competition remains likely," the competitive significance of network externalities, and the importance of admitting the entrant, are reduced).

111. Verizon Commc'ns v. Law Offices of Curtis V. Trinko, LLP, 540 U.S. 398, 407–08 (2004); *see also* Daniel F. Spulber & Christopher S. Yoo, *Mandating Access to Telecom and the Internet: The Hidden Side of Trinko*, 107 COLUM. L. REV. 1822, 1865 (2007).

112. *Trinko*, 540 U.S. at 407-08.

113. *See* Daniel F. Spulber & Christopher S. Yoo, *On the Regulation of Networks as Complex Systems: A Graph Theory Approach*, 99 NW. U. L. REV. 1687, 1689 (2005).

114. *Id.* at 1692.

These non-neutrality issues may arise whenever customers or suppliers are denied access.[115]

In addition, competition can be enhanced for compatible products if networks are compatible or if standardization is achieved.[116] When systems are compatible, competition exists for components of the network. Furthermore, standardization, by avoiding "tipping" to one network (rapid obsolescence of other networks when one network reaches a critical size), may allow multiple networks to exist. Standards that are established early in the development of a network, however, may result in less competition to provide the best technology.[117] The existence of networks involving "two-sided" markets makes the market power analyses of networks even more complex.[118]

Much debate remains on the extent of network market power. The Court of Appeals for the D.C. Circuit wrote in *Microsoft*:

> As an initial matter, we note that there is no consensus among commentators on the question of whether, and to what extent, current monopolization doctrine should be amended to account for competition in technologically dynamic markets characterized by network effects.[119]

---

115. *See* Christopher S. Yoo, *Network Neutrality and the Economics of Congestion*, 94 GEO. L.J. 1847 (2006).

116. *See, e.g.*, William H. Page & John E. Lopatka, *Network Externalities, in* ENCYCLOPEDIA OF LAW AND ECONOMICS 952, 963 (Boudewijn Bouckaert & Gerrit De Geest eds., 2000).

117. *See* Separate Statement of Commissioner Delrahim, ANTITRUST MODERNIZATION COMM'N, REPORT AND RECOMMENDATIONS 403, 407 (April 2007), *available at* http://govinfo.library.unt.edu/amc/-report_recommendation/toc.htm.

118. For a discussion of market power in two-sided markets, see *supra*, ch. V.

119. United States v. Microsoft Corp., 253 F.3d 34, 50 (D.C. Cir. 2001) (comparing Steven C. Salop & R. Craig Romaine, *Preserving Monopoly: Economic Analysis, Legal Standards, and Microsoft*, 7 GEO. MASON L. REV. 617, 654-55, 663-64 (1999) (arguing that exclusionary conduct in high-tech networked industries deserves heightened antitrust scrutiny in part because it may threaten to deter innovation), with Ronald A. Cass & Keith N. Hylton, *Preserving Competition: Economic Analysis, Legal Standards and Microsoft*, 8 GEO. MASON L. REV. 1, 36-39 (1999) (equivocating on the antitrust implications of network effects and noting that the presence of network externalities may actually encourage innovation by guaranteeing more durable monopolies to innovating winners)).

Whether market power in a network industry can be addressed through regulating price, guaranteeing access, creating standards, or changing the industry's structure is largely unresolved.

E. Conclusion

The different types of markets discussed in this Chapter present very different challenges to the antitrust analyst. In all these cases, defining markets and assessing market power will require a detailed, fact-intensive inquiry into the competitive conditions. The one common thread is that the ability to exercise market power will depend largely on purchasers' ability and willingness to turn to substitute products.

CHAPTER VII

BARRIERS TO ENTRY

A. Introduction

The economic concept of entry barriers plays a critical role in determining whether market power exists. Both the courts[1] and the

---

1. For consideration of barriers to entry in merger cases, see, for example, Chicago Bridge & Iron Co. v. FTC, 534 F.3d 410, 427-29 (5th Cir. 2008) (finding high barriers to entry and upholding Commission decision that merger violated Clayton Act Action 7 and FTC Act Section 5); FTC v. H.J. Heinz Co., 246 F.3d 708, 717 (D.C. Cir. 2001) (finding high barriers to market entry would enhance anticompetitive effects of a merger in baby food market in which there were no significant new entries in decades); United States v. Baker Hughes Inc., 908 F.2d 981, 988-89 (D.C. Cir. 1990) (upholding merger of firms after finding that "entry . . . would likely avert anticompetitive effects"); United States v. Syufy Enters., 903 F.2d 659, 664-65 (9th Cir. 1990) (upholding lower court's finding that entry into movie market was easy and lack of entry barriers undermined claim of market power); Cal. v. Am. Stores Co., 872 F.2d 837, 842 (9th Cir. 1989) ("An absence of entry barriers into a market constrains anticompetitive conduct, irrespective of the market's degree of concentration."), rev'd on other grounds, 495 U.S. 271 (1990); United States v. Waste Mgmt., 743 F.2d 976, 981-83 (2d Cir. 1984) (holding merger creating firm with 48.8 percent market share would not likely result in anticompetitive effects due to easy entry); FTC v. CCC Holdings, Inc., 605 F. Supp. 2d 26, 47-60 (D.D.C. 2009) (finding evidence of new entry "too speculative to reply upon" and issuing FTC requested injunction blocking merger); United States v. Country Lake Foods, 754 F. Supp. 669, 675, 679 (D. Minn. 1990) (finding lack of entry barriers for distant dairies to enter fluid milk processing market, which would prevent existing competitors from exerting market power); United States v. Calmar Inc., 612 F. Supp. 1298, 1306-07 (D.N.J. 1985) (finding ease of entry would prevent postmerger exercise of market power despite fact that merger would result in leading firm with over 75 percent of two markets and HHIs over 6400); Op. of the Commission, Polypore Int'l, No. 9327 (F.T.C. Dec. 13, 2010), slip op. at 33-35, *available at* http://www.ftc.gov/os/adjpro/d9327/101213polyporeopinion.pdf; Echlin Mfg. Co., 105 F.T.C. 410, 485-92 (1985) (finding absence of entry

---

163

economic literature[2] recognize that incumbent firms will be unable to

---

barriers into the assembly and sale of carburetor kits eliminates possibility of a substantial anticompetitive effect). For consideration of barriers to entry in monopolization cases, see Nobody In Particular Presents, Inc. v. Clear Channel Comm'ns, Inc., 311 F. Supp. 2d 1048, 1103-1105 (D. Colo. 2004) (finding sufficient evidence on summary judgment to show dangerous probability of monopolization of live concert market when evidence showed a rapid increase in market share from 45 percent to 50 percent over three years and the existence of significant entry barriers in the form of the incumbent's economies of scale in rock radio); Concord Boat Corp. v. Brunswick Corp., 207 F.3d 1039, 1059 (8th Cir. 2000) (finding recent entry into boat motor market undermined claim that firm, even monopoly firm, could charge supracompetitive prices); Handicomp, Inc. v. U.S. Golf Ass'n, No. 99-5372, 2000 WL 426245, at *4 (3d Cir. 2000) (finding no entry barriers into market for databases providing information for handicapping golf courses means that high market share did not prove monopoly power); Ball Mem'l Hosp. v. Mut. Hosp. Ins., 784 F.2d 1325, 1335-36 (7th Cir. 1986) (finding easy entry matters even though defendant has high market share); United States v. AT&T, 524 F. Supp. 1336, 1347-48 (D.D.C. 1981) (finding "persuasive showing" of monopoly power was made through evidence of "barriers to entry, such as the creation of bottlenecks, entrenched customer preferences, the regulatory process, large capital requirements, access to technical information, and disparities in risk") (internal citations omitted).

2. There is broad acceptance in the economics literature of the notion that markets will behave competitively if entry is easy. *See, e.g.*, F.M. SCHERER & DAVID ROSS, INDUSTRIAL MARKET STRUCTURE AND ECONOMIC PERFORMANCE 18 (3d ed. 1990) ("[S]ellers have little or no enduring power over price when entry barriers are nonexistent"). Entry is also emphasized in the "contestable market" theory, which argues that potential competition is as effective as actual competition in disciplining prices when "hit and run" entry is feasible. *See, e.g.*, WILLIAM J. BAUMOL ET AL., CONTESTABLE MARKETS AND THE THEORY OF INDUSTRY STRUCTURE ch. 2 (1982). However, there has been substantial debate over the circumstances in which the contestable market theory applies. *See, e.g.*, Midwestern Mach. Co. v. Northwest Airlines, 392 F.3d 265 (8th Cir. 2004) (Gibson, J. dissenting) (criticizing now "disproved" theory of contestability and noting that theory allowed airline mergers under the presumption that new carriers could easily enter new markets because airplanes are highly mobile, ignoring the difficulty of relocating or obtaining other essentials to airline operations). A number of scholars have suggested that there are many circumstances in which potential

exercise market power if any attempt to do so would be thwarted by entry of new firms. Despite a theoretical consensus among economists, attorneys, and policy makers regarding this fundamental proposition, significant disagreement remains regarding the proper definition of entry barriers and the appropriate application of the concept of entry barriers in antitrust cases.

This Chapter introduces the concept of entry barriers, the debate among economists about the appropriate definition, and some of the subtleties giving rise to the debate. It then discusses various sources of entry barriers in light of those debates. It concludes with the key analytical concepts and methodology described in the *Merger Guidelines*, including its emphasis on the timeliness, likelihood and sufficiency of entry.

B. The Debate over Defining Entry Barriers

1. Early Economic Literature

The economic literature on entry barriers began with Joe Bain's book *Barriers to New Competition*.[3] Bain's focus was how firms could be profitable in the long run without attracting entry.[4] Bain defined an entry

---

competition is less effective than actual competition. *See, e.g.*, William G. Shepherd, *Contestability vs. Competition—Once More*, 71 LAND ECON. 299, 303-07 (1995); Richard J. Gilbert, *The Role of Potential Competition in Industrial Organization*, 3 J. ECON. PERSP. 107, 123 (1989) ("[P]otential competition is important, but not as powerful as the theory of contestable markets implies."); Gloria J. Hurdle et al., *Concentration, Potential Entry, and Performance in the Airline Industry*, 38 J. INDUS. ECON. 119, 137 (1989) (rejecting theory of perfect contestability in airline industry); Steven A. Morrison & Clifford Winston, *Empirical Implications and Tests of the Contestability Hypothesis*, 30 J.L. & ECON. 53 (1987); Joseph E. Stiglitz, *Technological Change, Sunk Costs, and Competition, in* 3 BROOKINGS PAPERS ON ECON. ACTIVITY 883 (1987); Marius Schwartz, *The Nature and Scope of Contestability Theory*, 38 OXFORD ECON. PAPERS 37 (1986); Michael Spence, *Contestable Markets and the Theory of Industry Structure: A Review Article*, 21 J. ECON. LIT. 981 (1983); William A. Brock, *Contestable Markets and the Theory of Industry Structure: A Review Article*, 91 J. POL. ECON. 1055 (1983).

3. *See* JOE S. BAIN, BARRIERS TO NEW COMPETITION: THEIR CHARACTER AND CONSEQUENCES IN MANUFACTURING INDUSTRIES (1956).

4. *Id.* at 4.

barrier as a condition of a market that allows incumbents to earn economic profits in the long run without attracting entry. Bain identified what he considered to be three sources of entry barriers: scale economies, product differentiation, and cost disadvantages for entrants relative to incumbents.[5]

George Stigler criticized Bain's approach and Stigler's criticism of Bain often is misconstrued as being over his definition of an entry barrier. A better characterization is that Stigler disagreed with Bain's analysis of what gives rise to entry barriers. Stigler argued that the only possible source of entry barriers could be a cost borne by an entrant that incumbents do not have to bear.[6] As is discussed in more detail below, Stigler disagreed with Bain that scale economies could be an entry barrier.[7]

2. *Refining Entry Analysis*

Whether the Bain-Stigler disagreement concerned the definition of an entry barrier or the conditions that meet the definition, economists continue to debate both. McAfee, Mialon, and Williams identify seven distinct definitions in the literature before adding four of their own.[8] As to what constitutes an entry barrier, the substantial literature has failed to result in general agreement over whether fixed costs alone, sunk costs alone,[9] or the combination of the two constitute an entry barrier.[10]

For antitrust professionals looking to the economics profession for clear insight, this debate among economists is no doubt frustrating. However, as Dennis Carlton has observed: "[A] large part of the

---

5.   *See id.* at 12. Bain listed absolute capital requirements as a source of cost disadvantages for entrants. *Id.* at 146. However, because established firms with ready access to capital markets can be potential entrants, capital requirements generally are not a source of entry barriers based on cost disadvantage. *See* R. Preston McAfee et al., *What Is a Barrier to Entry?*, 94 AM. ECON. REV. 461, 464 (2004).

6.   GEORGE J. STIGLER, THE ORGANIZATION OF INDUSTRY 67-70 (1968).

7.   This argument foreshadowed the contestability literature discussed, *supra*, note 2.

8.   McAfee et al., *supra* note 5, at 461-62.

9.   *See infra* pt. C.2.

10.   *See* McAfee et al., *supra* note 5; Dennis W. Carlton *Why Barriers to Entry Are Barriers to Understanding*, 94 AM. ECON. REV. 466 (2004); Richard Schmalensee, *Sunk Costs and Antitrust Barriers to Entry*, 94 AM. ECON. REV. 471 (2004); BAUMOL ET AL., *supra* note 2, at 289.

confusion [about entry barriers] has arisen because authors are often unclear about the precise consequences of a 'barrier to entry.'"[11] By focusing on what is at issue in an antitrust case, much (if not all) of the conceptual confusion can be resolved. The plaintiff's theory in any antitrust case necessarily rests on an alleged anticompetitive harm (such as an increase in price above competitive levels). The key question one should ask with respect to entry is whether the threat of entry would prevent the alleged anticompetitive harm from occurring.[12]

One implication of focusing on the antitrust issues is that there might be entry barriers for antitrust purposes that do not meet Bain's definition or some of the others that have been proposed. McAfee, Mialon, and Williams distinguish "antitrust barriers" from "economic barriers."[13] In particular, Bain's focus was the determinants of long run profitability. However, as Carlton has explained:

> as a practical matter, the long run may be of little interest. It may take so long to get there that the persistence of supracompetitive profits in the transition period as the market adjusts to a long-run equilibrium turns out to be the fact of practical importance, not that these excess profits going forward will be eliminated in some far-off year.[14]

Moreover, not only might the categorization of entry barriers differ between antitrust and other applications, it might vary among classes of antitrust cases. Consider, for example, a market in which a dominant firm had established brand loyalty through extensive advertising. Is the need to advertise a barrier to entry? While plaintiffs in a Section 2 case might allege that the advertising was an act of monopolization to raise entry barriers, defendants would generally be on solid ground claiming that the advertising was a form of competition, not an entry barrier. However,

---

11. Carlton, *supra* note 10, at 466.
12. This question applies in most, but not all, theories of antitrust harm. For example, because price fixing is illegal per se, entry issues do not arise. The implausibility of successfully conspiring to raise prices because of the ease of entry is not a defense (though it may affect the determination of whether the alleged conspiracy existed at all). The inapplicability of entry, however, does not apply to all per se rules. The market power screen in the per se ban on tying under Sherman Act Section 1 means that there must be entry barriers into the tying good to trigger the rule.
13. McAfee et al., *supra* note 5, at 463.
14 Dennis W. Carlton, *Barriers to Entry, in* 1 ABA SECTION OF ANTITRUST LAW, ISSUES IN COMPETITION LAW AND POLICY 601, 605 (2008).

suppose a second firm also established a reputation for quality through extensive advertising and the competition between the two lowered prices. Further, suppose the two then proposed to merge. Absent entry, the merger would likely reverse the price reduction brought about by competition among the two merging firms; and the need to invest heavily in advertising to be a viable competitor may be a strong factor in considering whether the threat of further entry would prevent the price increase. Although disagreement over how to characterize this entry barrier may exist,[15] disagreement over the labels should not obscure agreement in the economic analysis of whether the threat of entry would necessarily prevent the merging firms from increasing their price.

This variance in the characterization of entry barriers, however, is not the only source of confusion. Another is that the term "entry barrier" in common parlance is not an appropriate definition for antitrust. McAfee, Mialon, and Williams distinguish "antitrust barriers" from "economic barriers."[16] In common parlance, a "barrier to entry" might seem to refer to any condition that makes entry unlikely. But, not only is such a definition imprecise, it can result in fundamental error. In antitrust, an entry barrier is a condition of the market that prevents entry from occurring *if incumbents in the market behave anticompetitively*.[17] If incumbents behave more competitively, they might make entry less attractive and, therefore, less likely. If so, the behavior is the result of competitive forces rather than barriers to entry in an antitrust sense.[18]

One sometimes sees claims that certain types of behavior (such as advertising in the above example) are barriers to entry. Bain conceived of barriers as being "structural," meaning that they are an inherent feature of the product itself or the technology of production. If barriers are entirely structural, then barriers are present in some industries but not others. However, even in Bain's analysis, the success of a structural barrier required that firms take appropriate action (such as a level of output). As the literature has developed, theories of entry barriers and deterrence generally have reflected a mix of underlying structural

---

15.   Arguments can be made for both "product differentiation" and "scale economies."

16.   McAfee et al., *supra* note 5, at 463.

17.   *See* U.S. DEP'T OF JUSTICE & FED. TRADE COMM'N, HORIZONTAL MERGER GUIDELINES § 9 (2010), *available at* http://www.justice.gov/atr/-public/guidelines/hmg-2010.html [hereinafter MERGER GUIDELINES].

18.   *See* FRANKLIN M. FISHER ET AL., FOLDED, SPINDLED, AND MUTILATED: ECONOMIC ANALYSIS AND *U.S. V. IBM* ch. 3 (1983).

assumptions about costs and demand and about the behavior that enables or reinforces the underlying conditions.[19]

On a related note, considering conduct or industry facts that do not constitute barriers to entry is also important. First, the need to produce a product cannot by itself be a barrier to entry. While such a suggestion might seem absurd at first, statements, such as "The need to build an oil refinery is a barrier to entry into the market for refined gasoline," can find their way into antitrust proceedings. Even though oil refineries are expensive, they are a cost of production. Competitive market prices compensate firms for necessary costs of production. If the costs of production are "high," competitive prices must also be "high." For an entry barrier into gasoline refining to exist, then entry would have to be unprofitable even if the price for gasoline was higher than needed to compensate producers for the cost of production.[20]

Further, when the issue in an antitrust case entails exclusionary conduct, plaintiffs might be tempted to label the allegedly anticompetitive behavior as an entry barrier. But doing so misconstrues the role that entry barrier analysis plays in some cases. Consider predatory pricing. Under *Matsushita*[21] and *Brooke Group*,[22] antitrust doctrine treats predatory pricing claims with a great deal of skepticism. As a result, plaintiffs must demonstrate a dangerous probability that defendant could successfully raise prices and recoup the cost of predation. This in turn requires a barrier to entry. As a matter of pure logic, entry may be deterred by the belief that incumbents will behave

---

19. Steven Salop introduced the distinction between "innocent" and "strategic" entry barriers. Innocent entry barriers are purely structural. Entry is deterred even if the incumbents simply maximize profits without regard to any effect their actions have on the threat of entry. "Strategic entry barriers" require that firms take actions they would not otherwise take except to deter entry. *See* Steven C. Salop, *Strategic Entry Deterrence*, 69 AM. ECON. REV. 335 (1979).

20. Oil refineries might well have features that give rise to entry barriers. Siting requirements might be a legal barrier to entry. As will be discussed below, time to entry can be an antitrust entry barrier. If it takes five years to plan and build an oil refinery, one might say that the five years it takes to build an oil refinery is an entry barrier. But the feature of the input that creates the entry barrier has to be something other than simply being expensive.

21. Matsushita Elec. Indus. Co. v. Zenith Radio Corp., 475 U.S. 574 (1986).

22. Brooke Group v. Brown & Williamson Tobacco Corp., 509 U.S. 209 (1993).

predatorily whenever entry occurs, and a history of below-cost pricing might make potential entrants fear similar behavior in the future. But, if fear of predatory pricing is the only entry barrier present, the recoupment test loses its teeth because the behavior that makes one ask whether a dangerous probability of success is present would be sufficient to resolve the question.[23]

In summary, the analysis of entry barriers is subtle and substantial disagreement over how to define an entry barrier and what satisfies the definition exist. Nevertheless, one can often avoid confusion by framing the question of whether entry barriers are present in terms of whether the threat of entry would prevent (or quickly nullify) the anticompetitive harm at issue in a the case at hand. Such focus can help analysts avoid the common pitfalls in entry analysis.

C. Sources of Entry Barriers

Given the controversy over how to define an entry barrier, naturally some controversy exists over what constitutes an entry barrier. Below, we discuss some of the more commonly considered entry barriers raised in the literature, along with an assessment of how controversial they are.

1. Legal and Regulatory Barriers

There is essentially no controversy that regulatory and legal requirements can constitute barriers to entry. If the government bans entry, the threat of entry cannot prevent incumbents from exercising market power; to the extent a government imposes limitations on entry short of an outright ban, it weakens the competitive threat from entry.[24] Examples of potential regulatory and legal entry barriers include patents, trademarks, mandatory licensing requirements, permitting for government-owned scarce resources, trade barriers, and various other types of regulations (e.g., regulations involving franchising or distribution requirements).

The magnitude of regulatory or legal requirements as entry barriers depends on the factual circumstances that exist in the market of potential

---

23.   Even though assertions that certain types of behavior by themselves constitute entry barriers may not be supported, conduct can strengthen structural entry barriers. See, for example, the discussion of long-term contracts in pt. C.6.a., *infra*.

24.   *See* MERGER GUIDELINES, *supra* note 17, § 9.

concern. In some cases, regulatory barriers effectively preclude entry. For example, the need to obtain FDA approval for a firm to market and sell prescription drugs in the United States is often viewed as an entry barrier in antitrust cases involving pharmaceuticals.[25] Similarly, patents can potentially preclude entry of competing products,[26] although this may not be the case if potential competitors can design around existing patents or if the patents are perceived to be invalid or unenforceable.[27]

In other situations, entry may occur despite the existence of regulatory or legal barriers, but such impediments may discourage entry. For example, certificate of need (CON) regulations generally require that certain health care providers apply for state government approval in order to build a new health care facility or make significant capital investments in an existing facility.[28] Because the severity of CON laws varies considerably by state, the potential entry impact of CON laws varies as well. Similarly, environmental and zoning regulations can vary considerably by geographic area and, thus, may or may not serve to deter entry. The key question is the impact of such regulations on the cost and timing of entry. Significant regulatory requirements may be sufficiently costly that entry is unlikely to be profitable. Regulatory requirements may also significantly delay entry.

---

25. *See, e.g.,* Complaint, Barr Pharms., No. C-4171 (F.T.C. Oct. 19, 2006), *available* at http://www.ftc.gov/os/caselist/0610217barrcomplaint.pdf; Complaint, Pfizer, Inc., No. C-3957 (F.T.C. Jun. 19, 2000), *available at* http://www.ftc.gov/os/2000/06/pfizercmp.htm.
26. *See, e.g.,* FED. TRADE COMM'N, TO PROMOTE INNOVATION: THE PROPER BALANCE OF COMPETITION AND PATENT LAW AND POLICY 48-55 (2003), *available at* http://www.ftc.gov/os/2003/innovationrpt.pdf.
27. In tying cases under Sherman Act Section 1, a necessary condition to trigger the per se ban is market power in the tying good, which in turn requires that there be an entry barrier into the tying good. Under *Jefferson Parish Hosp. Dist. No. 2 v. Hyde*, 466 U.S. 2 (1984), a patent on the tying good was taken as the basis for a presumption of the requisite market power. The Supreme Court overturned that presumption in *Illinois Tool Works, Inc. v. Indep. Ink.*, 547 U.S. 28 (2006).
28. *See, e.g.,* Admin. Compl. ¶ 34, *In re* Inova Health Sys. Found., No. 9326 (F.T.C. May 8, 2008), *available at* http://www.ftc.gov/os/adjpro/d9326/-080509admincomplaint.pdf.

2. *Fixed Costs, Sunk Costs, and Economies of Scale*

Economists continue to debate whether sunk costs alone, fixed costs alone, or the combination of the two are entry barriers. The debate might seem odd at first as the terms "sunk costs" and "fixed costs" often are used interchangeably. The terms are quite different, however. Fixed costs are costs that do not vary with the level of output even in the long run, whereas sunk costs are costs that, once incurred, cannot be recovered.[29] The two essential features of sunk costs are that they are durable and that they are devoted to a particular use. To illustrate the distinction with practical examples, an oil refinery is a sunk cost (because it is durable and cannot be used for anything other than oil refining),[30] but it is not fixed because oil refiners need additional refining capacity to refine more oil. The cost of developing a new drug is an example of a fixed cost as it does not depend on the quantity of the drug ultimately produced. Fixed costs give rise to economies of scale, which occur when long run average costs of production and/or distribution fall as output rises.

Bain argued that scale economies are a barrier to entry because they force an entrant to produce at large scale.[31] Even if the pre-entry price were above competitive levels, entry at such scale could drive price below competitive levels and make the entry unprofitable. Note that under this argument, what matters is the extent of scale economies relative to the market. To be a substantial entry barrier, scale economies must be large enough relative to the market that entry necessarily results in a substantial price reduction.[32]

The argument that scale economies are not an entry barrier is that absent sunk costs, an entrant could completely replace the incumbent, which would exit the industry. This is the argument underlying the "contestable markets hypothesis."[33]

29.	*See* BAUMOL ET AL., *supra* note 2, ch. 10.
30.	The fact that a refinery can be sold does not prevent it from being a sunk cost. When the purchase price for a used asset is far below the original cost (or, more accurately, what the company anticipated the net asset value would), the company still loses a substantial portion of the cost.
31.	BAIN, *supra* note 3, at 54-55.
32.	Scale economies are measured by minimum efficient scale (MES) or minimum viable scale (MVS).
33.	For cites to the economic literature on contestable markets, see *supra* note 2.

When costs are sunk as well as fixed, entry that forces the price below the competitive level would not necessarily induce the incumbent to exit. If so, the need to enter at large scale implies that entry can cause a sufficient reduction in price to make entry unprofitable. Thus, the combination of sunk and fixed costs does create the possibility that entry could not be relied upon to prevent prices from rising above competitive levels.[34]

Thus, the debate should be resolved as the combination of fixed and sunk costs constituting entry barriers when the purpose of entry analysis—identifying those barriers that would prevent prices rising above competitive levels—is properly considered.

3. Product Differentiation

As with the general definition of the term "entry barrier," a "product differentiation" entry barrier is different from the term "product differentiation" in common parlance. Restaurants and women's dresses are both differentiated products, but the facts that menus vary or that fashion plays a role in clothing choice does not create an entry barrier for antitrust or in any other economically meaningful sense.

The economics literature has identified several ways in which product differentiation can be an entry barrier. The first is what Richard Schmalensee called the "product differentiation advantage of pioneering brands."[35] When a consumer has to use a good or incur some other cost to ascertain whether it works, the "pioneer" has an advantage over subsequent entrants. Consumers might be willing to accept the risk of buying the pioneer's good because of the promise that it meets an unmet need. Once consumers do so and find a good that works, there is less benefit from finding a second good that works. A small price discount by an entrant may not be sufficient to induce consumers to try its brand.

A second type of product differentiation entry barrier, also formalized by Schmalensee, is brand proliferation.[36] Formulated in the context of the FTC's suit against the ready-to-eat breakfast cereal

---

34. *See, e.g.*, A. Michael Spence, *Entry, Capacity, Investment and Oligopolistic Pricing*, 8 BELL J. ECON. 534 (1977); Avinash Dixit, *The Role of Investment in Entry-Deterrence*, 90 ECON. J. 95, 106 (1980).

35. Richard Schmalensee, *Product Differentiation Advantages of Pioneering Brands*, 72 AM. ECON. REV. 349, 349 (1982).

36. *See* Richard L. Schmalensee, *Entry Deterrence in the Ready-to-Eat Breakfast Cereal Industry,* 9 BELL J. ECON. 305 (1978).

manufacturers for joint monopolization,[37] the Schmalensee model sought to explain important features of the industry. First, the industry was dominated by a small number of firms that were highly profitable. The firms themselves had a large number of brands. Yet, entry had not been successful. In the Schmalensee model, the brand introductions by the incumbents were part of a strategy to make entry unprofitable. An essential feature of the Schmalensee model was that a new brand with specific characteristics (such as sweetness, crunchiness, and vitamin content) would compete only against cereals with similar characteristics.[38] This "localized" competition meant that any specific brand would have to compete within a specific market niche.[39] The brand proliferation strategy was allegedly designed to make each niche too small for entry to be profitable.

A general issue raised by both Schmalensee product differentiation models is whether "branding" is a barrier to entry. The issue remains a matter of debate in part because what consumers learn from branding is not clear. Consumers plainly respond to brands; they pay a premium for a wide range of branded products over apparently comparable unbranded

---

37.   *See In re* Kellogg Co., 99 F.T.C. 8 (1982). The FTC alleged that the cereal companies avoided price competition in favor of brand rivalry because product proliferation deterred entry and protected profits. However, the administrative law judge in the case ruled that the behavior of the cereal companies was not anticompetitive.

38.   The assumptions about demand in the Schmalensee model do not plausibly apply to every market in which products are differentiated. For example, it probably would not apply to restaurants. A high-end French restaurant on a particular block in Manhattan would not compete just against high-end French restaurants on the same block. It would compete against similarly located restaurants of all types, including other Manhattan French restaurants (high-end and mid-level) and high-end restaurants with cuisines other than French.

39.   Similar models describe competition between firms in multidimensional geographic space. Although this discussion focuses on competition in product space, the results are similar in principle to situations that involve geographic space. *See, e.g.*, D.A. Hay, *Sequential Entry and Entry-Deterring Strategies in Spatial Competition*, 28 Oxford Econ. Papers 240 (1976); Edward C. Prescott & Michael Visscher, *Sequential Location Among Firms with Foresight*, 8 Bell J. Econ. 378 (1977); B. Curtis Eaton & Richard G. Lipsey, *The Theory of Market Pre-Emption: The Persistence of Excess Capacity and Monopoly in Growing Spatial Markets*, 46 Economica 149, 149 (1979).

products. In some cases, as with over-the-counter pharmaceuticals, consumers appear to take branding as a signal of quality. In other cases, different brands have known product characteristics. In either case, companies can invest in establishing a brand (most notably through advertising). So is advertising simply a cost, or can it be an entry barrier?

As discussed above, a necessary cost cannot by itself be a barrier to entry. This is just as true of the need to make a product's features known to customers as it is of production costs. However, advertising costs may have special features that indeed make them entry barriers. First of all, they might be sources of scale economies. If the most efficient form of advertising for a product is national television advertising, which can be expensive, the per unit cost of advertising might be prohibitive for smaller competitors. Also, a company's success in establishing a reputation for its brand might depend on how its advertising expenditures compare with its rivals. If so, incumbents might choose such high levels of advertising so as to increase the amount of advertising required of an entrant. To the extent that they do so, they raise entry barriers.[40]

As noted above, Schmalensee developed one of his models of entry barriers in the context of the FTC's case against the ready-to-eat breakfast cereal manufacturers. He developed the other with respect to the *ReaLemon* case, in which the Sixth Circuit affirmed the FTC's order finding that Borden used unfair methods in the sale of reconstituted lemon juice.[41] Both cases were problematic—the problem with both was the allegations of precisely what actions were anticompetitive. Introducing new brands to meet diverse customer tastes would generally be considered a form of competition.[42] Similarly, to the extent that consumers trusted the ReaLemon brand and were not willing to save a few pennies for store brand lemon juice, it is not clear why Borden (the owner of ReaLemon) could be said to be at fault.

---

40. JOHN SUTTON, SUNK COSTS AND MARKET STRUCTURE: PRICE COMPETITION, ADVERTISING, AND THE EVOLUTION OF CONCENTRATION ch. 10 (1991).

41. *See* Borden, Inc. v. FTC, 674 F.2d 498 (1982) (affirming the FTC's order).

42. The administrative law judge in the case ruled that the behavior of the cereal companies was not anticompetitive. *See* Initial Decision, *In re* Kellogg Co., 99 F.T.C. 8 (1982).

4. Access to Specialized or Low Cost Resources

In some cases, firms may not be able to obtain access to a key resource necessary to enter a market (e.g., a natural resource such as land, oil and gas, diamonds, etc.). In particular, other firms' control over key resources can deter entry. In other cases, resources may only be available at a substantially higher cost compared to the cost charged to incumbent firms. In these cases, potential entrants may be put at a significant cost disadvantage such that entry is unlikely to be profitable.

5. Network Externalities

A type of entry barrier that, while not new, has played an increasingly important role in major antitrust cases is network externalities. A positive network externality or network effect arises when one person's use of a good or service makes the good or service more valuable to other users.[43] Typical examples of positive network externalities include phones, some types of computer software,[44] and DVD players. For example, the value of a telephone increases with the number of other people one can call on that phone.

Network externalities can be a source of entry barriers because they can limit the potential inroads that new entrants can make or otherwise make new entry prohibitively costly. The first company that establishes a

---

43.   Economic articles discussing network externalities include Michael L. Katz & Carl Shapiro, *Network Externalities, Competition, and Compatibility*, 75 AM. ECON. REV. 424 (1985); Joseph Farrell & Garth Saloner, *Standardization, Compatibility, and Innovation*, 16 RAND J. ECON. 70 (1985); Nicholas Economides, *Desirability of Compatibility in the Absence of Network Externalities*, 79 AM. ECON. REV. 1165 (1988). For a discussion of network externalities as applied to the *Microsoft* antitrust case, see DAVID S. EVANS ET AL., DID MICROSOFT HARM CONSUMERS? TWO OPPOSING VIEWS (2000).

44.   Word processing programs have positive network externalities to the extent that people can more readily share files with people who use the same program. Any sort of "platform," such as a computer operating system, can have positive network externalities to the extent that the availability of applications for the platform are a function of how many people adopt the platform. On the other extreme, there is no particular reason why the value of a screen saver to one computer user is greater because others have the same screen saver.

network might find itself insulated against entry even if it simply maximizes short-run profits and has sufficient lead time.

As with product differentiation, when network externalities are present, firms might take actions that insulate themselves from entry. For example, at the early stages of competition in a network industry, a firm might compete more aggressively (on price, for example) than it otherwise would have in order to establish itself as the industry standard. Also, once a firm establishes itself as a standard, it might have to decide whether to make itself compatible with the products of its competitors. Consider, for example, competing telephone networks, one of which is larger than the other; and suppose the two companies can interconnect their networks (if both agree to do so). All else equal, interconnecting the smaller network with the larger one would make the larger network more valuable to its subscribers because they would be able to call more people. However, interconnection would increase the relative attractiveness of the smaller network even more. The larger network might choose not to interconnect so as to avoid helping its rival.

Whether it would be anticompetitive for the larger network to refuse to interconnect with the smaller network is subject to substantial debate.[45] However, the debate should not be about whether the presence of network economies is an entry barrier, but about what constitutes anticompetitive behavior in the presence of network externalities (although, they may be related). When network externalities are present, an entrant that offers consumers better value absent the network effects might be unable to enter successfully.[46] As a result, the threat of entry does not create the same pressure on an incumbent to keep prices down and quality up as would be the case if network economies were not present.

6. Behavioral Enhancements

The list of behaviors that have been alleged to create entry barriers is potentially quite long and include long-term contracts, excessively rapid

---

45. *See* Joseph Farrell & Philip J. Weiser, *Modularity, Vertical Integration, and Open Access Policies: Towards a Convergence of Antitrust and Regulation in the Internet Age*, 17 HARV. J.L. & TECH. 85, 117-18 & 117 n.141 (2003).

46. Better value might be due to a lower price for a good of comparable quality, a good of higher quality for the same price, or some other price-quality combination that consumers prefer.

introduction of new products, exclusive dealing contracts, tying, all-units discounts, and bundled discounts.[47] The analysis of all of these has a common thread. By themselves, they cannot be antitrust entry barriers. However, when structural barriers are present, they can reinforce them. Two examples illustrate the point.

a.   Long-Term Contracts

When a firm enters into a long-term contract with one of its customers, an entrant cannot compete for that customer's business until the contract is up. Although this might appear to preclude entry or at least make it harder, it is not sufficient to be an antitrust entry barrier because it does not give the incumbent the power to exercise market power without attracting entry. The customer enters into the long-term contract voluntarily. Absent any other entry barrier, it would only do so on terms that it finds competitive. The contract then protects it against anticompetitive behavior during the life of the contract (after which entry becomes feasible).

When scale economies are significant, however, then long-term contracts can reinforce entry barriers, making entry even harder. Suppose a successful entrant would need to get 10 percent of the market to be able to operate successfully. If the incumbent entered into five-year contracts and spaced out the starting dates evenly over time, such that only 20 percent of the market is available for contracting at any given time, a successful entrant would have to get 50 percent of the contracts that are subject to negotiation at the time it enters. This might be far less likely than being able to get 10 percent of all the contracts that are contestable at a point in time, as would be the case if no long-term contracts existed.[48] Alternatively, key customers may be willing to support the incumbent by signing long-term contracts if they will receive better prices for the product.[49] Although long-term contracts may serve as an entry barrier in these situations, customers may also use long-term

47.   *See, e.g.*, LePage's Inc. v. 3M, 324 F.3d 141, 155-57 (3d Cir. 2003) (describing exclusionary harms of bundled rebates and the strong incentive they provide to buyers, especially where the rebater's competitors cannot offer similar rebates).

48.   *See, e.g.*, Phillipe Aghion & Patrick Bolton, *Contracts as a Barrier to Entry*, 77 AM. ECON. REV. 388, 388-89 (1987).

49.   Steven C. Salop & David T. Scheffman, *Raising Rivals' Costs*, 73 AM. ECON. REV. 267-71 (1983).

contracts to encourage entry by assuring that new entrants can enter with sufficient business to be profitable.

b. Rapid Product Introduction

Suppose an industry is served by a monopolist whose product is covered by a patent, and the opportunity exists to engage in research and development leading to a patent on a superior good that would compete with the monopolist's offerings. Who has more of an incentive to develop the new technology, the incumbent monopolist or an entrant?

At first, it might appear that the incumbent would have little incentive to develop the new product, which would primarily compete with and therefore "cannibalize" its existing product. In contrast, any sales the entrant would garner from successful development would be incremental. If so, it might appear that the entrant has the stronger incentive.

However, if the incumbent recognizes the entrant's incentive to compete, its incentive to innovate and preempt the competition exceeds the entrant's incentive.[50] As long as the incumbent can preserve its monopoly by innovating first and the entrant would face some residual competition from the incumbent, the incumbent's incentive is stronger.

Does this analysis imply that innovation can be a barrier to entry? The entire analysis is premised on the possibility that patents can preclude entry into the market. Thus, the argument that behavior can raise entry barriers only makes sense in the presence of a structural barrier. Given the structural barrier, however, this type of preemptive innovation behavior can make entry harder.

The question then becomes whether the behavior is anticompetitive because it raises entry barriers. As with product introduction and advertising, the issue is less about what constitutes an entry barrier and more about what counts as anticompetitive. Predatory pricing doctrine reflects a reluctance to mislabel what would normally be considered competitive behavior as anticompetitive. Allegations of predatory innovation are problematic for precisely the same reason.

---

50. Richard J. Gilbert & David M.G. Newbery, *Preemptive Patenting and the Persistence of Monopoly*, 72 AM. ECON. REV. 514, 514 (1982).

D. Evaluation of Entry in the *Merger Guidelines*

The *Merger Guidelines* outline a basic framework with which to analyze entry in merger cases. The *Guidelines* embrace many of the key economic principles discussed previously regarding entry barriers and also attempt to put forth a practical framework for analyzing entry barriers in antitrust cases.

The sections on entry in both the *Merger Guidelines*[51] and the FTC and DOJ's 2006 *Commentary on the Horizontal Merger Guidelines*[52] reflect the role of entry analysis in antitrust. Like virtually all antitrust cases, merger cases reflect a concern about some anticompetitive harm, the most common one being an increase in price.

In evaluating entry, the *Merger Guidelines* focus on whether entry is "timely, likely and sufficient in its magnitude, character, and scope to deter or counteract the competitive effects of concern."[53] Regarding the timeliness of entry, "entry must be rapid enough to make unprofitable overall the actions causing those [competitive effects of concern] and thus leading to entry . . . ."[54] In many cases, it is the combination of many factors that leads to the conclusion that profitable entry will not occur in a timely fashion (i.e., typically viewed as being more than two years).[55]

Entry is considered "likely" under the *Merger Guidelines* if an entry alternative:

51.   MERGER GUIDELINES, *supra* note 17, § 9.
52.   FED. TRADE COMM'N & U.S. DEP'T OF JUSTICE, COMMENTARY ON THE HORIZONTAL MERGER GUIDELINES 37-49 (2006), *available at* http://www.ftc.gov/os/2006/031CommendaryontheHorizontalMergerGui delinesMarch2006.pdf [hereinafter MERGER GUIDELINES COMMENTARY].
53.   MERGER GUIDELINES, *supra* note 17, § 9.
54.   *Id.* § 9.1.
55.   For example, entry might be delayed due to regulatory requirements. Entry can also be delayed due to practical complications in the entry process. In some industries, entry may be significantly delayed because the new entrant must construct a new plant or expand an existing plant in order to sell product. New entrants may also need to design and test products before selling them into the market. In some industries, entrants may need to engage in a period of pre-marketing before product can be effectively sold into the market.

would be profitable, accounting for the assets, capabilities, and capital needed and the risks involved, including the need for the entrant to incur costs that would not be recovered if the entrant later exits.[56]

As a practical matter, this means that entry is "unlikely" under a *Guidelines* approach when there are significant fixed costs that are unlikely to be recovered by the entering firm so as to achieve a reasonable rate of return.[57] Entry would also not be likely if government regulations prevent or significantly limit potential entry or if the entrant is not able to gain access to essential inputs.[58]

The third entry criterion under the *Merger Guidelines*, "sufficiency," is focused on whether entry will be of a character and magnitude to "counteract the competitive effect of concern."[59] Under the *Guidelines*, entry is not sufficient if the "products offered by entrants are not close enough substitutes to the products offered by the merged firm to render a price increase by the merged firm unprofitable."[60] Further, "[e]ntry may also be insufficient due to constraints that limit entrants' competitive effectiveness, such as limitations on the capabilities of the firms best placed to enter or reputational barriers to rapid expansion by new entrants."[61] At the heart of the "sufficiency" analysis is the notion that different types of entry have different economic impacts and some types of entry may not be sufficient to offset potential anticompetitive effects even if they are both "timely" and "likely."[62]

---

56. *Id.* § 9.2.
57. *See* MERGER GUIDELINES COMMENTARY, *supra* note 52, at 37.
58. *See* MERGER GUIDELINES, *supra* note 17, § 9. As a practical matter, the federal enforcement agencies will also focus on cost disadvantages of entry in determining whether entry is likely. *Id.* ("Recent examples of entry . . . can be informative regarding the scale necessary for an entrant to be successful . . . ."). According to the agencies, the most common reason for a cost disadvantage is "the presence of economies of scale and scope." MERGER GUIDELINES COMMENTARY, *supra* note 52, at 45.
59. MERGER GUIDELINES, *supra* note 17, § 9.3.
60. *Id.*
61. *Id.*
62. The *Guidelines* explain:

> Entry by a single firm that will replicate at least the scale and strength of one of the merging firms is sufficient. Entry by one or more firms operating at a smaller scale may be sufficient if such firms are not at a significant competitive disadvantage.

The analysis of whether entry will be timely, likely, and sufficient considers a variety of evidence under a *Guidelines* approach. Perhaps the most important evidence relates to the presence of ongoing entry and exit and the history of entry and exit in an industry. Successful historical entry may provide evidence to support the argument that entry is easy. Recognizing the limitations of this evidence is important. Such evidence does not prove that entry will likely occur following a merger or that it will be sufficient to prevent anticompetitive effects.[63] On the other hand, a history of failed entry may bolster the case that entry barriers exist, although entry could still be easy despite a history of failed entry. Generally, evidence of past entry most strongly suggests that future entry will be easy when future entry conditions after a merger are likely to be similar to past entry conditions. Similarly, a history of failed entry might not suggest entry barriers if entry conditions have sufficiently changed so that entry is substantially easier and more likely compared to the past.[64]

Another factor that enters both the *Merger Guidelines* and the *Commentary* is the existence of substantial sunk costs. The *Merger Guidelines* distinguish "rapid entrants" from other entrants. Rapid entrants do not have substantial sunk entry costs (because they can redeploy the assets they would use for entry to some other use if they subsequently exit).[65] Their apparent logic is that entry almost always entails some risk of failure. As a result, the presence of sunk costs creates

---

Id.

63.   *See* MERGER GUIDELINES COMMENTARY, *supra* note 52, at 39.

64.   Notably, the elimination of a competitor through merger may sufficiently change market circumstances to make previously unprofitable entry profitable. *See* United States v. Baker Hughes Inc., 908 F.2d 981, 989 n.9 (D.C. Cir. 1990) ("[I]f prices reach supracompetitive levels, a company that has failed to enter in the past could become competitive.").

65.   MERGER GUIDELINES, *supra* note 17, § 5.1. The term "rapid entrant" is new in the 2010 *Merger Guidelines*, but it appears to be synonymous with what the previous *Merger Guidelines* called "uncommitted entry," and defined as firms that could enter with insignificant sunk costs. U.S. DEP'T OF JUSTICE & FED. TRADE COMM'N, HORIZONTAL MERGER GUIDELINES § 3.0 n.25 (1992), *available at* http://www.justice.gov/atr/public/guidelines/hmg.htm. Entrants that are not "rapid" appear to correspond to what the previous *Merger Guidelines* call "committed entrants," which were defined as new competitors that required "expenditure of significant sunk costs of entry and exit." *Id.* § 3.0.

the risk that entry would not be profitable (in an expected value sense) even if the market is profitable for incumbents.

E. Conclusion

Entry entails a practical assessment of a wide range of evidence with the underpinning of sound economic theory. The economic theories of entry barriers initially developed by Bain and Stigler have been refined over time and economic theory now provides a sound basis for evaluating the existence of entry barriers or lack thereof. The fundamental economic issue in evaluating entry barriers is to identify the factors that would prevent some firm currently outside the market from taking advantage of the profit opportunity that would result if anticompetitive behavior were attempted. The *Merger Guidelines* take this approach in their focus on the timing, likelihood and sufficiency of entry. Overall, many potential sources of entry barriers need to be carefully evaluated in order to determine whether a valid economic argument for entry barriers exist.

TABLE OF CASES

A

B

C

D

E

F

G

M

R

R.J. Reynolds Tobacco Co. v. Philip Morris Inc., 199 F. Supp. 2d 362 (M.D.N.C. 2002), 106, 108

R.R. Donnelley & Sons Co., 120 F.T.C. 36 (1995) (citing *H.J., Inc.*, 867 F.2d at 1537), 62, 72

In re RSR Corp., 88 F.T.C. 800 (1976), *aff'd*, 602 F.2d 1317 (9th Cir. 1979), 113

RSR Corp. v. FTC, 602 F.2d 1317 (9th Cir. 1979), 79, 81

Reazin v. Blue Cross & Blue Shield, Inc., 899 F.2d 951 (10th Cir. 1990), 9, 16, 109

Rebel Oil Co. v. Atl. Richfield Co., 51 F.3d 1421 (9th Cir. 1995), 21, 23, 24, 25, 62, 66, 69

Republic Tobacco v. North Atl. Trading, 381 F.3d 717 (7th Cir. 2004), 77, 81

Reynolds Metals Co. v. FTC, 309 F.2d 223 (D.C. Cir. 1962), 113

Richter Concrete Corp. v. Hilltop Concrete Corp., 691 F.2d 818 (8th Cir. 1982), 20, 23

Rome Ambulatory Surgical Ctr. v. Rome Mem'l Hosp., 349 F. Supp. 2d 389 (N.D.N.Y. 2004), 78

Rothery Storage & Van Co. v. Atlas Van Lines, Inc., 792 F.2d 210 (D.C. Cir. 1986), 6, 65, 81, 106, 138

S

SCFC ILC, Inc. v. Visa USA, Inc., 36 F.3d 958 (10th Cir. 1994), 6, 15, 17, 154

S. Pac. Commc'ns v. AT&T, 740 F.2d 980 (D.C. Cir. 1984), 25

Santa Cruz Med. Clinic v. Dominican Santa Cruz Hosp., No. C93-20613, 1995 WL 853037 (N.D. Cal. 1995), 74, 79

Schering-Plough Corp. v. FTC, 402 F.3d 1056 (11th Cir. 2005), 17

Sci. Prods. Co. v. Chevron Chem. Co., 384 F. Supp. 793 (N.D. Ill. 1974), 67

Sheridan v. Marathon Petroleum Co., 530 F.3d 590 (7th Cir. 2008), 10

Slocomb Indus. v. Chelsea Indus., No. 82-2546, 1984 WL 2945 (E.D. Pa. 1984), 68

SmithKline Corp. v. Eli Lilly & Co., 575 F.2d 1056 (3d Cir. 1978), 63, 65

Spanish Broad. Sys. v. Clear Channel Commc'ns, 376 F.3d 1065 (11th Cir. 2004), 63

Spectrum Sports v. McQuillan, 506 U.S. 447 (1993), 8, 21

Spirit Airlines v. Northwest Airlines, 431 F.3d 917 (6th Cir. 2005), 9, 83

United States v. Rockford Mem'l Corp., 717 F. Supp. 1251 (N.D. Ill. 1989), *aff'd*, 898 F.2d 1278 (7th Cir. 1990), 78
United States v. Rockford Mem'l Corp., 898 F.2d 1278 (7th Cir. 1990), 72, 78
United States v. Rockwell Int'l, No. 80-1401, 1980 WL 2000 (W.D. Pa. 1980), 138
United States v. Socony-Vacuum Oil Co., 310 U.S. 150 (1940), 14
United States v. Sungard Data Sys., 172 F. Supp. 2d 172 (D.D.C. 2001), 85
United States v. Syufy Enters., 712 F. Supp. 1386 (N.D. Cal. 1989), *aff'd*, 903 F.2d 659 (9th Cir. 1990), 67
United States v. Syufy Enters., 903 F.2d 659 (9th Cir. 1990), 20, 163
United States v. Tidewater Marine Serv., 284 F. Supp. 324 (E.D. La. 1968), 29
United States v. UPM-Kymmene Oyj, No. 03-C-2528, 2003 WL 21781902 (N.D. Ill. 2003), 85
United States v. United Shoe Mach., 110 F. Supp. 295 (D. Mass. 1953), 25, 143
United States v. Visa U.S.A., Inc., 163 F. Supp. 2d 322 (S.D.N.Y. 2001), *aff'd*, 344 F.3d 229 (2d Cir. 2003), 85
United States v. Visa U.S.A., Inc., 344 F.3d 229 (2d Cir. 2003), 13, 121, 154, 158
United States v. Waste Mgmt., 743 F.2d 976 (2d Cir. 1984), 29, 31, 76, 77, 163
United States v. Waste Mgmt., No. 03-CV-1409, 68 Fed. Reg. 47 (2003), 80
United States. v. WorldCom, Inc., No. 00-01526 (D.D.C. June 26, 2000), 154, 155

V

Valley Liquors v. Renfield Imps., 822 F.2d 656 (7th Cir. 1987), 10, 18
Valley Products Co. v. Landmark, 128 F.3d 398 (6th Cir. 1997), 107
Verizon Commc'ns v. Law Offices of Curtis V. Trinko, 540 U.S. 398 (2004), 7, 48, 159
Virtual Maint. v. Prime Computer, 11 F.3d 660 (6th Cir. 1993), 18, 64, 66, 107
Volvo Trucks N. Am. v. Reeder-Simco GMC, Inc., 546 U.S. 164 (2006), 27

W

X

Y

Z

ABA SECTION OF ANTITRUST LAW COMMITMENT TO QUALITY

The Section of Antitrust Law is committed to the highest standards of scholarship and continuing legal education. To that end, each of our books and treatises is subjected to rigorous quality control mechanisms throughout the design, drafting, editing, and peer review processes. Each Section publication is drafted and edited by leading experts on the topics covered and then rigorously peer reviewed by the Section's Books and Treatises Committee, at least two Council members, and then other officers and experts. Because the Section's quality commitment does not stop at publication, we encourage you to provide any comments or suggestions you may have for future editions of this book or other publications.